Open Text Metastorm ProVision® 6.2 Strategy Implementation

Create and implement a successful business strategy for improved performance throughout the whole enterprise

Bill Aronson

[PACKT] enterprise

PUBLISHING

BIRMINGHAM - MUMBAI

Open Text Metastorm ProVision® 6.2
Strategy Implementation

First published: March 2011

Production Reference: 1150311

Published by Packt Publishing Ltd.
32 Lincoln Road
Olton
Birmingham, B27 6PA, UK.

ISBN 978-1-849682-52-7

www.packtpub.com

Cover Image by Artie Ng (artherng@yahoo.com.au)

Credits

Author
Bill Aronson

Reviewers
Tom Foster

Ted Lefkovitz

Acquisition Editor
Stephanie Moss

Development Editor
Alina Lewis

Technical Editor
Gaurav Datar

Indexer
Rekha Nair

Editorial Team Leader
Vinodhan Nair

Project Team Leader
Lata Basantani

Project Coordinator
Leena Purkait

Proofreader
Kelly Hutchinson

Graphics
Geetanjali Sawant

Production Coordinator
Alwin Roy

Cover Work
Alwin Roy

Foreword

Look around you. Everything that is made has been designed, with one exception: we don't design the very organizations that make the things you see, hear, feel, touch and taste. This is a very curious omission.

Now all this is changing. Visionary organizations have started to do just that – they are designing their companies, with amazing results. One of the tools used to do this is made by the company that I work for, and is called Open Text ProVision®. It's a complete platform for designing and modeling any business. Just as a new design of a building or jet is modeled inside a wind tunnel and simulated on a computer, so you too can now re-design a business and understand and foresee many of the impacts those designs have before the changes ever see the light of day. We are very proud of what we have achieved.

This book's purpose is to enable you to explain the benefits and give you a road map of how you might implement a well designed business. The author draws on the experience of existing users around the world to help you get the very best from the tool, understand some of the challenges you might face, and how to overcome them.

I recommend this book to all current and intending users of the toolset.

Ken Goerg
Open Text Inc.
Director, EA Product Management

Every organization is designed. However, most are designed unconsciously. It is beliefs which shape the way the business appears to the world.

"This is the right way to do things", perhaps?

"We have always done it like this", probably not.

Beliefs are necessary. They serve an important purpose and they add tremendous value. When an organization knows its beliefs, it can get on with the job confidently. However, the world is changing rapidly. From time to time we need to examine our beliefs and see if they need replacing or updating.

I am an enterprise designer based in the US. Enterprise design gives me a framework and methodology for classifying important business information. Then I use ProVision® to model organizations. The challenge I find is, not so much how to use the tool, but how to get everyone on the same page. This is what this book is all about. It's the first book ever published on ProVision® that focuses on how to design a strategy and get it implemented.

Using this book you will be able to design a "conscious" organization and get everyone involved. You will be able to hold company beliefs up to the light of day and see if they continue to serve the purpose for which they were intended.

Tom Foster
Owner, Business Views LLC

Good managers have four core capabilities. They consult, train, mentor and facilitate. Great managers have five: they coach their team. Once you add coaching to your kit bag of skills, you cross an invisible line and become a leader. Leaders coach and manage the team's energy, and hold the corporate vision.

ProVision® lets you visualize your business and ensure that everything you do aligns to that vision. It's an enabler. This book will fast track your ability to get the most from it, and I highly recommend it.

Andrew Mackenzie
CEO, Shirlaws Australia
www.shirlaws.com.au

My passion is designing businesses from the customer's point of view. I call this "outside-in". Inside the gates everyone has their own introspective view of the world. It is hard to see the organization the way the client does. We forget that processes start way before we know anything about them.

This book is a great contribution to changing that blinkered thinking. The author provides the Chief Information Architect with a blueprint for designing an organization that is truly customer centric.

Ray Brown
Founder, www.ClienteerHub.com

Business is emotional and rational, both an organism and mechanical. We cannot design an organization the same way that we design a car. Forget about the metaphors of engineering and architecture; a business is a community of people with dreams and hopes. Every one of us wants to live, to love, to learn and leave a legacy. We will only engage in our workplace if we care, and this engagement is a conversation around creating new meaning, not solving old problems.

When we care, we see new possibilities and opportunities, and we co -create a shared future together. The most successful organizations on the planet are those that are designed with this in mind and they are constructed to engage the critical emotional connections in organizations to continuously create a better world.

This book breaks new ground. It shows you how to design a business that will find and engage the critical connections in your organization to move beyond the "red ocean" of survival and into the "blue ocean" space of abundance and meaning.

Jeremy Scrivens
Founder, TheEmotionalEconomy.com

About the Author

Bill Aronson is a business coach with global coaching firm Shirlaws (`www.Shirlaws.com.au`). He lives with his wife and daughter in Tasmania, Australia, one of the most beautiful places on earth. His job is to help businesses gain clarity. He helps them increase revenue, get more time, and reduce stress.

Bill has been coaching, mentoring, training, and teaching for more than 35 years. Using modern technology, he works remotely with clients around the world.

Bill is recognized as a global expert on ProVision® and has written a number of technical books for users that have been published by `www.Lulu.com`.

Bill is the founder of `www.EnterpriseDesigner.com`, whose mission is to show organizations how to design their businesses to make better decisions now.

Bill is also the author of `www.TurningUpForLife.com`, his contribution to making the planet a little bit of a better place to live.

A number of people have contributed to the success of this book. First, I wish to thank all of the people who generously shared their wit and wisdom. Some cannot be named for reasons of confidentiality. Those who can, include Jeremy Scrivens of `www.TheEmotionalEconomy.com`, Gordon Lescinsky of `www.Ioctane.com`, and Ray Brown of `www.ClienteerHub.com`.

Next, I have been fortunate to have had a whole editorial team supporting me this time. My thanks to Stephanie Moss, Leena Purkait, Alina Lewis, and the unsung heroes at Packt Publishing. My thanks also to Tom Foster and Ted Lefkovitz, who took on the noble and thankless task of proofreading, and suggested many ideas for improvement.

I wish to acknowledge Darren Shirlaw for creating one of the best strategic thinking frameworks available, and for making an important contribution to the discipline of coaching.

As always thanks to Bob Farrell, Ken Goerg, Neil Hudspeth, Mike Cawsey, and all the people at Open Text Metastorm.

My special thanks to my wife Catherine and daughter Zoe, whom I love dearly. It's not easy living with a writer.

Finally, to you dear reader. I do hope you find this book valuable. If you do, then please contact me at `baronson@shirlaws.com.au` and start a conversation.

About the Reviewers

Tom Foster is a business consultant and managing member of Business Views LLC. He has extensive experience assisting customer organizations with business strategy, business requirements, process improvement, and end-user business readiness. He has provided services to the mortgage and commercial banking industries, as well as numerous public sector clients. Tom is an Enterprise Designer with the Enterprise Designer Institute, and is a ProVision® user. Additionally, he is a certified TOGAF 8 practitioner with the Open Group. Tom graduated from the University of Toledo with an MBA degree and a BBA degree in Finance.

Ted Lefkovitz uses his experience with some of the leading enterprise architecture and business process frameworks and modeling tools, in order to provide vendor-independent consulting and mentoring services. He is skilled in the definition of business rules, vocabularies, and taxonomies, and is capable of integrating a wide range of methodologies to design business improvement solutions that deliver bottom-line results.

Ted has served clients in a variety of industries in the US, the UK, and Canada including GM, GE, HP, Shell, JP Morgan Chase, ING, E*Trade, Ameritrade, Delta Air Lines, BellSouth, Export Development Canada, and many others. He keeps current with industry thought leadership and innovations through communities of practice such as Enterprise Designer, ARIS North America User Group, BPMN, and Rules World. As an early practitioner of object-oriented technology, Ted was a member of the Object Management Group (OMG) representing Coopers & Lybrand, and participated in the research captured in the book *Patterns for Effective Use Cases* (Addison Wesley, 2002).

Ted holds an undergraduate degree in Computer Science and an MBA with Organizational Design concentration from York University in Toronto. He currently lives in Atlanta and can be reached at tlefkovitz@gmail.com.

www.PacktPub.com

Support files, eBooks, discount offers and more

You might want to visit www.PacktPub.com for support files and downloads related to your book.

Did you know that Packt offers eBook versions of every book published, with PDF and ePub files available? You can upgrade to the eBook version at www.PacktPub.com and as a print book customer, you are entitled to a discount on the eBook copy. Get in touch with us at service@packtpub.com for more details.

At www.PacktPub.com, you can also read a collection of free technical articles, sign up for a range of free newsletters and receive exclusive discounts and offers on Packt books and eBooks.

![PACKT]

http://PacktLib.PacktPub.com

Do you need instant solutions to your IT questions? PacktLib is Packt's online digital book library. Here, you can access, read and search across Packt's entire library of books.

Why Subscribe?

- Fully searchable across every book published by Packt
- Copy & paste, print and bookmark content
- On demand and accessible via web browser

Free Access for Packt account holders

If you have an account with Packt at www.PacktPub.com, you can use this to access PacktLib today and view nine entirely free books. Simply use your login credentials for immediate access.

Instant Updates on New Packt Books

Get notified! Find out when new books are published by following @PacktEnterprise on Twitter, or the Packt Enterprise Facebook page.

Table of Contents

Preface

I had a conversation the other day with the head of IT in a globally known organization. He was trying to justify the expense of buying ProVision®. He told me that the IT department really understood the point of it, but people in the business side were lukewarm. He asked me whether he should hold off buying the software until the business was supportive, or get started and wait for them to catch up. I told him that if he started without their support they would never catch up. If he waited for them to catch up he would be waiting for ever.

Then there was a third option.

I asked him, "What's the biggest issue in the business right now?" He said, "We never have enough time."

So then I asked him, "How long does it take to make a major decision?" He paused for a moment. "I suppose it takes at least six months, sometimes longer."

So then I said, "If there was a way to make the same decision in six weeks, perhaps even a better decision, how would that feel." His eyes lit up. "Oh, that would be fantastic. People get so frustrated by how long it takes to get decisions made. It would be wonderful."

So then I said, "What would you get if all the decisions you made took less than six weeks, rather than more than six months?" He thought about it awhile. I could see he was struggling. "I'm not sure what you mean", he said eventually.

"Well", I said, "You just told me that the biggest issue around here is the lack of time. What do you get more of if decisions take six weeks or less?" He smiled. "We would get more time."

We grinned at each other, "Exactly", I said. "The reason you don't have any time is that the decision-making process is sucking all the oxygen. So, how can you accelerate the decision-making process? First you have to give up the belief that a slow decision is a good decision and a fast decision is necessarily a bad one. It has nothing to do with speed. So let's examine why the decision making process is so slow."

"We are very concerned about our reputation. We want to do everything of the highest quality. We usually take years to plan some of the things that we do. There are a lot of people to consult."

"I am guessing. So you arrange a meeting and then it gets cancelled because a key person can't be there?"

"Oh yes, that happens all the time. And when a meeting gets cancelled it can take a month or two before everyone's diaries are free."

"When you make a decision, you need to have a shared understanding of what it is that you want to do. That is what all those meetings are about, trying to ensure that everyone is on the same page. To do this you construct models. The thing is that the models that you make are inside your head.

There are a few problems with this. Nobody can see your models. They are invisible to the world and as you get new information you change the models at a moment's notice and nobody will know.

When you are examining the models you may forget details or you may be distracted. As a result your models are incomplete and distorted.

In a large and complex organization you can't understand everything. You have your own unique perspective. So, even if you are operating at your best, your models are incomplete and inaccurate.

If you go on leave, or are away for some reason, then nobody has access to your models. If you quit the organization, the models walk out the door inside your head. Your successor has to start all over again constructing their models. While they may be able to recover the information they may never get the same insights. The process takes months, sometimes years. You don't have a choice about whether to make models or not. You have to use models to make decisions. There is no other way. Your only choice is whether you make those models visible or invisible, shared or individual.

What you call a meeting is a group of people sitting around trying to synchronize their mental models. Until this is done you can't begin to make a decision. What happens is that politics and psychology come into play. It is human nature. I try and persuade you that my mental model is better than yours. You get offended. You then try and coerce me to accept your model. And so it goes on. The whole human soap opera continues and in the meanwhile the decision gets delayed.

Now if you take all the key information and put it into a centrally-managed model, the game changes. Vital information that was scattered now becomes accessible. It doesn't replace mental models. However, everyone is responsible for synchronizing their mental models to the common shared model. When a decision needs to be made you print out the relevant models for everyone to see and discuss. If someone can't be there then it doesn't matter because their knowledge is embedded in the central model. If they want to attend the meeting but are away then they can participate remotely.

The trick is not to overload the central model. You need to put just enough information in to enable a better decision to be made than would have happened otherwise. The more information you add, the more you have to maintain. Too little, and the information is insufficient. Too much, and the information is too hard to manage and interpret."

He paused for a moment. This was a lot to take in.

Eventually he said, "So what you are saying is that I need to demonstrate that ProVision® can be used to save time. We need to treat the decision-making process like any other. We make a model of how it runs right now and then show how we can simplify and improve it."

"Yes."

"If the business sees the tool as some kind of technical thing then they will never show any interest. If they see it as part of a strategy to make better decisions now then they will see the point."

"That's about the size of it."

"So, how do you build the model?"

"That's up to you. If you use the Enterprise Designer framework, it can be done in two weeks."

"Are you serious?"

"Yes."

"Only two weeks?"

"Yes. After that you add detail one project at a time. When you do a project you have to spend time thinking up front anyway. It doesn't take any more effort to put it into the central repository. In fact it takes less."

[This conversation is reprinted from *Turning up for Life – the lost manuscript* by Bill Aronson.]

About this book

This book is a practical guide for architects and CIOs working in large organizations, who want to get the most from ProVision®. It covers all the relevant broad areas— designing a strategy, creating a business case, using a framework, adopting a methodology, implementing effective governance, understanding the toolset, and obtaining buy-in. Taken together, these areas provide a comprehensive strategy to deploy ProVision® successfully.

What this book covers

Chapter 1, Designing a Strategy, will show you a five-layer strategy framework. This framework has been developed by global business coaching company Shirlaws `www.shirlaws.com.au`. It can be applied to any business issue that you want to understand in greater detail.

Chapter 2, Making a Business Case, explains some general principles of modeling, and the key benefits of using the ProVision® modeling solution specifically.

This chapter explains the limitations of drawing, and why modeling is not only a best practice and essential to support a sustainable strategy, but also has a lower TCO (total cost of ownership). The reader can use this information to make their business case compelling and get the funds that they need to do the job properly.

Chapter 3, Using a Framework, explains what a business framework is. A business framework is not an enterprise architecture framework. The original idea of enterprise architecture was exactly that—to capture all of the information about the whole enterprise. However this has proven to be too hard for most businesses. A business framework is the highest level framework that provides a context for all other frameworks. It describes the organization's primary goals, who are the customers, what are the products and services, what are the key processes and major elements. ProVision® is designed to support industry standard enterprise architecture and business frameworks. The user can modify a framework or create their own. To do this they need to understand the key components of any framework and why it has been developed.

Chapter 4, Adopting a Methodology, shows you how to build a business framework. What parts of the organization must be modeled. What is the correct sequence? To what level of detail should the modeler go? There has to be a trade-off between too much detail and too little. This chapter proposes a sequence in which to build models and helps you define to what level of detail you need to go.

Chapter 5, Implementing Effective Governance, describes how to design a governance structure that will support the creation and maintenance of modeling. Too often modeling is seen as a technical function and is conducted in a vacuum. Getting the governance right is a key to successful strategy. By ensuring that all key stakeholders are involved, the models will reflect the higher needs of the business.

Chapter 6, Understanding the Toolset, provides a high-level view of the features and functionality of ProVision®. The purpose is to provide information that can be used to introduce the tool to modelers and explain what it can be used for. As this is not a technical book, this chapter is designed to explain to the people developing the strategy what the tool is capable of so that they have realistic expectations.

Chapter 7, Obtaining Buy-in, reminds us that business is emotional. The purpose of this chapter is to reinforce the message that a successful strategy depends on the buy-in of people across the whole organization. We will explore techniques that win hearts and minds, and ensure alignment between the commercial and cultural aspects of the business.

The *appendix, References,* contains website references where you may find more information.

Conclusion

So often an organization invests in a modeling tool for a specific project and then, when the project is complete, the team disperses and the tool gets forgotten. When a new project starts the team may favor another tool. Very quickly the work done on the previous project becomes out of date and impossible to integrate into the current initiative.

This is not because of any technical reason, as most tools have comprehensive import and export features. It is because the organization does not have a common strategy, a common framework for managing information, a consistent methodology for gathering information, and a governance structure that manages and motivates users.

By the end of this book you will have a simple and effective way to do things differently.

What you need for this book

Much of this book is intended to help you with your strategy. So, if you just wish to get a high-level understanding, a copy of the software is not strictly essential. If you intend to delve a little deeper, you will need a current Microsoft Windows platform with ProVision® Enterprise Edition 6.2 or later. Most modern computers will have sufficient memory and speed to run the application. If your organization has Knowledge Exchange® 6.2, that is a bonus but not essential to get value from the book. It is also useful to have Microsoft Excel.

Who this book is for

If you are a business architect or CIO in a large organization who wants to implement a successful strategy using ProVision®, then this book is for you. It will also be of interest if you are an enterprise designer or architect. It might be that you already have working knowledge of ProVision®, but do not yet have the skill to implement it in the right context; this book will help you get there.

Conventions

In this book, you will find a number of styles of text that distinguish between different kinds of information. Here are some examples of these styles, and an explanation of their meaning.

New terms and **important words** are shown in bold. Words that you see on the screen, in menus or dialog boxes for example, appear in the text like this: "In the following example screenshot, the business class **Medical Plan** is an integral part of the **Benefit Plan** package:"

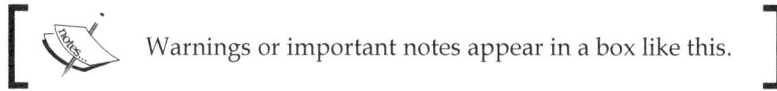

> Warnings or important notes appear in a box like this.

> Tips and tricks appear like this.

Reader feedback

Feedback from our readers is always welcome. Let us know what you think about this book—what you liked or may have disliked. Reader feedback is important for us to develop titles that you really get the most out of.

To send us general feedback, simply send an e-mail to feedback@packtpub.com, and mention the book title via the subject of your message.

If there is a book that you need and would like to see us publish, please send us a note in the **SUGGEST A TITLE** form on www.packtpub.com or e-mail suggest@packtpub.com.

If there is a topic that you have expertise in and you are interested in either writing or contributing to a book, see our author guide on www.packtpub.com/authors.

Customer support

Now that you are the proud owner of a Packt book, we have a number of things to help you to get the most from your purchase.

Errata

Although we have taken every care to ensure the accuracy of our content, mistakes do happen. If you find a mistake in one of our books—maybe a mistake in the text or the code—we would be grateful if you would report this to us. By doing so, you can save other readers from frustration and help us improve subsequent versions of this book. If you find any errata, please report them by visiting http://www.packtpub.com/support, selecting your book, clicking on the errata submission form link, and entering the details of your errata. Once your errata are verified, your submission will be accepted and the errata will be uploaded on our website, or added to any list of existing errata, under the Errata section of that title. Any existing errata can be viewed by selecting your title from http://www.packtpub.com/support.

Piracy

Piracy of copyright material on the Internet is an ongoing problem across all media. At Packt, we take the protection of our copyright and licenses very seriously. If you come across any illegal copies of our works, in any form, on the Internet, please provide us with the location address or website name immediately so that we can pursue a remedy.

Please contact us at copyright@packtpub.com with a link to the suspected pirated material.

We appreciate your help in protecting our authors, and our ability to bring you valuable content.

Questions

You can contact us at questions@packtpub.com if you are having a problem with any aspect of the book, and we will do our best to address it.

1
Designing a Strategy

Where do we start to build a strategy? Let's start with a working definition. A strategy is a plan to achieve a goal. Every situation may require different strategies and different plans. However, it is possible to apply a consistent way to design a strategy. The benefit of doing so is that everyone involved learns a consistent language.

In this first chapter I will show you a five-layer strategy framework, developed by global business coaching company Shirlaws (www.shirlaws.com.au). It can be applied to any business issue that you want to understand in greater detail. The five levels are:

- **Context**: What is the context for deploying ProVision® in your organization?
- **Strategy**: How will you develop a fully documented strategy for the deployment?
- **Implementation**: How will you implement the first deployment across the business?
- **Next Phase**: How will you mentor and pre-plan the next phase?
- **Leverage**: How will you leverage what you have learned across the organization?

Typically, organizations do not pay sufficient attention to the second level and jump straight from Level 1 (context) to Level 3 (implementation). Level 2 (strategy) requires the organization to slow down in order to speed up. As a result, they do not get the full benefits and are unable to leverage.

Why choose ProVision®

Before we examine the context level in detail, here is a quick summary of why organizations select ProVision®. You can read more about the application in *Chapter 6, Understanding the Toolset*.

The world is changing faster. Anecdotal evidence indicates that a key aspect of your environment will change every quarter. Within the business it might be a new product line, a new service offering, a change in a process or the departure of a key manager. Outside of the business it might be the entry of a new competitor, the release of disruptive technology or a change in legislation. Whatever it might be, it will impact your work and the ability to do your job. The environment in which you operate is not stable.

The larger or more diverse your organization is, the greater these changes will impact you. To know what to do, and how to respond, you need to know more. Some observers argue that the rate of change is increasing exponentially. Therefore the situation is not going to get any better.

How do we gather this information? We talk, we browse, we research, we request, we listen. From numerous sources, a picture forms. Our co-workers do the same. We compare notes, we gossip, we text, we e-mail, we meet, we argue, and we fight. A rough consensus emerges — very rough. If we are honest, we will see that the picture is not complete, accurate or current. It is a mental model. It resides inside our heads. Our memory plays tricks. We forget and we distort. So does everyone else.

Important information is written down in reports, memos, websites, minutes, proposals, manuals, e-mails, and numerous forms. Not everyone knows how to write. Not everyone knows how to read. Workplaces employ people from various cultures where English is not always their first language. Even if it were, English is a pastiche, with layer upon layer of meaning laid down over centuries, like bark rings.

Creating pictures and diagrams is a good way to supplement the written word. Pictures offer an alternative way to grasp a hierarchy, process or workflow. Pictures are a universal language.

However, as the rate of change increases exponentially, we need a way to manage and maintain pictures easily. The same object might need to appear on multiple diagrams. How will we remember where they all are? How will we update them all?

This is the problem that ProVision® solves.

- It is a visual relational database.
- An object can be created once and used in multiple places.
- Any changes made to one instance of the object instantly update all others.

- Where several people are creating models, they can share them without overwriting each others' work.

- ProVision® can import and export information to other sources. It can reference information stored in documents, websites, and the intranet.

- It is a tool that will help you visualize and understand your business. Using it, you can collaborate with others to make better decisions now.

One could argue that these points apply equally to other modeling suites. The key differences that separate ProVision® from the rest of the pack are:

- **Ease of use**
- **Scalability**
- **Breadth of use**

ProVision® is a product aimed at the top of the market, designed to manage thousands of objects, used by many different modelers. It has been used in numerous industries across the world. This means that local support is likely to be available. You will probably be able to find people with relevant experience and expertise to help you on your journey. Because it is relatively easy to use, organizations can get started
fairly easily.

Personal context

One might argue that the *context* of any set of actions is more significant than the *content*. Our day to day experience is content-based and so we tend to be unaware of the context of our actions. If the context is not articulated, then different people will have different contexts. When this happens, we perceive others as having hidden agendas. Our own context seems obvious to us, and we assume that it must be obvious to others.

Context simply means *why*? Why are you contemplating ProVision® or implementing it? It is a piece of software, albeit a very flexible one. It is easy to make the mistake that the tool itself will provide you with a strategy for its implementation. In fact, context precedes strategy and strategy precedes implementation. That is why this chapter does not provide any details of ProVision's features and functionality. There are three key contexts that affect how you approach ProVision®—**time**, **responsibility**, and **scope**.

Time

A lifecycle is characterized by three states—past, present, and future. Where are you in the lifecycle? What is your knowledge and experience?

- You are thinking of using ProVision® (future user)
- You already are using it and want to make better use of it (present user)
- You used it and are no longer doing so (past user)

Each of these user groups has a different context. The *future* users have a vision and perhaps little or no experience. Their expectations may not match what is realistic. Their vision is an idealized view of what the tool offers. The present users have experience and thus their expectations are different. They are better able to distinguish between the promise and the performance. The *past* users will have formed an opinion or judgment, either positive or negative. If they believed that the tool was a panacea, then they may have a jaundiced view.

Responsibility

The second context concerns your position within the company. In order for you to implement ProVision® effectively you need three things to be a part of your job description:

- Responsibility for implementation
- Accountability for implementation
- Authority to implement

In my view, the true meaning of responsibility includes accountability and authority. Let's clarify what we mean by these in more detail. This doesn't just apply to implementing ProVision® of course. It applies to all work. If you understand the distinction then you will dramatically improve your ability to do your job. If you educate others within your business then you will dramatically improve the effectiveness of your organization.

Responsibility means that it is part of your job description to make this piece of work happen. Responsibility doesn't mean that you do the work, although you might. Responsibility means that you are the one who is ultimately meant to make it happen. Can you delegate responsibility? Yes.

What happens when you delegate responsibility? Does that mean that if something goes wrong then you can blame the person to whom you delegated? No. Let's see why not.

If you have responsibility for a piece of work it means that you are also accountable. Simply put, accountability means that there is a clear and objective test as to whether the piece of work has been done. By designing this test before the work is undertaken you can review whether it was done to the appropriate standard. What happens when you delegate responsibility for a piece of work? The delegate is now accountable. However, the accountability has not been passed from one person to the other. Rather, a new accountability has come into existence. You have created it out of nothing. You are 100% accountable, they are also 100% accountable.

The alternative approach doesn't work. How can you say that you are 20% accountable and that the delegate is 80%? These divisions are meaningless. You can no more be 20% accountable than you can be 20% pregnant. While responsibility can be delegated, accountability cannot. The blame game can only happen when accountability is split.

Finally, authority means that you are able to do what you think is the best thing to do in order to get the work done. You have the funds, the people, the equipment and the decision making ability. You can make it happen. Your level of authority has to match both your level of responsibility and accountability. If, at one extreme, you have authority that is greater than your accountability then you are a dictator. If, at the other extreme, you have insufficient authority then you are a helpless victim.

Well run companies ensure that everyone's roles clearly define responsibility, accountability and authority. Great managers make it their business to ensure that these are well understood. Great salesmen discover quickly if they are talking to a person who has responsibility, accountability and authority. If not, they know they are wasting their time, trying to sell to someone who will never be in a position to buy.

So ask yourself these three questions:

- Am I *responsible*, or have I been delegated to, implement ProVision®?
- Am I *accountable* to implement ProVision® successfully?
- Do I have sufficient *authority* to implement ProVision®?

If the answer is no to any of these three questions, then the only way that you will succeed is by pure luck. Many organizations delegate responsibility for a piece of work but do not give the delegate the authority that they need. If you are the manager and are not prepared to give the delegate the authority that they need, then it is better that you do the job yourself. Of course that then begs the questions why you don't trust them? You are meant to be a manager, right?

When you take responsibility at a *context* level, your focus is on how you can empower others around you to become responsible. You understand that responsibility simply means being 'able to respond'. If you talk to someone who is taking context-based responsibility, key words to listen out for are enjoyment, easy, excitement and play.

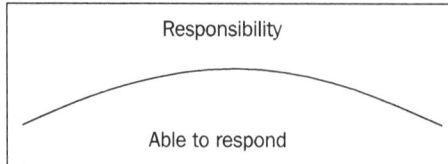

When you take responsibility at a *content* level, your focus is on how you can do everything yourself. You equate responsibility with having to do everything, so it becomes a burden. If you talk to someone who is taking content based responsibility, key words to listen out for are serious, duty, obligation, and work.

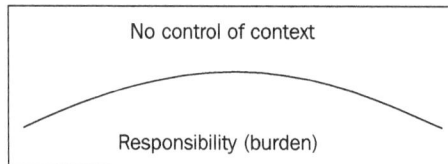

Often, it is hard to tell the context that you are operating under as it is often unconscious. A simple way to discover your context is to look around you. The way that people work with you correlates exactly to your context. If you are the only one who is being held responsible, and you work in an organization that has a blame culture, that is what you have created. If you transform your context, then everyone around you will start to transform theirs as well.

Scope

There are two types of scope that are relevant here. You might be running a specific project and think that ProVision® will be useful. Alternatively, you are responsible for managing all of the corporate knowledge of itself. Let's examine each scope.

Project scope

In this scenario, you are only responsible for a specific project and select ProVision® because you can see that it would make sense, from the whole of the organization's point of view. However you don't have the mandate to implement a central repository so you are trying to influence outside of your area of authority. This **bottom up** approach may or may not be successful. There are numerous examples of users pushing an organization in a direction that they didn't think of or plan for. Many organizations did not have a conscious strategy to implement Microsoft SharePoint. Users found it easy to do and they didn't have to wait for the IT department to build them a website. Suddenly the IT department found that there were numerous SharePoint sites that had been built under the radar.

The probability is that this approach will not work when implementing ProVision®. The key quality of bottom up is that it is frictionless. The change has to be so easy and smooth that it spreads like a virus. ProVision® requires training and a change of mindset.

So take the time to engage the people who are responsible for the enterprise. Get their agreement that your project will be the first phase of implementing an enterprise-wide strategy.

Enterprise scope

You are responsible for implementing a central repository and have selected, or are considering, ProVision® to do the job.

You have the opposite challenge from the person responsible running a project. How will you get users to put information into the central repository? How will you get them to change their behavior? How will you get them to see that it is worth having a central repository?

Fortunately, the solution is the same. The best way to build a central repository is one project at a time. Every project has to take time upfront to think, plan, and decide. The first project that is used to populate the central repository may take slightly longer than normal. However, as each project follows, the process gets faster and faster. More and more information that the project team will need access to, will be found in the central repository left there by the previous project team. It may need some updating but it is far easier to update information than to start from scratch.

Business context

We have described three contexts that apply to you personally. In addition to you as an individual, the business will have its own context. This will probably be different to yours. You may have been selected to be responsible because of prior experience and expertise. Your understanding may even be far ahead of the rest of the organization.

The business may not have an understanding that ProVision® is an enterprise tool. Its success is dependent on an enterprise-wide implementation strategy. The strategy comes first. The tool is not a panacea. Does the business understand that its most valuable asset, perhaps, is its knowledge of itself?

Let me provide a metaphor. You want to build a picket fence and have not done so before. You are buying tools and are thinking a lot about whether to get a nail gun or just use a hammer you already own. You think so much about this issue that you come to believe that the success of the project depends on buying the nail gun. The nail gun is a good tool and will make the job easier. However if you don't know what type of wood to use, how deep to dig the holes for your posts, or how far apart they should be spaced, having a nail gun is not going to result in the best outcome.

When selecting a modeling 'nail gun', large organizations often send out detailed questionnaires to vendors. Can it do this? Can it do that? Is it compliant with this standard? Can it export in XML? Does it comply with **TOGAF**? Can I customize the application?

They assemble all the answers and then pick the tool that they can afford which gets the most ticks.

They then look at Gartner and Forrester, and gather reports on the vendors. ProVision® is consistently a leader in these reports. However the information is of limited value. The research organizations test products in the lab not in the real world. The people who test have only a limited amount of time to conduct their review.

This process is an essential prerequisite and yet more is required to lead to the best outcome. The success of enterprise modeling is not just about features and functionality. ProVision® is a good enterprise solution. There are other products which have similar features and functionality. Success occurs when you understand your context and create the appropriate strategy.

Recommendation

- Before developing a strategy, first document your personal and business context for implementing ProVision®.

- Get agreement on the context with all the key stakeholders. It is our view that the context in which success is most likely is one in which ProVision® is recognized as a tool for modeling the *whole* enterprise. This means that there has to be a commitment by senior business managers to create a central repository. Individual projects can then be used to populate the central repository, so that it gets built one project at a time.

Context is the big picture. The context document should only be one or two pages long and written in plain English. Here is an example of what it might look like:

Our organization operates in a complex world in which the rate of change is increasing. It is no longer possible for any one person to have a complete understanding of our business. Different parts of the business have developed their own specialized languages. Sometimes the same word means different things to different people. The word 'service' does not mean the same thing when used by a programmer as when used by a customer. While these special languages are essential, it makes it harder to have a shared understanding of who we are, where we are going and how we will get there, or simply communicate with each other and with our customers.

When people leave the business they take knowledge with them. As a result of all of these issues, decisions can be made without understanding the implications for other parts of the business. At the same time, it is simply not possible to document every piece of knowledge, so a balance must be struck. Therefore the business context for creating a central repository of knowledge about our business is that we want to make better decisions now.

We accept that better is more realistic than perfect. We will populate the central repository with just the information that is needed to make key business decisions. We will ensure that the information is current so that the decisions we need to make now are informed by the central repository.

In crafting this document, the language that you use will have a big impact. For example, we try not to use the word *architecture*. When you use the word architecture it conjures up images of buildings. This reflects the origins of enterprise architecture which examined how complex buildings and airplanes are maintained over many years. A jumbo jet might be in service for fifty years. During that time many parts will need to be replaced. The technology will change. The replacement part must fit precisely. The high level context of air travel is safety. How do you keep track of a million parts over fifty years?

Organizations are not buildings. They are people in conversation. Employees are not *resources* but people with lives outside of the business. As soon as you use the term *architecture* you are creating a mechanistic view of a business. Recent research by Gartner shows that emotional engagement is four times more important than rational engagement. By measuring how valued an employee feels by their line manager, you can predict accurately how long they will stay with the company. Lack of emotional engagement costs money. Most employees would prefer to be praised than get a pay rise.

In the first decade of the 21st century we saw the convergence of maps and data. Who can imagine not using Google Maps now? Over the next decade, we will see the emergence of tools that add an emotional layer to datasets. In ten years time, we will not just model how a process runs, we will visualize how stakeholders feel. We will redesign processes not to make them more logical and efficient, but to make them more enjoyable.

Strategy

Organizations, even ones that have been in existence for decades, sometimes argue that they are not mature enough to take a particular course.

The Capability Maturity Model describes the maturity of organizational processes. Five levels of maturity are defined starting at the initial or chaotic, repeatable, defined, managed, and optimized: `http://en.wikipedia.org/wiki/Capability_Maturity_Model`.

This is very curious. I don't know any individual who runs a company who publicly acknowledges that they are not mature enough to do their job. How is it that an organization that is run by mature individuals can argue that it is immature? If it really is immature, why is this said with a shrug? Surely the recognition of immaturity should be treated as a major crisis!

This issue around immaturity is now being addressed by business coaching. Coaching provides an organization with a common language and set of frameworks. It enables an organization to reflect on the causes of the immaturity and discover ways to transform them.

Once an organization has agreed a context, it is very tempting to jump straight into implementation. By taking the time to craft a strategy, the implementation phase will go more smoothly. It does mean that you have to slow down to speed up, and this can feel frustrating. We know what the problem is. Why not just jump in and fix things along the way?

Context answers the *why* question. Strategy answers the *what* question: what are we going to do differently? Implementation answers the *how* question.

In the remainder of this book, we will describe the key aspects of the strategy in more detail. The strategy document can be divided into sections in accordance with the key aspects of the strategy, namely:

- Making a business case
- Using a Framework
- Adopting a Methodology
- Implementing effective Governance
- Understanding the Toolset

Here is an example of what a strategy overview might look like:

The business case

ABC Co. has three wholesale divisions that sell electricity, gas and telecommunications. The telecommunications and gas businesses were acquired. Currently the organization has difficulties in responding to customers because each division is a silo. Customer information is not centrally available and we are not able to cross-sell effectively. In effect we are three separate companies.

The framework and methodology

This project will create a central repository of information about the organization in order to understand who we are today and how we can become one company. The Board has selected the Enterprise Designer framework and methodology to capture the key information. Population of the central repository will be done one project at a time. All major projects will contribute to, and extract information from, the central repository.

The toolset

ProVision® is the tool that will be used to capture, maintain and present the information. This toolset has been selected as it is capable of capturing all the key information about the organization relatively quickly. As we gain greater expertise, we can add ProVision's server-based repository, Knowledge Exchange®, to enable greater communication and collaboration. We can also bring the models into Metastorm Open Text Business Process Execution. This will allow us to describe a process in ProVision® and then track individual process instances in real time.

Governance

The Program Management Office that reports directly to the Board will have overall responsibility, accountability and authority for this initiative. The Board has appointed global business coaching company Shirlaws to advise them on implementation strategy.

Implementation

Once the strategy is agreed, the Program Management Office, or equivalent, can determine the sequence of projects that will be used to populate the central repository. A typical project should take no more than three months from start to finish. The initial project will be to gather core information that will be required by all subsequent projects. In the Enterprise Designer framework this core information is defined as:

- Who are the Customers?
- What are the Products and Services we provide to them?
- What are the Critical Processes required to produce these Products and Services?
- What are the Critical Elements that drive the Critical Processes?
- What are the Key Goals of the Organization?

Lists

As you can see, these are all **lists** of components and they are normally arranged into **hierarchies**.

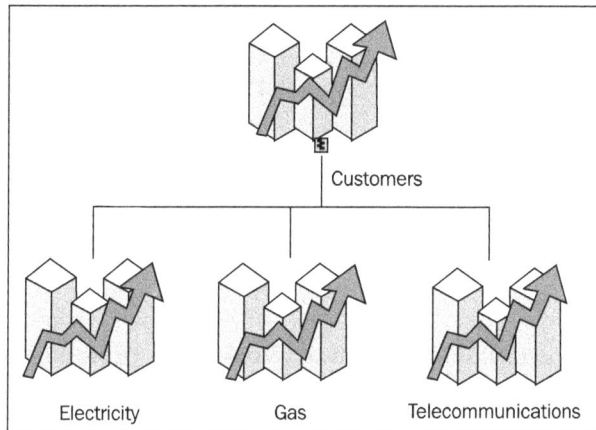

In the example above, we see that a type of ProVision® object called a market has been used to describe three major customer groupings: Electricity, Gas and Telecommunications. These major groupings can decompose down further into sub-customer groupings as required. As we create a model and add objects to it, ProVision® updates the object inventory. There is no need to add objects to the object inventory first. We can create them 'on the fly'.

ProVision® provides a toolkit of common objects, such as markets, organizations, processes, elements and goals, out of the box. If necessary, you can create custom objects to extend the standard set or you can rename objects to match your corporate language. For example, in the Enterprise Designer modeling language, we have re-named the *Business Domain* object and called it *Product*.

So, before you begin to create more complex models, you need to create lists of the objects that might be required in many different situations.

Building your lists

There are several issues around building lists:

* Who is responsible for initially gathering the information?
* How do you name objects?
* Who ensures that the object is maintained?
* Where is the object stored?

- What is the publishing process?
- How much detail does the object require?
- How do you get the information from another system into ProVision®?
- How do you prevent duplicate objects and what do you do when you find them?

As you can see, building and maintaining a list is not as easy it might seem at first. Besides the technical issues, there are issues around maintenance, governance and standards. Let's look at these issues more closely.

Who is responsible for initially gathering the information

Many organizations start off with a team of two or three professional modelers. Their background is likely to be business analyst, system architect, business architect, or enterprise architect. They will either have a business process or technical background.

Part of their job is to work with subject matter experts who have the best appreciation of what each list should contain. The subject matter experts will not normally learn how to use ProVision®. One approach is for the modeler to have a conversation with the subject matter expert and extract the relevant information. The problem with this approach is that it transfers ownership from the subject matter expert to the modeler. When changes occur, the modeler may not find out.

The alternative approach is for the modeler to create an Excel spreadsheet template and help the subject matter expert populate the information. The benefit of this approach is that the subject matter expert can maintain the list, using Excel, a tool with which they are familiar. The modeler can then import the list to ProVision® on a regular basis, catching any changes.

Because ProVision® stores an object once, any changes will update instantly in all of the models in which the object appears.

How do you name objects

ProVision® does not enforce a naming convention. The organization must define their own and put in place a mechanism by which all users adhere to.

ProVision® offers the option to number objects. These numbers are not part of the object name but appear as if they are. Thus the same object can have different numbers in different models. For example an activity in one model might have the prefix 1.03 in one model and 6.4.1 in another. This can create confusion.

Therefore, we recommend that objects either have no numerical prefix, or the numbers are hard-coded and are part of the object's name. In this way they will appear in a consistent order in any list.

The key point to remember is to treat the number as a unique identifier, not as a sequence number.

The benefit of putting a unique ID at the start of any name is that the text that appears afterwards can change, without it losing its unique character.

For example, imagine that you have an activity object called *Undertake Assessment*. When you look in the object inventory it will appear with other activities that start with the letter 'u'. If you decide to change its name to *Perform Assessment* then it will now appear alongside the activities that start with the letter 'p'. Another modeler, unaware of the name change, may not find it. However if you call the activity *36112 Undertake Assessment*, you can change it to *36112 Perform Assessment* without it changing its position.

The disadvantage of using a numerical prefix is that all objects now appear in numerical order in the object inventory.

We recommend that you have an upfront discussion about the naming convention, document your choice, and ensure that everyone follows the same convention. One compromise that is worth considering is to use number prefixes for all key objects. Individual modelers are not permitted to create new key objects. They can, however, create child objects which do not have a numerical prefix.

Who ensures that the object is maintained

This discussion about naming conventions reveals the need for a role that is responsible for managing the central repository. We need to distinguish between the technical and business aspects of this role. If there is a large team then the role might be split. The technical aspects of the role include:

- Overall responsibility for defining, explaining and ensuring that the naming convention is followed
- Overall responsibility for ensuring that models and objects are kept current
- Overall responsibility for defining and managing the publication of models

Where is the object stored

ProVision® stores information in **repositories**. Within each repository the modeler can create multiple **notebooks**, models and objects are created inside notebooks. A metaphor you might use is that a repository is a bookshelf, a notebook is a book on a shelf, a model is a chapter in the book and an object is a word in the chapter.

In a small team, where there are just one or two modelers, the working repository will be stored on a local drive with appropriate backup strategies in place. A static published version might be stored on the corporate intranet.

However, once you start to have larger teams, the recommended approach is to upgrade ProVision® by adding the server-side component **Knowledge Exchange®**. This enables several different modelers to work together through formal version control procedures. If one person is updating a model, the objects therein are 'checked out' to that person. This prevents other modelers from overwriting changes. Meanwhile, if they need to use the same objects, they can check them out as 'read-only'.

As objects are checked back in, Knowledge Exchange® automatically makes a web version of the current state of the repository. Interested parties can watch the models change over time using Internet Explorer. They can even be given rights to comment on the models and add details, directly from their browser.

Once Knowledge Exchange® is installed it is best to store these lists on the server. The latest version of the application allows the user to store objects remotely on the server and then reference them in the local repository.

What is the publishing process for models

We recommend using a three-step process. In the first step the modeler creates a notebook on their local hard disk and builds models. This notebook will contain models and objects that are not for publication. For example, they may sketch a model and discover it is not useful. Once a model is ready for review it is transferred to the **QA repository**. This is an easy process. If Knowledge Exchange® is not installed the modeler drags the model from one location to the other. If Knowledge Exchange® is installed they check the model into the QA repository and notify the person responsible.

The QA repository administrator reviews the model and determines if it is ready for publication. The stakeholders check the model and either accept it or request changes. Once the model is approved, the QA administrator transfers the model to the Production repository where it is visible to anyone who has been given rights to view it.

The process might look like this:

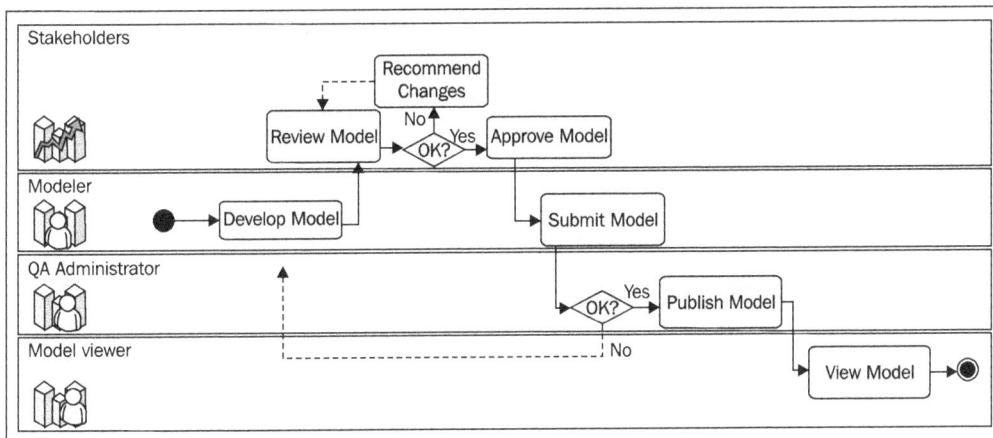

How much detail does the object require

The bare minimum is the name of the object and its type. There is no requirement to add any further information. To keep objects looking clean and simple onscreen, all the detail is stored in hidden tabs, which can be accessed if required. We recommend that all objects that are published include a short description.

How do you move the information from another system to ProVision®

ProVision® supports a number of ways to transfer information and is compliant with standards such as XML. The simplest way to transfer information is to import it from an Excel spreadsheet that has been formatted to comply with the ProVision® data structure. There are a number of wizards which will aid the import process from other products, such as Visio. If these manual and semi-automated methods are not suitable, a developer can create a custom routine which would take information from another system and import/export it automatically. This routine would ensure that the information about the object remains consistent in both places.

It is not always essential to create an object in ProVision®. If the other source is a document or web page, it may be far easier to use the artifact feature. This is essentially a hyperlink. The user clicks the link and it opens up the relevant page. This approach eliminates the need to synchronize the two locations as the external source becomes the master and ProVision® becomes the slave.

Use artifacts to link to manuals, procedures, business rules and similar documents that may be stored on the corporate intranet.

How do you prevent duplicate objects and what do you do when you find them?

If you define a naming convention, and ensure that everyone understands and follows it, you will reduce the chance of duplicate objects. It will still happen. ProVision® treats object names as *case sensitive*. Thus an organization object called *Finance* is not the same object as *finance* or *FINANCE*. Therefore, your naming convention will need to decide on the correct format to try and reduce duplicates. Activity objects should follow a convention such as [Verb] + [optional adjective] + [Noun].

Project management methodology

Good project management methodology suggests that, before the project starts, you define the outputs, the outcomes, and the measures by which you will know if you have completed the work successfully.

Once the project is complete you conduct a post-implementation review to confirm that the work was done properly.

Despite this, many projects do not define the measures and never get round to doing a post-implementation review.

Many people are also confused about the difference between an **output** and an **outcome**. They use the two words interchangeably. Perhaps it is because the words are so similar. The purpose of a project is not to deliver outputs but outcomes. (If the people doing the work don't understand the outcomes, then they will not be able to do the best job possible.) Outputs are tangible 'things'. They are nouns. Outcomes are intangible. They are adjectives that usually end in 'er'. All outcomes, whatever the word used, come down to three key changes: better, faster, and cheaper.

For this first project the outputs that you will deliver are the strategy and a series of hierarchical lists of the key objects.

> The strategy is the documented business case, framework, methodology, and governance structure as discussed earlier.

These outputs are enablers. All that you have done is gathered information, most of which was known already. However, now it is inside ProVision®, and you can use of these standard objects to start building the models that you will use to make 'better decisions now'. Because you have done this preparatory work, the process of building the models will be better (you have lists of all the key objects at your disposal), faster (you can just use them, rather than have to create them from scratch) and cheaper (there will be a significant time saving in doing the second and subsequent projects).

Build sequence

The five key components of a business framework are defined as **customers**, **products** and **service**, **critical processes**, **critical elements**, and **goals**. We recommend that you build the lists in that order.

Customers

Customers come first, without customers you don't have a business. Therefore, you must start by defining who your customers are. There is another important reason. When creating models of your business, try to see what you do from the outside looking in. This is hard because our everyday experience is the opposite. We place our organization at the centre of the universe and our customers on the periphery. The more we can create a relationship with our customers, the greater the level of trust. Focus on the relationship and allow the customer to buy from you rather than sell to them. If you are not going to be building models yourself, but just want to understand the general principles, you can skip over the technical tips.

Use the *market* object to represent classes of customer, and the *organization* object to represent specific organizations with which you do business. Place these objects on an Organization Model, with market objects at the top of the hierarchy and organization objects below. You don't need to represent every single individual customer and if you have many that might be impractical. Focus on general market categories, particularly as individual customers may come and go, thus creating a maintenance headache.

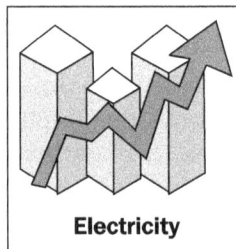

Electricity

Products and services

Products and services come next, because these are the tangible things that cause our customers to come to us in the first place.

> Use the *business domain* object to represent products and the *deliverable* object to represent component parts. Please note that if you use the Enterprise Designer modeling language then business domain is automatically renamed *product* and the deliverable is called *receivable*. Represent products and services in a hierarchy on a Process Model.

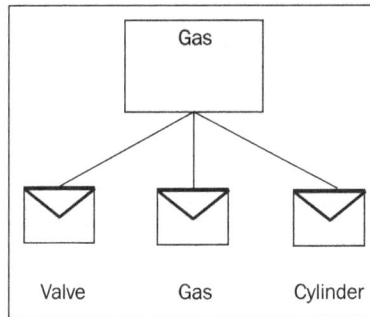

Critical processes

The only way that we can deliver products and services in a consistent way is to put in place processes. Not all processes are critical to maintaining a good relationship with a customer. You may already have a methodology in place that you can use to rank processes. If not, in *Chapter 4, Adopting a Methodology*, we will look at a way to decide which processes are the most important.

Represent processes on a process model. The process model permits you to use *business domain, process* and *activity* objects in a hierarchy. *Business domain* objects are used to represent the high level product or service that the process delivers. Because the *activity* object is more powerful, we recommend that you use it rather than the more obvious *process* object. Activity objects can appear in workflow models and be simulated. Since ProVision® does not permit activity objects to be linked to business domains directly, make a process object with the same name to act as a link. When you are publishing models, hide the process object as it might cause confusion.

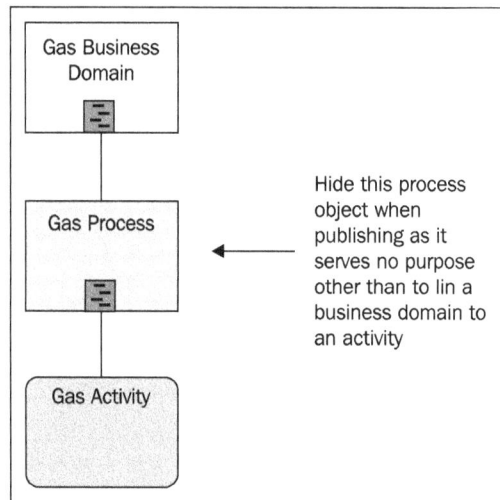

Gas Business Domain

Gas Process

Hide this process object when publishing as it serves no purpose other than to lin a business domain to an activity

Gas Activity

Critical elements

Once we have identified the critical processes, we can then see what elements are the most critical to make these processes run.

In the Enterprise Designer framework we identify seven elements that are used to run processes. They are (in alphabetical order):

Actors

Actors are people performing work manually. Internally, you will start by creating a hierarchical list of business units, position descriptions, and roles. Externally, you will start by creating objects for suppliers, customers, regulators, and competitors.

Use the *organization* model and *organization* objects to create an 'org chart' of the business. Use the *person* object to represent positions within business units. If there are more than one of any type of position, use one object to represent them all. Do not use the *role* object on an *organization* model. Later, you will use the *role* object in *workflow* models.

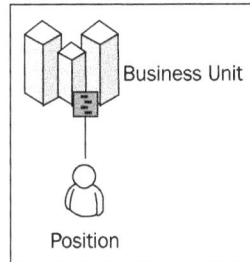

Business rules

As a process runs, the way that the work is done will be shaped and influenced by rules, legislation and practice. By documenting rules, you will help simplify and standardize business practice.

Use the *rule* object on a *business rule* model to represent specific business rules. Use the *standards* object on a *standards* model to represent legislation, standards, and less specific advice and guidance. Typically, business rules are set internally and standards are part of the environment in which the business operates.

Best practice for rule specification is to include the following elements in each rule statement:

- Rule Subject (what the rule is about)
- Rule Keyword (for example, must, may not, is)
- Rule Qualifier (for example, if, when) — optional
- Literal — optional

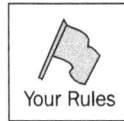

Your Rules

Computer systems

Increasingly repetitive work is done automatically. Some processes are now completely automated (such as requesting a bank balance at the ATM). Others are partially automated (obtaining cash from the ATM). Some are primarily manual (getting financial advice from your bank). ProVision® is very good at modeling business processes and can even simulate them running.

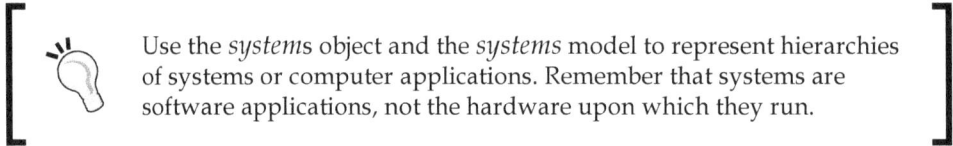

Use the *systems* object and the *systems* model to represent hierarchies of systems or computer applications. Remember that systems are software applications, not the hardware upon which they run.

Your computer systems (applications)

Data

Processes consume data. At each step, data might be created, read, updated or deleted. Information is the lifeblood of a process.

Start off by using the *business class* object on a *business class* model. Later, you may wish to explore *package* objects and models, and *subtype* models for more sophisticated data modeling.

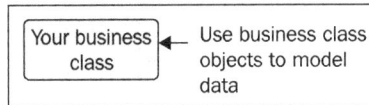

Your business class ←— Use business class objects to model data

Events

All processes are triggered by events. Within each process, the individual activities are also triggered by events. Typically, the completion of the previous activity is the trigger. This is how BPMN classifies events:

- **By type**: message, timer, error, escalation, termination, and so on
- **By origin** (in relation to the process participant): external (for example, message), internal (for example, signal)
- **By timing** (in relation to the process): start, intermediate, and end events
- **By role**: send (throw) a result, listen for (catch) triggers
- **By effect** (on the process): interrupting, non-interrupting
- **By scope of influence**: all the internal workings of a process or activity, or just the flow on which they are placed
- **By trigger configuration**: multiple events — only one required, multiple events — all required

This is an example of a *request* event. Time events such as *end of day* or *end of financial year* start a process irrespective of what has happened. Threshold events trigger an action when a certain point is reached. For example, *start manufacturing when we get 50 orders*.

[💡 Start off by using the *event* object on the *event* model.]

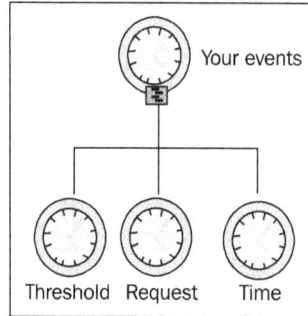

Facilities

All processes take place in specific locations. Even if the process is fully automated, there is still a place, albeit a server rather than a specific office.

[💡 Use the *location* model and represent places with the *location* object, and specific offices, factories and other buildings with the *facilities* object. If necessary, represent specific pieces of gear, such as servers, as children of facilities using the *equipment* object.]

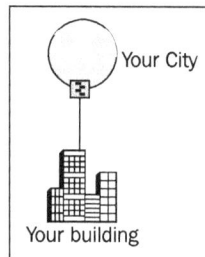

Gear (equipment)

Many processes rely on gear or equipment being available to support the actors. They use these tools (furniture, equipment, computers, mobile phones, and so on) to get the job done.

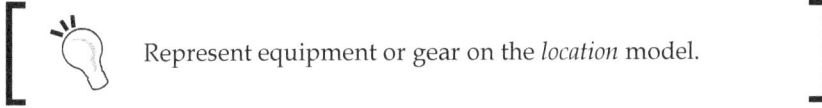

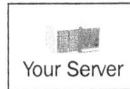

Represent equipment or gear on the *location* model.

Your Server

Goals

Goals come last, not because they are least important, but because they are the hardest to gain consensus on. When an organization changes its goals, people can lose their jobs or be assigned work which has less responsibility. Naturally, goals are political and, depending on who you speak to, you may get different answers, when trying to define them. Later, we will show you a way to define goals which does not depend on a personal point of view. In effect the goals of an organization can be reverse engineered.

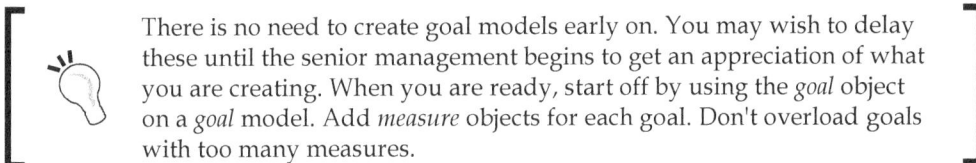

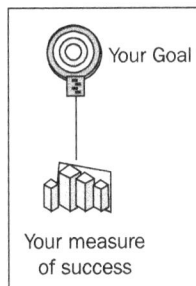

There is no need to create goal models early on. You may wish to delay these until the senior management begins to get an appreciation of what you are creating. When you are ready, start off by using the *goal* object on a *goal* model. Add *measure* objects for each goal. Don't overload goals with too many measures.

Your Goal

Your measure of success

Next phase

Congratulations! If you have made it this far you have designed a strategy and got it approved. You now have a business case, an agreed framework, methodology, and governance structure. You have created repositories and developed a process by which you can publish your models. You have populated the repository with key components that will be used again and again. In alphabetical order, these critical components are hierarchical lists of the following business objects:

- Actors
- Business rules
- Computer systems
- Customers
- Data
- Events
- Facilities
- Gear
- Goals
- Processes
- Products and services

They may not look like much. After all, you did not need to purchase ProVision® just to make lists. You could have done that in Microsoft Word or Excel. These lists are the building blocks from which you will start to assemble models. So now what do you do, to create value?

We recommend that the first model you build to show to stakeholders is a **Client Service** model. (If you sell products to customers, then you may wish to call it a **Customer Product** model.) Throughout this book we will use the terms interchangeably. This model is often overlooked. It visualizes which clients get which services. In an outside-in view of the world, the customer comes first. Therefore it is essential that you have a way to express the relationship between who your clients are and what they get.

> Use the navigator model to build the *Client Service* model. Populate the model with the customer and product objects you created previously. Use communication links to express the relationship. You can remove any objects from the model which do not add clarity without breaking the relationships. Senior managers must own this work. Once the *Client Service* model is complete, do not proceed to the next step until they have approved it.

You now have a bare bones repository of information about your business. The next step will be determined by the priorities of the business. There will be specific projects that will be candidates as the 'first cab off the rank'.

In determining which projects to select, we recommend that you choose the ones which are mission critical. It is tempting to choose a project that is low profile and low impact. It is also tempting to choose a project because the project manager is happy to have your help. This way you can iron out the bugs, build skill, expertise, and confidence in a safe environment.

Please resist this temptation. Remember that something significant in your environment will change within three months. This might be that the champion goes off to do another job or even leaves the company. Their replacement may not like what you do at all!

Therefore, each modeling project must demonstrate value to the business every three months. Making lists of processes is important and essential. It does not demonstrate to anyone outside of the modeling team that your costs are worthwhile.

So, within the first quarter, make it your business to model the benefits that a key business project will have. If it is a critical project then the senior managers will know that it is critical. If it is technical in nature, they might have little understanding of what is actually being done. By creating models that visually demonstrate what the project is about, you can help that project team and the senior management team. In some cases your models will actually enable the senior managers to understand the project for the first time.

Leverage

Each project you model from now on needs to be critical, in the eyes of senior management, and related to the previous projects. In this way, much of the information that would normally need to be gathered is already populated. This does two things. First, it saves time, speeding up the work of the project team. Second, it provides a mechanism to validate and update the previous data. Information goes stale, so that even if it was correct three months ago, it might not be now.

Sample development program

Project #1 captures the complete list of products and services of the company and the critical processes which underpin the key products and services.

Some benefits: The complete list of products and services can then be mapped against the corporate website. This will identify gaps. Products and services that don't appear on the website can be added based on the old adage that if you don't tell you won't sell. Redundant products and services can be removed from the website.

Business interaction models provide a clearer image of what the business is about, improving induction training.

Project #2 develops *workflow* models for the critical processes.

Some benefits: You discover differences in the way that the same process is done in different divisions. There is no need for these variations, which have emerged over time due to silos in the business. Using **appreciative inquiry**, you identify the best known way to run the processes. This creates a cost reduction of 20% and the process time is cut in half. Because you used appreciative inquiry, the staff involved feel energized by the change.

Project #3 develops *system interaction* models of the systems that underpin the critical processes identified in Project #2.

Some benefits: The IT department now has a complete list of critical systems. They know who the process owners are in case of a system failure. They leverage this to form the basis of their business continuity plan.

Project #4 develops a *business class* model of the information that is created, read, updated, and deleted in the critical processes identified in Project #2.

Some benefits: Now the business can see where information is stored in different formats across different systems. By standardizing, the business can have a shared understanding of the customer. Before this project, the same customer might appear in two different systems, and it was nearly impossible to know that they were the same.

Project #5 develops an organization model of the business units and positions that participate in the critical processes. Combining this with the information that came from the workflow models in Project #3, it is now possible to create a grid which maps position descriptions to roles.

Some benefits: Instead of a position description being purely descriptive, it can now be expressed as a collection of roles. If a position needs to change, you can immediately see all the processes that will be impacted. In a business continuity event you can query the repository for all other positions which have the necessary skills.

Each project reveals information in a way that was never available before. Each project builds on the previous ones and makes the repository richer.

Summary

You have learned a five-layer framework. Typically, organizations do not pay sufficient attention to the second level and jump straight from Level 1 (context) to Level 3 (implementation). Level 2 (strategy) requires the organization to slow down in order to speed up.

You have learned that the *context* of any set of actions is more significant than the *content*. What is the context for deploying ProVision® in your organization? Context precedes strategy, and strategy precedes implementation.

You have also learned that the business may have a different context to your personal one. The business may not have an understanding that ProVision® is an enterprise tool. ProVision® is a good enterprise solution. Before developing a strategy, first document your personal and business context for implementing ProVision® and get agreement on the business context.

You now understand the key parts of a strategy document. The strategy document consists of six sections that are described in more detail in the following chapters:

- Making a business case
- Using a Framework
- Adopting a Methodology
- Implementing effective Governance
- Understanding the Toolset

The initial project will be to gather core information that will be required irrespective of what the second and subsequent project is.

Good project management methodology suggests that, before the project starts, you define the outputs, the outcomes, and the measures by which you will know if you have completed the work successfully.

You now have a business case, an agreed framework, methodology, and governance structure. You have created repositories and developed a process by which you can publish your models. You have populated the repository with key components that will be used again and again.

You now have a bare bones repository of information about your business.

Each project you model from now on needs to be critical, in the eyes of senior management, and related to the previous projects. In this way, much of the information that would normally need to be gathered is already populated.

2
Making a Business Case

In this chapter, I will explain some general principles of modeling and the key benefits of using the ProVision® modeling solution, specifically to support business strategy. You can use this information to support your business case.

Recently, I had a meeting with the directors of a major household brand. They had just finished completing a strategic review of the business, which had been signed off by the board. They had numerous stakeholders to satisfy, and naturally the final result was a compromise, which was reached after months of meetings. I was with an experienced business coach who asked the CEO, "So, how will you know if you have succeeded?". The CEO had difficulty in answering the question. One of his senior managers in the room jumped to his rescue: "Oh, we are working out what we want to measure. We have agreed on some of the measures, but haven't yet put any numbers against them."

The coach asked: "How do people in the organization feel about the new strategy?"

The manager replied saying, "It's a good question. There are a lot of people who feel that it was a waste of time and they just want to get back to the real work. We have a team of very passionate and committed people, but they see strategy as navel gazing."

We realized that the strategy was doomed. It seems logical to define the goals and then identify the measures. In practice, it is often easier to do it the other way round, even though that is counter-intuitive. First, define the measures of success and then articulate these measures as goals. The employees were right to be dubious.

There are various ways to create, read, update, and delete information. These solutions fall into two major approaches—**drawing** and **modeling**. Drawing is still the approach adopted by many organizations because it is cheaper. Most companies that have considered using ProVision® have Microsoft Visio installed on every user desktop. As far as a project manager is concerned, Visio is a free resource. The project manager doesn't need to ask for funds, and if they do, then the manager will ask why they aren't using Visio. This chapter explains the limitations of drawing and why modeling is best practice and essential to support a sustainable strategy. The reader can use this information to make their business case compelling and get the funds that they need to do the job properly. Areas covered also include:

- The benefits of moving to a central repository. (What needs to be stored and how users can access it.)

- Are we building architecture or doing design? (The importance of language in getting your message across.)

- Better decisions now. (The purpose and notion of good enough architecture.)

- ProVision® and Metastorm BPM. (Is this Metastorm's unique selling point?)

Finally, we will meet Sandra, a veteran architect who has implemented enterprise modeling in telecommunications, banking, and the food sector in the UK. Sandra has a very important message: *Stay focused on modeling for strategy and don't get lost in the detail.* She works with the management team to visualize the measures and goals.

The benefits of moving to a central repository

It is important to understand the difference between a drawing tool and a visual relational database such as ProVision®. The outputs can look identical. Because drawing tools are so much cheaper, why would you invest in ProVision®?

There are a number of drawing packages available, Microsoft Visio is the key player in this market. It is a drawing package that is optimized for business diagrams. Modelers can select pre-built stencils to create models rapidly. As Visio is often installed already, it is the tool of choice of many business analysts.

Designed to scale

If all you need to do is visually represent an aspect of a business, then there is nothing wrong with Visio. However, its limitations soon become apparent. To understand the key differences, I need to explain some basic concepts about ProVision® as you will see them mentioned throughout this book. I mentioned them in the first chapter of the book and will now examine them in more detail. These concepts are the reason why you can manage hundreds of models in ProVision®. It has been designed to scale. The core concepts are:

- Object
- Link
- Model
- Notebook/File
- Repository

Object

ProVision® uses **objects** to represent business concepts. Everything you see—a role, system, process, or a goal is an object. Every object has a name and an icon. After that, it is up to you how much more detail you want to add. All objects can have associations with other objects. These associations will vary, according to the type of object.

Link

A **link** is a special type of object. It is displayed as a line that connects two objects. You can modify the way the line displays, that is, change its color, thickness, or arrow shape. Links appear in their own area in the object inventory. Some types of link can have a **payload** (a deliverable) and events associated with them. For example, the link between two activities is called a **workflow link**. This link can display the deliverable that is passed as an output from one activity to the other. It can also display the event that triggers the deliverable. Both deliverables and events are optional. In many cases, it is obvious what the deliverable or event would be. To distinguish between an event and a deliverable, ProVision® places the name of the event inside double quotation marks.

In the example shown in the following figure, once the event named "**Model ready to review**" is triggered, the deliverable called **Draft Model** becomes the input for the **Review Model** activity:

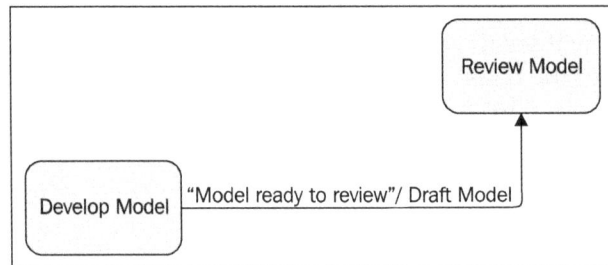

Model

A **model** is a special kind of object that contains other objects. Every model must have an object that is designated as the **subject** of the model. ProVision® provides three types of model—**hierarchical**, **non-hierarchical**, and **navigator**. Hierarchical models typically allow only one object type to appear. For example, a Systems model can be used to create only the hierarchical relationships of systems. No other object type can be added. Even if you create a custom object, you will not be permitted to add it to a hierarchical model.

Non-hierarchical models permit more than one object type to appear, so that you can show predefined relationships other than parent-child relationships between these objects. For example, a Systems Interaction model will allow you to demonstrate relationships between systems and hardware.

The Navigator model is a special model that you can use when you are unable to express the relationships that you want using one of the other model types. You can use virtually any object type on a Navigator model. This is both its strength and weakness. As any object can be used, you can become overwhelmed by the choices. The Navigator model is the only model type that allows you to display models as well as objects. By default, these display as thumbnails of the full model. In the following example, a Navigator model shows a thumbnail of the **Approval Process** workflow model. The subject of the workflow model is the activity called *Approval Process*. It has been placed to the right to demonstrate the difference.

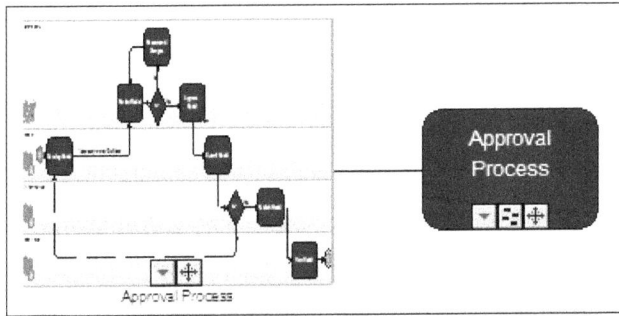

The Navigator model has one more purpose. You can use it to visually express indirect relationships. For example, a goal may be realized by delivering a product or service to a customer group. The product requires processes. Each process decomposes down into a series of activities, some of which might require certain computer systems to be in a running state. There is no direct relationship between the goal and the computer system. There is an indirect relationship, which you can visualize using a Navigator model.

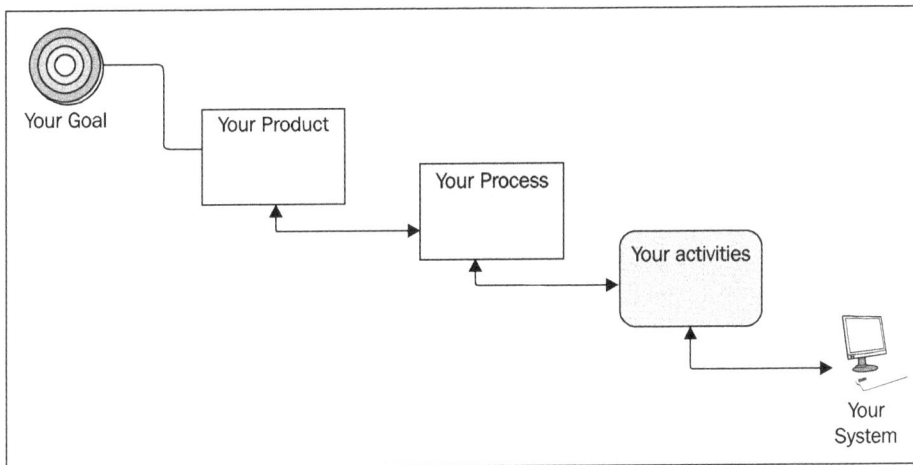

Notebook and file

Objects, links, and models are stored in **Notebooks**. If you think of a Notebook as a physical book, then the models are equivalent to chapters. Each model tells a story. Inside each story, there are words. Objects are equivalent to words. Links create phrases.

Several Notebooks can be stored together. They share a common modeling language that changes the look and feel of objects, links, and models. Other than that, each Notebook is independent. So, it is possible to have two objects in different notebooks that have the same name and type but are completely different. Objects and models can be dragged from one Notebook to another. You can save a Notebook under a different name and thus use the first Notebook as a template for the second.

A **File** is the logical equivalent of a Notebook. The main difference is that a File can be saved anywhere on a computer and then e-mailed or copied onto a memory stick for transfer. So, Files are used to share and exchange Notebooks with other users.

Only one Repository can be open at any one time. Only one Notebook can be open within the Repository. In the example shown in the next diagram, the **Sample** Repository appears in bold writing to highlight that it is open. Also, the **PackT** Notebook has a different icon to distinguish that it is the Notebook being viewed.

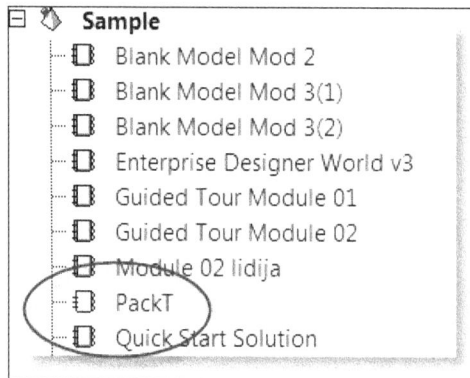

```
☐ ◊  Sample
    ─ ▯  Blank Model Mod 2
    ─ ▯  Blank Model Mod 3(1)
    ─ ▯  Blank Model Mod 3(2)
    ─ ▯  Enterprise Designer World v3
    ─ ▯  Guided Tour Module 01
    ─ ▯  Guided Tour Module 02
    ─ ▯  Module 02 lidija
    ─ ▯  PackT
    ─ ▯  Quick Start Solution
```

Repository

All Notebooks are stored in **Repositories**. A Repository can contain many Notebooks (in practice most users would be unlikely to have more than 50, and typically around 10). The modeling language is associated with a Repository, and once it is made the default language, it changes the names, look and feel of all objects, links, and models, irrespective of which Notebook they are in. In the following example, the **Sample** Repository is bold to indicate that it is open. The **POC Repository** has a world icon to represent that it is stored on a remote server and accessed via Knowledge Exchange®. By contrast, local Repositories have a pyramid icon.

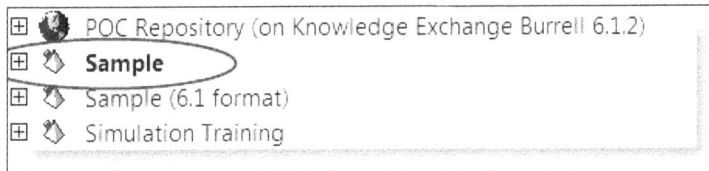

Now that you have understood these basic concepts, let's see how ProVision® varies from a drawing package such as Visio.

Store once, reuse many times

Imagine that you build a model, which is an organization chart. On the chart is an object used to represent the **Accounts Department**.

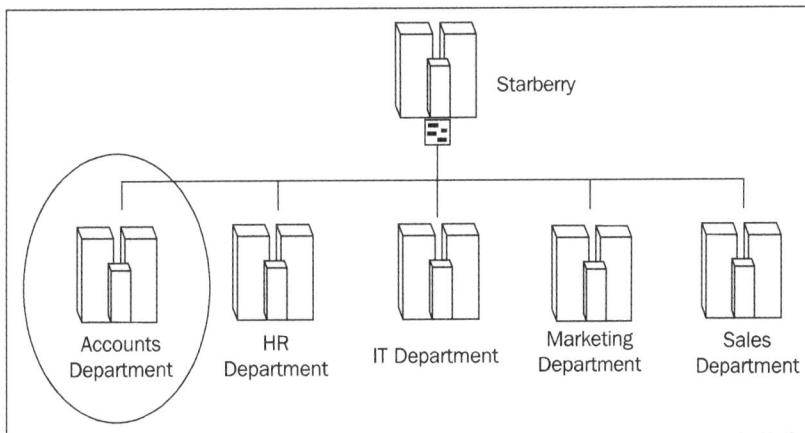

Now you build a separate model, which is a workflow. One of the swim lanes is the **Accounts Department**.

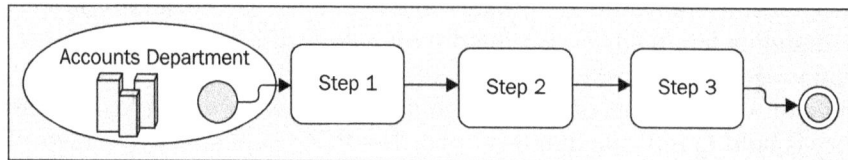

After a restructure, the Accounts Department is now called the Finance Department. You will now need to find every instance of the old *Accounts Department* object and rename it as *Finance Department*. In this simple example, there are only two models. Assume that there are 50 models! How would you keep track of them all?

To try and get round this maintenance issue, Visio modelers create huge diagrams so that everything is on the one page. System diagrams are a common example. The maintenance issue is solved, but now the drawing is so detailed and complex that only the modeler actually understands it. Cramming everything into one Visio model also makes it a major time-consuming challenge to modify the model after receiving user input. So, while Visio appears cheaper, the cost has just shifted to pay an extra salary.

The main purpose of modeling is to visually explain something, which might otherwise require several pages of text. Successful modeling simplifies and tells a story. I recommend that no model should have more than 15 objects on it. The more objects, the more complex it becomes. If the viewer doesn't understand the story, then the model is of little value as a communication tool.

When you draw a model using ProVision®, the object is stored in the object inventory. Any changes to one instance automatically update all other instances of the same object. There is no need to create and edit objects in the object inventory. The act of adding, updating, or deleting an object that is displayed on the current model automatically corrects the object inventory. This means that there is no chance of accidentally forgetting to update a specific model.

When you examine the object inventory, you can see all the places in which an object is used. Naturally, you can also rename or delete objects directly from within the object inventory. In the following example, we can see that the activity object called **Approve Model** is used only in the **Approval Process** workflow model:

```
Object Inventory
  ⊟ ⬔ Objects
      ⊟ ⬔ Activities (10)
          ⊞ ■ Approval Process
          ⊟ ■ Approve Model
              ⊞ ◻ Component Models
              ⊟ ⬔ Where Used
                  └ ⬔ Approval Process(Workflow Modeler:)
          ⊞ ■ Develop Model
```

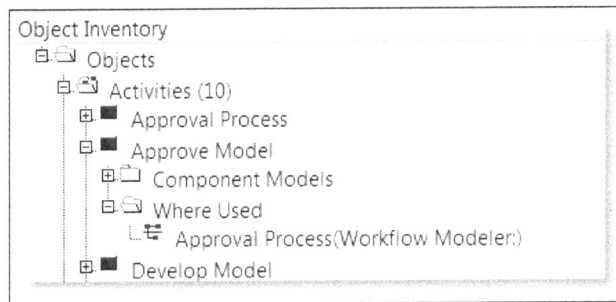

ProVision® enables the user to nest models. This is why you can create models that are simple to understand, in part because they do not contain more than 15 objects. Each object can become the subject of a child or nested model. If you need to see the detail, you can just click into the nested model. Like Russian dolls, each model can contain another model inside it.

As this is not possible in Visio, modelers have to change their mindset. The modelers are used to cramming everything onto the one model, so it takes time to understand that this is neither necessary nor desirable.

A drawing is not a model but is a static image. The objects that a drawing contains are drawn directly onto the blank sheet and that is where they remain. When you use ProVision®, you are using the model as a means to update the object inventory. Everything is stored centrally.

Working collaboratively

Knowledge of a business is scattered. Everyone knows a lot about the area for which they are responsible and less about the rest of the business. Creating a central repository requires communication and collaboration. So, what happens when two people need to make changes to the object inventory? In the previous example, the name of the Accounts Department had to be updated to become the Finance Department.

One person might be responsible for maintaining and updating the organizational chart. Another person keeps the workflow models up to date. The same object called *Accounts Department* appears in both models. How can one person make the changes without creating problems for the other?

ProVision® follows the same process that has been used by software developers for many years. Models and objects are stored in a central location and checked out when required. ProVision® locks the objects. The next person who wants to use those objects will find that they are now read-only. They will have to wait until the first person releases the objects by checking them back in.

It is quite common for several modelers to be working on the same information at the same time. Without this ability to lock and unlock objects, it would be easy for one person to accidentally overwrite the work of another. Needless to say, Visio does not have this capability.

In the latest version of the companion product, Knowledge Exchange®, the ability to share objects is taken to the next level. It is now possible to store objects in a central remote repository and then hyperlink to them. In this way, a master list of objects can be reused by many modelers working in multiple Notebooks. If the master object changes, this will be reflected across all the Notebooks.

Architecture or design

Enterprise Architecture is a response to increasing rates of change and complexity. Once a business reaches a certain size, it becomes increasingly difficult to remain responsive to the changing business environment. As a consequence, the systems and processes do not support the business objectives. This lack of alignment reduces the return on investment.

In order to write your business case, you need to have a high-level understanding of what Enterprise Architecture is.

When the founder of Enterprise Architecture, John Zachman, started to think about how to make models of a business, he looked at how engineers created and maintained models of large complex structures such as skyscrapers and jumbo jets. These constructs had to be managed and maintained over many years. They comprised hundreds of thousands of parts manufactured by different companies. As time passed, the technology used to create parts would change. Different groups wanted to see the information and hence filters were required. Zachman wondered, "How do they manage all of this?"

He thought that if it was possible to design systems to manufacture goods and services, would it not be possible to design the actual businesses themselves? In the late nineteenth century, there were numerous screw manufacturers. There was no standard of what a screw looked like. If you needed a replacement, you had to go back to the original company. While this was good for the company, it was bad for the growth of the industry. Fast forward 100 years and the idea of standard reusable parts is well established in manufacturing, and yet it is still hard to acquire, off the shelf, standard reusable business processes.

Much of what an organization does is the same as every other. Virtually all organizations hire staff, pay bills, and rent premises. Within each industry group, there are great similarities. Running one university is not so different from running another. All health clubs do similar things. What if an organization could just pick best practice business processes? This would mean they could focus on their competitive differences.

> Zachman's work, first published in 1987, has had a profound influence. Many other frameworks have been developed over the past two decades, which are modifications or refinements.

He applied the lessons that he learned and created an architectural framework. It has evolved over time. Information is classified by the six questions that we can ask about any area of enquiry: what, how, where, who, when, and why? The answers are stored at five levels, representing the different perspectives of context, concept, logical, physical, and detailed views. These levels align with different roles:

- The planner manages the context
- The owner manages the concept
- The designer manages the logical layer
- The builder manages the physical layer
- The sub-contractor provides the individual components

	What	How	Where	Who	When	Why
Planner (context)	Data List	Process Catalog	Geographical List	Organization List	Event List	Key goals
Owner (concept)	Entity Relationship Diagram	Process Model	Geographical Relationships	Organization Chart	Event Relationships	Goal Hierarchy
Designer (logical i.e. no reference to technical or physical)	Logical Data Models	High level Workflow model	Logical Infrastructure models	Role definitions and relationships	Logical event diagrams	Standards and Business Rules and relationships
Builder (physical expressions of the logical)	Physical Data Models expressed in technology specific formats	Technology and role specific Workflow models	Physical Infrastructure Components and their relationships	Role definitions at the work break down level	Specific Event states triggered by time, threshold and requests	Specific rules and tests applied at each step of the workflow
Sub-contractor (detailed specifications)	Data Details	Process Details	Location details	Role details	Event details	Rule details

Sometimes the framework shows a sixth row, which represents how the organization appears to the world.

The framework adheres to a set of rules. While the rows follow a logical sequence, the columns can be displayed in any order. The structure creates cells, each of which can store information only of a certain type at any level of detail. Thus, we say that each cell is normalized, with each column and each row having a specific and unique set of characteristics. The information in all of the cells is a complete expression of a business entity. You cannot add rows or columns. Zachman does not tell the modeler much about methodology:

- What is the sequence in which the framework should be built?
- What level of detail is adequate?
- Are there cells which are more important than others?

- Are some rows or columns more important than others?
- What process should we follow?

Zachman leaves it up to others to answer these questions.

TOGAF9

The Open Group Architecture Framework (TOGAF) is the best-known process. While it is called a framework, it actually also describes the process by which information is gathered, maintained, and used to make decisions. This process is called the **Architecture Development Method (ADM).** After defining the framework and principles, the ADM is a continuous loop, consisting of eight phases and a **Requirements Management** process:

1. Architecture Vision
2. Business Architecture
3. Information Systems Architectures
4. Technology Architecture
5. Opportunities and Solutions
6. Migration Planning
7. Implementation Governance
8. Architecture Change Management

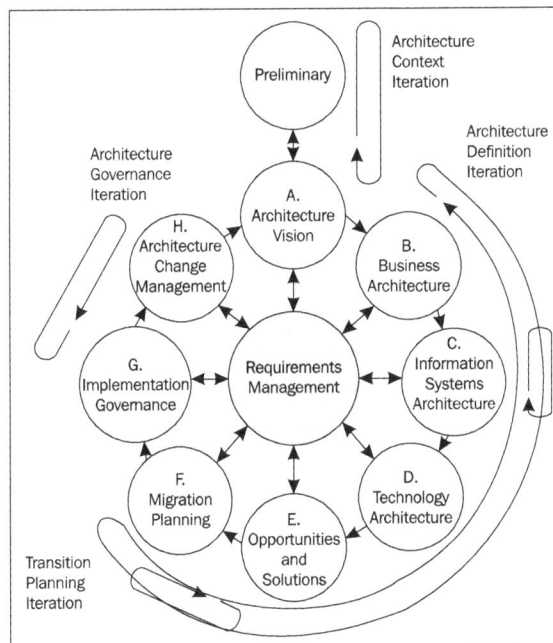

Consequently, many modelers combine Zachman, which gives them a consistent taxonomy, and TOGAF, which gives them a sequence in which to record the information. However, if you look at the language and origins of TOGAF, you can easily make out that it is a methodology for changing technology and systems. It is only in TOGAF 9 that we begin to see business architecture content. The TOGAF 9 user guide is 778 pages long, which in itself makes it difficult to execute. The original promise of Enterprise Architecture was that it would be a simple way to describe the whole enterprise, not just focus on the systems that support it. To be fair to the Open Group, they have invested significantly in ArchiMate—a lightweight agile framework that is business-focused.

Federal Enterprise Architecture

Since 2006, the **Federal Enterprise Architecture** (**FEA**) has attempted to create an integrated framework and methodology for one of the largest and most complex organizations on the planet—the US government.

The FEA divides business into core mission-area segments and business-services segments. Core segments reflect what the organization exists for. Business segments describe the functions, such as HR and Financial Management, that support the core mission for a specific agency. Enterprise services are functions that cross agency boundaries. For example, Records Management and Security is designated to be enterprise-wide.

The FEA includes five reference models that are designed to provide a common language across agencies. The purpose, of course, is to facilitate cooperation between Agencies. By creating a shared understanding, the FEA hopes to reduce waste and duplication.

The FEA has a four step process for preparing projects.

1. Analyze and demonstrate how the project aligns with the overall organizational plan.
2. Describe the future architectural state, the measures for success, options considered, and the proposed approach.
3. Look at project funding.
4. Produce a project plan with all the normal features.

Success is measured by how complete the architecture is, how extensively it is used to inform decisions, and how successful the programs are. The FEA color codes success using a traffic lights system (green, yellow, and red).

Refer to *A Comparison of the Top Four Enterprise-Architecture Methodologies* by Roger Sessions of ObjectWatch, Inc. for an excellent discussion on this topic: `http://msdn.microsoft.com/en-us/library/bb466232.aspx`.

Evidence

To my knowledge, there have been few comprehensive independent surveys of Enterprise Architecture to measure results. Hardly any are available in the public domain. One exception is *Enterprise Architecture as Platform for Connected Government* — the research done by the National University of Singapore in 2010. Its purpose is to understand the impact of Enterprise Architecture on connected government. It concludes that *Enterprise Architecture has attained the status of mainstream activity and is gaining further traction, and is a pre-condition for successful implementation of connected government*. The key areas that could help experience benefit were common infrastructure and interoperability, collaborative services and business operations, and public sector governance.

For more information, please refer to `http://unpan1.un.org/intradoc/groups/public/documents/unpan/unpan039390.pdf`.

South Korea is singled out as the best example of EA in action. Over a period of five years, it has moved to the number one position, on a number of measures, including participation of citizens in e-government. The report states that South Korea *does not have a proven model to follow. As a leader, it must continually innovate and create its own model.*

Anecdotal evidence suggests that, in other cases, architecture has not delivered significant results. The absence of proven models does not help.

There is no point in creating taxonomies and models for their own sake, so the absence of a consistent verifiable process to measure success is surprising

Again and again, the lifecycle of an Enterprise Architecture initiative follows this script:

- A visionary imagines a world in which all the information about the business is stored in one central repository. In this vision, the information is complete, accurate, and current.

- Somehow the visionary manages to get funding and put together a team to populate the repository. Week after week, they work to create this perfect vision.

- For some reason, when they explain the value of Enterprise Architecture to their dim-witted colleagues, there is a failure to understand how glorious the business will be when this work is complete.

- Realizing that they are not getting the interest and support they need, they work even harder, adding greater and greater detail. An air of despondency begins to set in.

- One day, a budget review examines the team's work and decides that there is not sufficient value to justify the project continuing.

- The team is disbanded.

In a world in which the rate of change is increasing, as is complexity, by the time the comprehensive model is built, it is too late. Our view is that the metaphor of architecture is flawed. Architecture implies structures that have certainty and consistency. The skyscraper does not change shape. It may need to flex but it is not expected to morph into something completely different. Building engineering principles have been developed and tested over centuries. Months, or years, of planning can result in comparatively short construction cycles. Once the plan is set, there is very little leeway for change.

Organizations, on the other hand, are collections of flesh and blood individuals. Calling people resources does not make them so. Applications are limited only by the inventiveness of their designers. As the global economy expands, work moves from one continent to another. The landscape changes daily.

Here are some pointers on the difference between purposeful and mechanistic views of organizations:

- **Processes**: A set of role interactions built on communication and synchronization of participants.

- The emphasis is on the **goal**, for example, satisfying customers, quality, and better long-term relationships.

- Technology solutions are targeted toward increasing the value proposition.

- Empowered workers make decisions at the front line.

- Employees seek to understand the entire process, growing their business acumen and learning.

- As people develop new ways of doing things, the organization can also learn.

Therefore, I replace the word *architecture* with *design* to reflect this more fluid and uncertain world. Architecture represents a context in which players must adapt to a pre-existing structure. Design represents enablers that a player can adopt if appropriate.

One way to explain the difference is in two different approaches to an unrelated field — traffic management. At an intersection, signs depict who has right of way and where each vehicle and pedestrian can travel. If accidents occur, the intersection is altered to force the participants to follow a particular behavior. For example, traffic lights are added and additional signs enforce the message.

The design approach might remove all signs and make right of way ambiguous. This counter-intuitive approach requires everyone to be more aware when approaching the intersection.

> *We glide into Drachten, a 17th-century village that has grown into a bustling town of more than 40,000. We pass by the performing arts center, and suddenly, there it is: the Intersection. It's the confluence of two busy two-lane roads that handle 20,000 cars a day, plus thousands of bicyclists and pedestrians. Several years ago, Monderman ripped out all the traditional instruments used by traffic engineers to influence driver behavior - traffic lights, road markings, and some pedestrian crossings - and in their place created a roundabout, or traffic circle. The circle is remarkable for what it doesn't contain: signs or signals telling drivers how fast to go, who has the right-of-way, or how to behave. There are no lane markers or curbs separating street and sidewalk, so it's unclear exactly where the car zone ends and the pedestrian zone begins. To an approaching driver, the intersection is utterly ambiguous — and that's the point.*

> *Monderman and I stand in silence by the side of the road a few minutes, watching the stream of motorists, cyclists, and pedestrians make their way through the circle, a giant concrete mixing bowl of transport. Somehow it all works. The drivers slow to gauge the intentions of crossing bicyclists and walkers. Negotiations over right-of-way are made through fleeting eye contact. Remarkably, traffic moves smoothly around the circle with hardly a brake screeching, horn honking, or obscene gesture. "I love it!" Monderman says at last. "Pedestrians and cyclists used to avoid this place, but now, as you see, the cars look out for the cyclists, the cyclists look out for the pedestrians, and everyone looks out for each other. You can't expect traffic signs and street markings to encourage that sort of behavior. You have to build it into the design of the road".*

The source is `http://www.tmforum.org/BusinessProcessFramework/1647/home.html`.

Enterprise Designer has the simplest and lightest of frameworks and methodologies for practitioners to focus on supporting business strategy. This Framework, and others, will be described in detail in *Chapter 3, Using a Framework.*

Open Text Metastorm's unique strengths

Business Process Analysis (BPA), **Enterprise Architecture (EA)**, and **Business Process Management (BPM)** are three separate but related disciplines. Open Text Metastorm Enterprise was the first vendor to bring all three together in one suite of applications and is a leader in all three areas. Business Process Analysis is sometimes called Business Process Mapping, but as this creates the same acronym as Business Process Management, I prefer not to use it. The purpose of BPA is to describe a process. A map, or a model, is one way to do this.

ProVision® is an Enterprise Architecture and BPA tool. There are two versions of the toolset. ProVision® for BPA is just a cut down version of ProVision®. Thus business analysts and enterprise architects can work on the same data.

Open Text Metastorm BPM

Open Text Metastorm BPM enables a business to describe and monitor instances of a process in real time. Each time a process is triggered, Open Text Metastorm BPM tracks its progress from start to finish. The statistical information gathered, such as how long each step takes, is then used to understand how well a process is running. The data can be brought into ProVision® and used to simulate alternative scenarios. For example, imagine that you are a law firm. One of the processes is *Client Onboarding* — the process by which the firm does due diligence on the client. Has the firm acted against them in the past? Is the firm already representing a client where there might be a conflict of interest? With hundreds, sometimes thousands of clients, checking the files and talking to partners is going to take some work. The firm can't afford to make a mistake, which at best might be embarrassing. Like many processes, part of this work is manual. This means it can get stuck if people are away, don't respond to requests, or are just too busy. It is very easy to overlook or forget something.

After implementing Open Text Metastorm BPM, every time a new client comes onboard, the application opens a new folder containing everything known about that specific instance. As each step of the process is completed, Open Text Metastorm BPM keeps an audit trail with dates, times, and the name of the person completing the step. If a folder gets stuck, it can be re-routed to someone less busy. Open Text Metastorm BPM integrates with other systems such as CRM, e-mail, and SMS. Managers can receive alerts before a delay becomes a drama, allowing them to intervene rather than react. They can be provided with consoles where they can monitor all the processes for which they are responsible.

As participants complete their tasks, they can tell Open Text Metastorm BPM by updating the folder. For example, the folder might be accessed via a website.

In many cases, users are unaware that they are using Open Text Metastorm BPM. A business manager might need to give an approval. Users might receive an e-mail asking them to select a yes or no button, and, depending on their response, the folder is routed in different ways. Open Text Metastorm BPM integrates with current editions of Office so that participants can run processes from within familiar applications such as MS Word.

Open Text Metastorm BPM competes with a number of other applications. Its strength is that it is very fast to implement, taking weeks where others might take over a year. It is aimed at processes that have a lot of manual steps.

Because Open Text Metastorm BPM sits above all steps, whether manual or automated, it is possible to switch out systems and processes underneath, without much work. So, for example, if you decide to change CRM vendors, Open Text Metastorm BPM can adjust without much effort.

Although a process model is efficient, and reflects accurately the best way to do the work, the world continues to change. While you can encourage or mandate participants, the probability is that the process model and reality will quickly diverge. The beauty of Open Text Metastorm BPM is that it ensures that the process is followed the way that it is intended, and, if a better way is discovered, the Open Text Metastorm BPM model is easy to adjust.

The competitive advantage

Competing modeling products to ProVision® also have simulation engines. However, without easy access to the live data, business analysts make guesses about how a process runs in practice. These guesses can be improved by surveys and conversations with suppliers and customers, which is both time and money consuming. One ProVision® competitive advantage is the integration of the modeling tool and the execution engine. Organizations that adopt ProVision® Enterprise can transfer process data between the modeling and execution applications, and back again. However, few organizations buy based on this point as it is regarded as too esoteric. From a customer's perspective, the purchase decision is usually made on ease of use, scalability, access to local expertise, and breadth of use.

Many organizations start by using ProVision® and, as they mature, acquire Open Text Metastorm BPM. Because of the cost of Open Text Metastorm BPM, it is usually applied to processes that are high volume, high value, or both.

> Refer to the case study, Sandra's story, at the end of the chapter for a better understanding on Enterprise Architecture implementation.

Better decisions now

The phrase, *better decisions now*, will be used throughout this book to ensure that we do not lose sight of why we do this work. This is the essence of your business case. Each word has been chosen with care.

Why **better**? In a world where change and complexity are increasing, it is not possible to know if a choice is the best possible one. Many organizations do not model their businesses. They rely on the experience and intelligence of their decision makers. Good decisions can be made without the use of models. Therefore, we can only argue that the decisions that are informed by modeling are better, not ideal or perfect.

I base this argument on the following points:

- All the key information needed to make a decision is stored centrally and thus available for review.
- The information can be displayed in multiple ways—visually, as text, as graphs and tables, to suit the intended audience.
- The information can be filtered to show the appropriate level of detail.
- The information typically comes from multiple sources and thus represents a collective view.
- To combine the different data sources, the information depends on a consistent framework and methodology.
- The information has been subjected to quality checks and is thus more likely to be complete, current, and accurate.
- The quality checks help demonstrate if there are gaps, thus reducing the chance of decisions being made based on false assumptions.

Without a central repository, each decision maker constructs mental models. These can change in an instant. They are stored inside our heads and are invisible. It is very difficult to know how complete, current, or consistent they are. If the person leaves the organization, or is temporarily unavailable, access to the information is very difficult. It might be ignored. Re-building the information is expensive and can take time.

Why **decisions**? When building a model of an organization, it is very easy to get lost in the detail. Adding detail to the model takes more time and increases the task of maintaining the model exponentially. The acid test is, *will this additional detail help the organization make better decisions*? There is an important distinction between information and decisions. More information does not correlate to better decisions. You need just enough information to make a better decision than you would if you had not had a central model.

Why **now**? Business leaders have to make decisions today. The world is changing rapidly and they have to make the best possible decision with the available facts. Sandra gave us a practical example.

> *When you get into a bid room, you only have between four and seven days to construct a bid. Unfortunately the M&A enterprise architect isn't allowed to talk to any of us during that seven day process. He is solely accountable for defining what is reusable, what we want to buy, what we don't want to buy, around the assets that we are purchasing. The more information that he has at his fingertips, the more accurate his guesses are going to be.*

The business case for implementing ProVision® is that it will enable the business to make better decisions now. As long as the team sticks to this mantra, they will succeed.

Case study: Sandra's story

Sandra Jones is a highly experienced architect, based in the UK, who has worked in telecommunications and banking, and is now a lead architect for a major multinational in the food sector. This case study describes her experience with Enterprise Architecture implementations in large organizations.

[This is not her real name. It is easier for some professionals to speak candidly if they are off the record.]

BA: How have you got into using ProVision® and what are some of the challenges and issues that you faced?

SJ: I will talk fairly generically as I have used other tools as well. What my sweet spot has ended up being is capability building, managing expensive people, and the other is around strategy and planning. My journey started in a telecommunications company, which was a business process management-driven shop. What I have been working on in my last two positions has been putting the top and the bottom on that BPM model. For the top, what we have been working on lately is getting the business strategy encapsulated in an easy way, not just to the processes (which is an operational view) but also to the assets and the asset strategy. So I developed a point of view that the business strategy is one thing. The strategy itself isn't delivered by process. It is delivered by other changes that we can make. The strongest link that we can make to business strategy is change events. Change events link to business process. They also link to assets and third-party relationships, which might deliver a combination of processes or assets, for example, business process outsourcing or software as a service.

So, this is where I have been focusing for the past three years, and it has been a lot of fun.

BA: So, when you are having conversations with other managers and trying to explain to them what it is that you are trying to achieve and why you are taking this enterprise approach, why is it worth investing the time and the money? What are the key messages that you find resonate with the business?

SJ: The first thing is that I don't try and sell the methodology. I am trying to sell the outputs of the methodology. We have five business units here. In one day, we were able to take their business strategies and map them in a uniform way. Then we went back to the business units and say, "We understand that you want to do these eight things and this other unit wants to do those eight other things. We are having a hard time understanding how you are going to measure the success of that."

That is where going from strategy to business case is really important. Behind the scenes, we are trying to use a meta-model to link the business strategic drivers to the business measures. Because we aren't able to do that successfully, it surfaces a quality issue for the inputs that we are trying to construct in that prototype model. We are going back to the business and saying, "Look, Unit A has shown us what they have done, and we have been able to map that in this particular way. We have mapped two of your eight drivers this way. We then don't understand how you are going to measure these other six." Generally, when we are having these kinds of conversations, we are doing it in terms of wanting to understand their business case and articulate the benefits better for their business case. So at each step, as we go through the lifecycle, we are shadowing the conversations of what people are saying. We are quietly applying the methodology, we are really focused on the outputs.

So, we have developed this language around data quality, data completeness, and data coverage. Previously, the language had only been around data quality and not the completeness and coverage. By coverage I mean the ability to link exhaustively. If I am trying to link a set of business functions to a set of business measures, I should have at least one measure for every business function.

By just taking that simple modeling construct, which the tool supports, we are using the semantic validation rule. We have business analysts out there gathering information into the model, or we have people uploading spreadsheets. Then we run simple semantic validation rules to see if all of the *minimum of one* or *minimum of two* checks are successful. Once the semantic checks are there, the meta-model really comes to life and really starts to affect the business planning side of things. That is what we are experiencing.

BA: The methodology that you have was developed over time or is it something that you have acquired?

SJ: It's a homogenization. At the telecommunications company, we were using the eTOM with a BPMN framework that was based heavily on BPTrends (methodology/architecture framework).

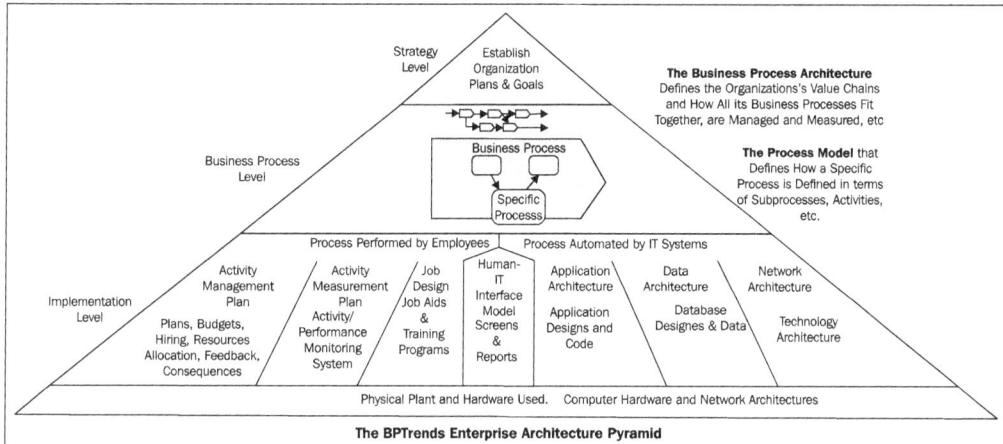

The BPTrends Enterprise Architecture Pyramid

The image is taken from `http://enterprisebusinessarchitect.com/BPTrendsEAPyramid.htm`.

All of the sites that I have worked at in the past four years have all been dipping their toe into process improvement methodologies such as LEAN, Six Sigma, and Kaizen. That is perhaps the other bit that you add and which gives you a shared language. A lot of organizations have been making significant investments in LEAN/Six Sigma and the continuous improvement stuff that has nothing to do with technology. It gives us a language and a glossary that we can use to connect what we are modeling as architects to what they want to achieve as a business unit.

BA: So you have picked and combined different frameworks, but the fundamental thing that you are focusing on is the way that you can identify measures, tie them into specific business functions, and then look for the gaps.

SJ: That is exactly right. Looking for the gaps is the unique thing that enterprise architects can offer. Because we take a systematic approach, we are exhaustively identifying gaps, rather than just doing something on a whiteboard and seeing where the gaps are. I term that as the engineering side of what we do. But it is not very time-consuming. Every time I work on a new business project, I have to take some time to look at the meta-model and the associated views to make sure that they are compatible with the business. But underneath all of that it is pretty simple what we are doing. It is not very time consuming to construct those validation rules. This is good because you can really focus on having the business conversation and getting the complete data.

BA: Can we talk a little bit about governance, how you create and manage this information, how you get buy in. As you know, there are different ways that people have tried this. One way is to get all the business analysts in one program office, very closely connected to senior business managers, so that there is very much a business focus. Another approach has been to put people into different units, a much more distributed approach. Then there is the approach that says that this is an IT function, this is only tangential to the business. All of this work will be done within the IT section of the organization. Who do think needs to be involved? Do you try and mandate, or do you try and gain consensus?

SJ: It is interesting. The three categories that you have just described, my last three roles have been one of each. I think what that tells me is that the approach you take to gain adoption of an enterprise model needs to be culturally sensitive to the business that you are in. Not just culturally, but also politically sensitive.

What I mean by that is that people don't care about data ownership until you try to take it off them. I think that is a pretty pragmatic way to look at the world. They will say, "I don't own it, I don't own it. Yes, I know that it's rubbish and I am not going to fix it." But the second you attempt to take it away and give custody to someone else they say "Wait, what are you doing with it? Give it back."

Where I am right now is a very interesting case in point. I am trying a hybrid approach. Across our business units, one has already made a $5m investment in documenting their processes, getting ISO certified, and building continuous improvement around them. The standard that they used is a very loose proprietary standard in iGraphx. Let's say I now come along and say "Our strategic partnership is with Oracle. The language that Oracle uses for process modeling is BPMN Version 2. From now on, at the governance level, I mandate all processes will be modeled using BPMN 2 in this repository." Obviously, that works for me, because if those processes go into the enterprise repository, then suddenly they are linkable.

Then the thirty continuous improvement people say, "Wait a minute. We have made this massive investment here. We have trained all these business people. They understand all the modeling constructs and views. We are going to continue with what we are doing."

So at that point, I can get my governance stick out and beat people. However, their point is valid. They have a continuous improvement agenda for their business unit. They have a standard and a method defined, everybody is trained and everyone is using it. They are delivering results. The only benefit of changing is that if they start to do it in the same way as everyone else then I can start to get that snowball effect connecting them into the rest of the business.

What I chose to do this year with them is accept that the leveling is all over the shop and their methodology is full of inconsistencies. Let's now give us nine months to build a process catalog. We won't re-do any process flows or procedural documents. Let's agree that we are going to create a process hierarchy using APQC within each of the two modeling repositories. Then, at least the taxonomy is same. We just won't sweat about the details. Then we start linking their processes to the strategic drivers. Obviously a lot of what they are doing is operational, so they have metrics where they measure the time taken for delivery, average operating cost per widget, among other things. We have implemented those slow changing metrics, the ones that are measured monthly or quarterly. It is not onerous for us to gather those and put them into the model.

> Leveling: Because a process breaks down into sub processes and tasks, it is important to get agreement on the characteristics of each level. Otherwise one model might contain sub processes that are designated level three and another model designates them as level five. When you try to connect the two models you get a leveling issue.

Now the business unit has a big transformation project coming up. They are seeing the other programs that we have got using our toolset, model, and methodology. So now an internal war has broken out in their business unit, between two camps, which is currently unresolved.

What will happen is that the rest of the business will adopt the new approach. The reason is that we have developed a certain amount of critical mass in the new repository. Just for context, we have about 240 solution architects and 200 business analysts using the toolset. That is a decent amount of intellectual property (IP) when you have 440 people working inside the model. When a lead architect launches a new project, we are just quietly modeling it in the tool. We are on the leadership teams of all major programs of work. We are leaving it to the leadership teams to decide if there is value. At the same time, the small group of us in enterprise architecture is quietly continuing to chip away, getting content into the model, regardless of where it is and what format it has been created in.

I suggest a guerilla warfare approach is the best way to do it. It either stands or falls on its merits. I don't believe that trying to use a stick to force enterprise modeling is the right approach. There has to be a need and a demand that is pulling it through. It is inherently abstract. You cannot get business people to understand the abstract. You can only get them to understand the benefits of the outputs, the views coming out of the model. When you start early, although the information you have at hand during the planning and strategy stage is less but it is of high value.

It is not until you get into design and the later stages, when you get into integration and data models. Getting adoption of modeling early in the lifecycle is the easiest way.

The other thing that we have mandated is that there has to be an enterprise architect on the leadership team of every program of work. The leadership team consists of five people – the director, the lead architect, the program management office person, and a couple of senior business people. We are making sure that the people on those leadership teams are champions of the model, not just in name but in practice. We have just moved six people out of those roles because they were not championing the cause. That is all within our own area of authority.

You have to be sensitive to the data ownership. We are only slaving much of the data, we aren't actually mastering it. For example, our Integration Catalog has 12,000 integrations. They are mastered in the Oracle Enterprise Repository. We just replicate that information.

BA: Presumably you are doing a similar thing with the continuous improvement documentation that you were talking about earlier. Are you just making hyperlinks?

SJ: Bingo! It works in about 80% of the cases. The problem is that the leveling concepts are so rotten because they don't actually have a rigorous methodology that can say things such as *your process can have a maximum of six steps.* There is no real rhyme or reason to how some of these processes have been modeled. They have been worked upon by untrained business analysts and subject matter experts. So, there are some quality issues with that, but it is the 80:20 rule.

BA: You are not alienating those people, because their work is still valued. You are also reducing the time that you need to take in maintenance because you are distributing that task amongst a wider group of people?

SJ: That is 100% right. That is really where the telecommunications company was interesting. We had a heavyweight modeling framework that we inherited. We had a mandate to use across the board. In the food sector company, we started with a blank sheet of paper. We were able to create the strategy in the tool. As the program rolled out, with the exception of a couple of bits of work that were won by IBM, we were the systems integrator in effect. In my current environment, the business is mature and fragmented. We have information being mastered in perhaps six or seven major repositories. Each of those has a mature governance process around it. This is the technical asset catalog and there is a whole bunch of passionate people, who are managing that catalog and the hierarchy and mapping and relationships for event monitoring between systems. So we are just replicating that information on a monthly basis.

Let's consider the high volume information sets that need to be in the enterprise model. It has been an active strategy of mine to seek out the people who are already managing that information in the business. I am, in effect, advertising the good work that they are doing. That has been very positive.

We have found two or three business units that are managing the same information in different ways. We have said to them, "We are not interested in creating a fourth way. If you want to come and have a look at how our toolset does it, you are most welcome." And then we are saying to them, "Would you go and talk to these other units who are doing something similar to you?"

So, we are driving the enterprise agenda, not the tooling agenda. As enterprise architects, that has been much more successful because we are getting people aligned and we are not sweating the small stuff around the tool. Of course that creates some headaches for us, such as the leveling issue I mentioned earlier. We have a few more quality issues, where this catalog has not used the same master data for application name or service name, so we are not getting automated mappings when we replicate. We are using a lot of the data warehouse principles to fix that information at source.

By getting the other groups to talk to each other and realize, "Oh, if I am really the master, then I have to ensure that everyone has a current version", is an idea liked by few. We aren't spending a huge amount of money. People are just doing this as we do our major programs of work.

BA: Would you say you are building the model one project at a time?

SJ: I distinguish between projects and programs. We have one program that mandates the use of the tool wall-to-wall. That's a billion dollar program. That is perhaps 50% of the company's investment spent. We have probably got about 80% of the company's investment spent using the toolset in the way that it was intended.

The challenge we have is that the company has been in business for more than a hundred years. Many of the IP assets have been there for forty or fifty years in one way, shape, or form. It really is that legacy environment and the non-technology areas such as continuous improvement within the business where we are taking this gentle approach. We don't want the operational guys to lose ownership of the status of the assets that they are responsible for. We want them to manage and maintain it themselves. It just so happens that they are doing that within another toolset, which is connected to a proprietary help desk. It makes consummate sense for them to use their own tools.

BA: So they are managing the information in their own toolsets, you are joining it up and publishing it, exposing information that perhaps people didn't know existed. The information managers are getting the kudos. Slowly you are bringing it all together. How long do you think it will be before it is complete?

SJ: We will never get there. The reason is that we are doing mergers and acquisitions (M&A). We are acquiring systems and business units faster than we are fixing them. So we will never win.

BA: Let me rephrase the question. Would you say that you wouldn't be able to do those mergers and acquisitions effectively if you were not doing enterprise modeling?

SJ: It is definitely one of the major benefits that have been flagged. We talk about the ability to accurately triage. When you get into a bid room, you have between four and seven days to construct a bid. Unfortunately the M&A enterprise architect isn't allowed to talk to any of us during that seven day process. He is solely accountable for defining what is reusable, what we want to buy, what we don't want to buy, around the assets that we are purchasing. The more information that he has at his fingertips, the more accurate his guesses are going to be. We do about two good-sized acquisitions a year, over the past few years. In the past year, as we have had the model, we have seen his guesses getting better.

BA: So am I right in saying that it is making the process far smoother, and giving you confidence, when you acquire a company?

SJ: Yes, it tells us what we can rely on. For example, we realized that the multi-brand thing is a big deal. A lot of systems were built for a single brand. Having that as an attribute, understanding it is important. Just because a system can support a business function doesn't mean that it can support it for a different brand. Think of something simple such as statement printing. So, having that as an attribute in the catalog where the architect can come in by business function and look at *accounts payable* or *accounts receivable*, for example. The entity we are thinking of acquiring has this function, with a certain number of people, and does a particular number of invoices a month. Can I plug that into whatever application of whoever outsourced partner we have running that business process? He has to be able to make that call in the bid room with no other information. That is where the accuracy of the information and our fine tuning some of the attributes is paying dividends.

We start with the catalog and we gradually grow the attributes. It is more important to have the catalog because that shows you fundamental gaps at the high-level. If you don't have a full set of business functions, then you don't know where your gaps are. So this is where having a framework for processes such as the APQC is so critical, even if you don't have the information underneath. But as you mature in different areas, that is where the understanding comes, by customizing the attributes to the specific questions that you will be asked time and again. That is really important. For us, *multibrand-aware* or *multibrand-capable* is one of those classic attributes. Generally, you won't find that in a standard meta-model for applications. However, it is one of those absolutely critical attributes for a group holding company like ours that is currently running about a dozen brands.

BA: One of the challenges of doing modeling work is the level of effort and detail that you go to. Too little detail and people can't see the point. Too much detail and you can get overwhelmed and create a rod for your back, as the amount of work in maintenance goes up dramatically. You have solved the problem by distributing the work. However, do you have a rule of thumb of where you draw the line?

SJ: For Enterprise Architecture, yes we do. We are cautiously encouraging others to use the toolset. We know that the more user communities are using it, the richer the data. So, yes, we have solved half of the problem by having people managing the data in their native environment. This is where I come back to this language of clarity, completeness, and coverage.

I can cover off completeness very quickly. This was a bit of an epiphany for me. This is why we focus on catalogs and taxonomies but not populating detail. For Enterprise Architecture, I don't need to do process simulation for a particular business unit.

If you are in the process flows world, for example, there are all of these additional attributes such as *number of transactions per hour* or *quality retries*. It makes for a very sexy demo of ProVision®. The rod gets created the moment you add these attributes, if it is not part of the production team's continuous improvement effort and they aren't going to monitor and maintain those metrics and round trip them back into the repository. Otherwise you don't continue to have an accurate reflection of the production state.

For me, all I care about is my eight business functions. Underneath that, I have my 600 process names. All I need are the organizations that provide those processes and the applications that support them. If you go to a BPTrends methodology, you will see that you are meant to link the business functions to the services. Suddenly that is one or two orders of magnitude more information that you are meant to collect. But for Enterprise Architecture, all I need to do is associate the applications to the functions. I don't need to go down to the services, which are thousands in number. Siebel has got 5,000 services. So, just one of the 1,100 applications that I am monitoring has 5,000 services. That is patently ridiculous to do that for the purposes of Enterprise Architecture. I can just associate the modules in Siebel with the business functions that are dependent upon them and I can do that in a day. The other important thing is how often do they change? When Siebel gets upgraded, how many web services change? The answer is quite a lot of them. How many modules change? They might add one. It is very rare that they take one away — easy for me to maintain accuracy and completeness at the EA level.

Let's come back to the data warehouse theory about slowly changing dimensions. The speed of change affects the way that you track those changes. There is a similar paradigm that hasn't been thought through with Enterprise Architecture. I want to master stuff only if: (a) nobody else is: (b) it is changing slowly; and (c) it is low volume.

BA: There are a couple of phrases that I use. One is that the purpose of modeling is to make *better decisions now*. I have used the term *better*, not perfect, as perfect is a mirage. Also, I have used *decisions*, not models, as we aren't modeling just for the sake of it. And finally I have said *now*, as six months time is too late. The other phrase is *good enough architecture*. Just enough to make the decisions and no more.

SJ: I concur with all of that. I think that the challenge is that some of the concepts are still abstract for a business owner. So for a business person, when I write up a brief to do an iteration of a business model, I ask them: "What are the top three questions that you need to answer? It doesn't matter if it is a strategy map, a business case, or anything else. Tell me your top three concerns".

For example, when making a business case, what is the benefit of changing the business function? On the debit side, what are the costs effort and risks? That is normal project management stuff. When I create a model, I will put the specific metrics into the PowerPoint slide. I will go to the effort of finding or building the views in the model that answer those specific questions. So I don't customize the meta-model itself, but for every business case I create a custom view. It seems like overkill but I don't care. The views come and go. They are volatile. The content within the model is well governed. The semantic checks and quality criteria are all there before it gets migrated out. There is something about being incredibly specific. Don't be abstract. State the question in business terms as though it came out of the mouth of a general manager. What is the question that the general manager wants to put proof on the table around when he is presenting his business case to the board? That makes it real.

BA: Can we talk about governance a little more. We have talked about operational governance. Is there a layer of governance that you need to put in place, to get really senior buy-in? Do you have a high-level governance committee with the CEO and other senior managers involved?

SJ: [laughs]

BA: So, you can't get that buy-in. Is that what you mean by a guerilla strategy?

SJ: Yes. You know all those old, wise, phrases such as *don't worry about what you can't control*. Anyone who thinks they can control the executive committee within a multinational is dreaming. An enterprise model, a method, a paradigm, will never be respected. You might get it to the forefront of their minds once when you want them to make a business decision. What I have done in the past eighteen months has been to counsel my teams against trying to get that senior stakeholder buy-in view. You need to have a sponsor. You need to have someone who passionately cares and can provide cover for you. In my case it is the Chief Information Officer (CIO). He talks about architecture as a competitive advantage, which our competitors don't have. The reason that he has developed such a point of view is that he trusted the head of architecture to go away and actually prove it to him. It was really a relational thing. He would mandate the first technology person on a program, when it was being planned, would be an enterprise architect. Before anyone from technology shows up, when you are putting a project together, it needs to be shaped by an enterprise architect. Why? Because they are the only people in the group who are thinking group wise. We now have principles that the company doesn't have, that we will make decisions for the benefit of the group, not for the benefit of the individual company.

Coming back to the culture, we are now able to use some of the guiding principles and behaviors for the group, to get some of these organizational things taken care of. The CEO doesn't care if we live or die, whether or not we are on a project, and neither does the executive group for any of the companies care about such things. We don't talk to them about architecture ever.

As long as you have someone protecting your back and budget, then you don't need to talk to them. We live and die on our merits. If I can't be one of the five people on the leadership team and make a fundamental difference to the paradigm of how they going about the project in the first four weeks, then I shouldn't be on the project. In that first four weeks, it is more about enterprise thinking, reuse, and some of those good architecture things that we believe in. It isn't about *look how good my model is*. You aren't even at that point. You are just talking about methods, gates, and the Gant chart in that first four weeks. But in that period, it is where you have set the mould as to whether you are going to be successful in an enterprise viewpoint of that work. I can now point back to ten group principles that we have created to drive alignment across the group because the different business groups were too fragmented. The pendulum has kind of swung in our favor in the last couple of years. In other companies that I have worked in, the pendulum swung the opposite way.

They split the organization into several independent companies, separate technologies, separate everything. So, it just depends on where you are in that enterprise-thinking lifecycle.

BA: Looking back over the last few years, are there some mistakes that you made where you feel you really learned a lesson, and would be happy to share that, so that other people don't make the same mistake as you.

SJ: Yes, I think the detail thing is important. I got too caught up in SOA being the center of the enterprise model. SOA is the web service catalog paradigm. In reality, if I come up three or four levels and really understand business strategy and the value tree, that happens much earlier and is much more strategic, and is a lot less effort, to be honest. It has a much bigger impact. It is helping people understand that if you have balanced drivers and you have only ten votes and you want to do twenty things. Let's weight them against each other. Let's use enterprise modeling as a method to prioritize and understand the impact on these competing things. In my own mind, I have woken up and stopped sweating the detail. I really focus on aiming the gun. If there is one thing that we can do is get the gun pointing towards the battlefield. Then, hopefully, we can make it aim quite accurately. But, once the gun is fired, once the projects have started, the controls that we have are very low. The project management office and the Steering Committees take over. If we haven't got the strategy and planning right from an enterprise point of view, then we have got nowhere.

In the past I have come in and tried stuff midway through the development cycle. I have come in and implemented process modeling. I have spent my life getting attacked by people asking me why I was implementing this heavyweight methodology.

In many cases that methodology is appropriate; it does accelerate the work and does reduce risk. But it is a much harder journey than getting them on the boat at the start of the journey. For me, it is about understanding the annual planning cycle. What are the windows of opportunity? How can I be strategic about planning and position to get models on the table and be able to say, "What if we were to do our strategic planning cycle this way, this year?" What I am doing is reflecting the entities and relationships in the meta-model out of ProVision®. I am explaining that this is the really mature way to do this. Maybe I have unplugged myself for a week, taken up last year's strategy, mocked it up in the tool, and shown them what it looks like and what some of the potential gaps are.

This is the other way of doing things—instead of saying, "This is the new way of doing things, this is the new methodology", we actually show the project management office, the real artifacts with real data that they will understand. If I sell them 10%, then they will buy 90%. I just need to show them something that is pretty compelling and solves a particular need at that time. So that is really it.

I have gone from building heavyweight models through to deploying them to focusing on Sales 101, but using real data and answering real questions. I don't wait to be asked, I'd rather say: "I care about this business. This is my business. My job as a senior employee is to grow this business. If I believe in enterprise modeling, then I need to use it for good and I need to use it now. Nobody else is as passionate about this as me. So why don't I just get on with it and do something real."

Summary

If all that you wish to do is draw pictures, then Visio will do the job. However, as soon as you want to create a model of the key parts of the enterprise, a drawing package is inadequate. It simply is just not designed for this purpose. You can't maintain thousands of objects, you can't collaborate, and you can't scale.

ProVision® is one of a handful of software packages that have been designed to help manage large, complex organizations.

ProVision® is part of the Open Text Metastorm business process execution suite. As your enterprise matures and grows, you may want to be able to automate the monitoring of high value or high volume processes. By adopting ProVision®, you give yourself the ability to transition to business process execution, without the need to switch platforms.

Of the tools that are designed to model the whole business, each has strengths and weaknesses. ProVision® is a good all round tool.

Sandra developed a point of view that the strongest link to business strategy is change events. Change events link to business process. They also link to assets and third-party relationships that might deliver a combination of processes or assets.

Many business leaders still struggle with the need for modeling. It is too abstract a concept. Therefore, if you can't convince them that modeling is a good idea, they won't see the benefits of a single environment in which to practice business process execution.

Why use ProVision®? Drawing packages such as Visio are not designed to support such a process, are not easy to maintain, and cannot scale. ProVision® is one of the simplest tools available with good overall coverage. Later, if the business wants to, there is the added bonus that it can transition to business process execution. ProVision® is an enabling technology. It supports decision makers to make better decisions now. It acts as a portal that collates information from multiple sources to create views of the business. These views inform strategy.

In the next chapter, we will examine business frameworks in more detail and understand how they help us develop strategy.

3
Using a Framework

The purpose of a framework is to get a consistent understanding by adopting a common language. By their nature, frameworks have strengths and weaknesses. Thus, the user needs to understand the problem that the framework was designed to solve. As we shall see, there is no perfect framework. In this chapter, we will cover:

- **What a business framework is**:

  In this section I will clarify the confusing relationship between various frameworks. I argue that frameworks are best understood as fitting into one of three levels. Once you understand the characteristics of each level, then you can select the right framework for the task. I will illustrate the power of using the right framework at the right time.

- **The Enterprise Designer framework (level 1)**:

  In this section, each of the 26 components of the Enterprise Designer framework are defined and explained in alphabetical order.

- **The ArchiMate framework (level 2)**:

  Because the Enterprise Designer framework is the base from which all other frameworks have been derived, we can now use it to examine the ArchiMate framework. In this section, I will describe the components of the Open Forum's ArchiMate framework and use Enterprise Designer to clarify the gaps.

- **eTOM (level 3)**:

  Top-level frameworks are practical and functional. eTOM is a framework that describes business processes. As with ArchiMate, there are logical inconsistencies that derive from creating a framework at this level.

What is a business framework

A business framework is not an exhaustive enterprise architecture framework. It has a higher context. The purpose of a business framework is to define the relationships between key business concepts so that everyone in the organization shares a high-level common language. Thus, when they communicate and collaborate, they are not using the same term to mean different things. When a database developer uses the word *customer*, it does not mean the same thing to a salesperson. For the database developer, the term *customer* is a field in a database. For the salesperson, it is someone with whom they are conducting business.

How frameworks can confuse

The original idea of enterprise architecture was to capture the information about the whole enterprise. However, this has proven to be too hard for most businesses. Over a period of time, the meaning of the term **enterprise architecture** has changed. I have seen discussions on `www.linkedin.com` where the meaning of the term has resulted in thousands of posts. This tells me that there isn't, and probably will never be, any agreement.

Given the diversity of opinions, Open Text Metastorm is intentionally neutral. It provides all options and lets the user decide. ProVision® is designed to support industry-standard enterprise architecture and business frameworks. The user can modify a framework or create their own.

To do this, they need to understand the key components of any framework and why it has been developed. We look at some of the key objects that the modeler will want to create, and propose suggestions of how these models can be created and linked together to give an end-to-end business-focused view of the whole organization.

The term **framework** is used to mean different things. As previously discussed, TOGAF is really a process methodology. The Zachman framework defines components in a grid but does not provide much assistance in the methodology to model them.

eTOM (The enhanced Telecom Operation Map) is an industry-specific framework that defines a comprehensive catalog of processes.

ArchiMate describes itself as (**refer to** `www.archimate.org`) a modeling technique (language) for describing enterprise architectures. It presents a clear set of concepts within and relationships between architecture domains, and offers a simple and uniform structure for describing the contents of these domain.

There are many more frameworks that focus on specific industries or business domains. Therefore, it is easy for the reader to become confused. However, if we introduce the concept of layers, and make a clear distinction between framework and methodology, the relationship between the different frameworks becomes clear. Moreover, advanced modelers can start to pick components of the various frameworks to enhance and support each other.

Making sense of frameworks

Understanding the framework can mean different things to different people; how do we resolve this? What we need is a framework of frameworks or, as John Zachman once called it, a meta-meta-meta model. Frameworks can be classified into three levels. This can be represented with the help of a table using a linguistic analogy:

Level	Metaphor	Framework	Methodology
3	sentence	Industry-specific frameworks such as eTOM	
2	word	Zachman, ArchiMate	
1	letter	Enterprise Designer	Enterprise Designer

Some other metaphors that you might find helpful include:

- **Machine code (level 1), Operating system (level 2) ,Application (level 3)**:

    All software consists of 0 and 1, and in the early stages of software development, holes were punched into cards to represent the ON/OFF states. Operating systems enable programmers to create platforms without the need to understand assembler. An operating system is of little use, unless there are applications that sit on top of it and help solve real world problems.

- **Physics (level 1), Chemistry (level 2), Biology (level 3)**:

    At the base level is the world of physics, where everything comprises of atoms (of course this is an oversimplification). Atoms combine together to form chemical compounds. At the biological level, we start to see living, functional systems.

Enterprise Designer will tell you all the core concepts that you need to describe a business, and will give you a methodology for determining which aspects of the business to model, and in what depth. It literally consists of 26 letters.

Once you understand what the available letters are, you can then move up a level and start combining them to form words. This is the strength of the Zachman and ArchiMate frameworks.

Industry or domain frameworks are a level above. Now the components appear as working processes, guiding the modeler on the business functions that are required to make the business run. This is the least abstract framework and thus the easiest to grasp. The advantage of using an industry framework is that many of the working processes are already provided, based on best practices. This avoids the need to build from the ground up.

When the highest-level framework is complete and consistent, there is no need to examine the deeper levels. However, as they may have been developed without reference to the lower levels, they may have logical inconsistencies that can be understood and resolved only at a lower level.

Therefore, letters are combined to form words. Words are combined to form sentences. It is only when you start to create sentences that you have a framework that is both useful and meaningful. However, if the words are misspelled or have missing letters, then the sentence will be ambiguous or confusing.

Once again, we can see the relationship of context and content. Each level sets the context for the level above.

Enterprise Designer classifies all processes into 10 types. In a particular organization, there might be hundreds or thousands of processes, each of which performs a specific function. If the product or service that they deliver is not working well, you can use the Enterprise Designer framework to classify all processes into the 10 categories. You might find that one of the 10 is either missing or poorly designed. You can then focus on fixing that class of process and not even touch the other nine classes.

Is it really possible to forget one of the 10 process types? Yes. It happens all the time. I once acted as a consultant to a large company that had a big team of modelers designing a brand new set of products and services. They had made hundreds of process models based on information gathered from focus groups.

We sat down together to do a review of their work to date. I looked at the models that they designed and used the 10 classifications as an overlay. After reviewing for 10 minutes I asked, "Where are your quit processes?", The team looked confused. "If someone wants to cancel the service, where are the processes that describe that?", I offered an explanation to my question.

There was a stunned silence. This was important as one could reasonably expect this to happen quite a few times in a year. It was not a trivial oversight. How had they forgotten? There were no focus groups of ex-customers, so the information never got captured.

This is the power of using the right framework at the right time.

Enterprise Designer framework

In *Chapter 1, Designing a Strategy*, we outlined the five core components that are needed to describe any organization, along with the sequence in which to capture them. Here is a quick reminder. Every business has *goals*. The way to achieve goals is to create *customers*. To retain those customers, offer *products and services* that the customers want. To provide these services in a consistent and repeatable way, design *processes*. These processes combine seven *elements* together. The five basic components are:

- Elements (seven elements that are used to configure a process)
- Processes (ten types of process and how they relate to each other)
- Products and services (how and why to create a model of products and services)
- Customers (how and why to create a model of customers)
- Goals (where the five types of goal fit into your business model)

Let's take a closer look at these five components. Each component breaks down into greater detail. In all, there are 26 components that can be used to describe any business at a high level. By assigning a letter of the alphabet to each component, it is easier to recall. Some of the words have been modified or invented for this purpose. Therefore, when having conversations with stakeholders, change the language to suit the audience. By adopting a framework that is simple and complete, you ensure that nothing gets overlooked.

The definitions of the 26 elements are based on the material, first published by Bill Aronson, in *Enterprise Designer – building a conscious organization* (Lulu 2008).

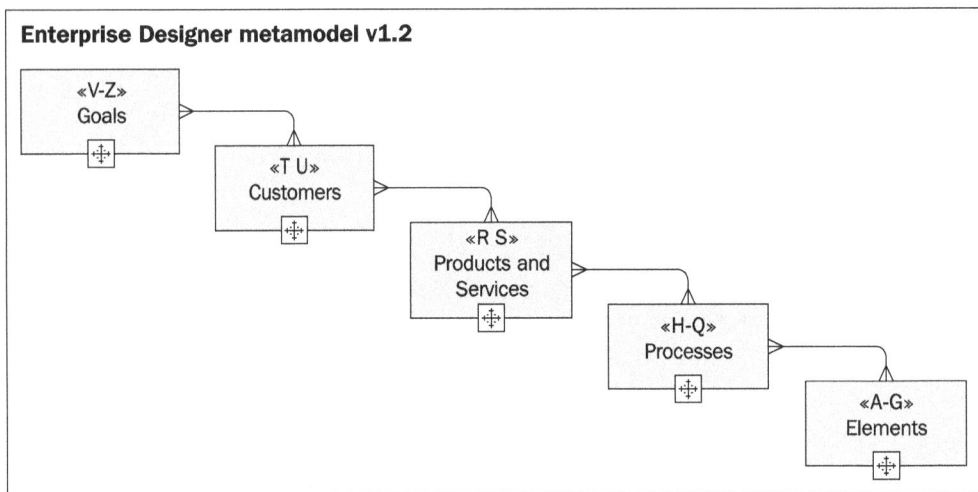

Enterprise Designer metamodel v1.2

How to read this section

Because this section is quite detailed, the following introduction explains the format. Because ProVision® allows any framework, the user must understand what objects they may use, and what they should not, so that the framework remains consistent.

While we use the Enterprise Designer framework, this issue applies to any framework. For example, the eTOM framework describes processes. Should the modeler use the process or activity object? There has to be consistency, otherwise one modeler may use one type of object while the other might use a different one.

Each time a modeler makes a choice like this, they open up possibilities and close off other choices. In this example, a process object cannot be simulated.

Component group	Letters assigned
Elements	A–G
Processes	H–Q
Products and services	R,S
Customers	T,U
Goals	V–Z

Each letter of the framework is preceded by a general explanation about the component group in which it falls. For example, the first seven letters of the alphabet are **elements**. The following table illustrates how each component is defined.

Component	Example	Comment
Component definition	Actor	The Enterprise Designer component.
Naming convention	Person or position	How the object is named in ProVision®.
Permitted objects	Market	The complete list of objects provided by ProVision®. Advice on which objects should be avoided.
Relationships	Position Role grid	How to associate and link objects to relate meaningful information.
Comments		General comments and illustrations.

Seven elements A–G

In the Enterprise Designer framework, seven elements are defined that can be combined to configure a process. **Actors** and **computer systems** perform work manually or automatically. In either case, they may be constrained by **business rules** as they perform activities. When a process is performed, **data** is created, read, updated, and deleted as the actors interact with the process. Each process, and each step within a process, is triggered by **events**, takes place in **facilities**, and the actors make use of **gear** and other equipments. The seven elements are complete. There is no eighth element. Thus, once you have captured information related to the seven elements, you know that nothing has been missed.

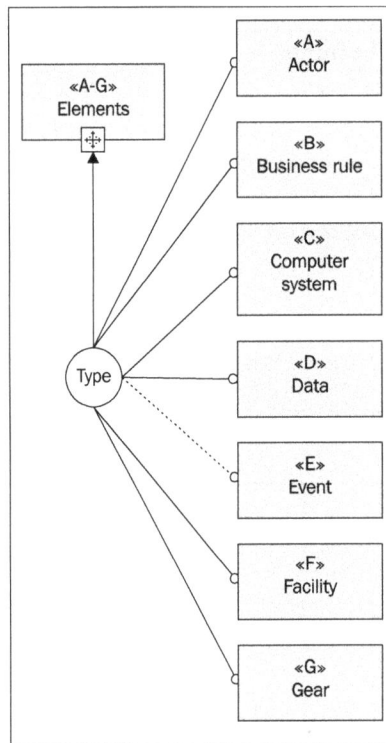

Actor

An actor is a person manually performing a role in a process.

Naming convention

ProVision® uses the object name **person** to represent a type of actor. Enterprise Designer renames the object to **position** in order to clarify that this is not an individual.

Permitted objects

ProVision® treats market, organization, role, and person as candidate (or type of) actor objects.

Permitted models

Actors can appear in any of the following models:

- Business Interaction (participant)
- Communication (subject or participant)
- Navigator (subject or participant)
- Organization (subject or participant)
- Use Case (participant)
- Workflow (swim lane)

Relationships

Many processes require people to perform a collection of roles. Enterprise Designer calls them actors. In this approach, each position description is the collection of roles that the actor performs in a set of workflows. Most organizations are hierarchical, so the position description identifies the person's place in the hierarchy, as well as what they do.

You can create organizational charts in ProVision®. These charts reflect business units that decompose down to positions. You can then create an Association Grid or Navigator Model that shows which positions do specific roles. This is where you will gain the benefit of flexibility. You will be able to see which other positions have the capacity to perform the same role. When you design a new process, you can see where the gaps are in terms of skill, training, and experience. In a business continuity event, you can identify what other position has the necessary skill to fill in for someone who is unavailable.

You can then associate positions with roles and enter the role as swim lanes.

We recommend that you do not use a position in a workflow swim lane. This is because a position being a collection of roles, if you use roles in swim lanes, then you will increase flexibility. For example, the role of proofreader is often done by many people (positions) in the organization, so in a swim lane you would want to have the proofreader role. However, there may be a position in the organization called *proofreader*. For this reason, we recommend that instead of using a noun for a role, you use the format verb noun. In this instance, the role might be *proofread documents*.

Thus a report can be generated that shows the positions that tie back to the workflows.

Comments

Organizations and markets can notionally be actors and are included for completeness. For example, a market might be the first swim lane in a workflow model. It is better to use positions rather than roles in an organizational chart, and roles rather than positions for swim lanes in a workflow. In the following diagram, we can see an organization model used as an organizational chart with business units and positions:

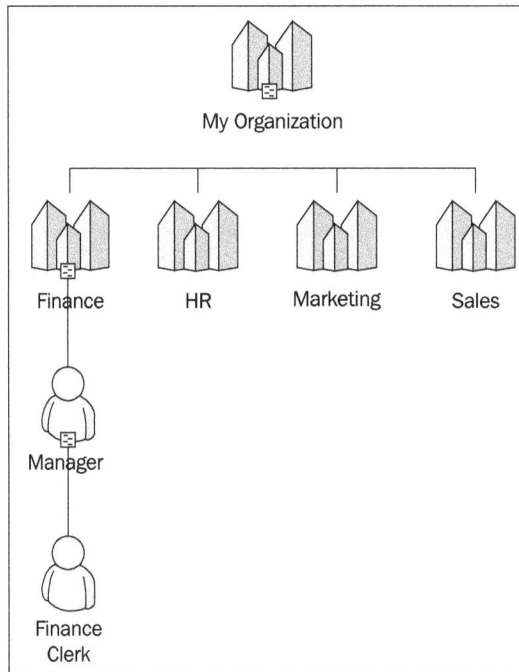

Business rules

As per www.businessrulesgroup.org:

> *A business rule is a statement that defines or constrains some aspect of the business. It is intended to assert business structure or to control or influence the behavior of the business.*

As a general rule, regulatory controls are imposed on the organization through legislation, standards are set by external bodies such as industry associations, code of conduct is dictated by the culture of the organization and other mechanisms, whereas business rules are defined by the organization through policies and guidelines. Regulation, standards, contracts, and other factors set the context for business rules.

Naming convention

Enterprise Designer renames the rule object as business rule to fit with its naming convention.

Permitted objects

The following objects may be used:

- Business Rule
- Standard

Permitted models

The following models may be used:

- Navigator (subject or participant)
- Rule (subject or participant)
- Standard (subject or participant)
- Strategy (subject or participant)

The Strategy model can also be used to visualize business rules, but standards are not a legal object—you can still make associations between business rules and standards in a Strategy model but not visualize them.

Relationships

If you start to treat business rules as an asset, then you will be able to simplify them and apply consistent business rules across all processes that drive products and services.

The easiest way is to associate business rules or standards for each workflow. Once you have made the relevant associations, you can see them in a Navigator model.

Comments

Business rules, legislation, policy, and custom shape the way a process runs. If these rules are articulated, they are easier to understand and easier to change. Older computer systems embed the business rules, making them hard to find. It is quite expensive and difficult to change these business rules. The trend is to uncouple each of the seven elements. Business rule engines provide rules to people or computer systems that require decision services. As they are separate, they are easier to maintain.

ProVision® also offers a standards object and model. Both business rules and standards require adherence. You can associate business rules to standards. You can associate business rules and standards to pretty much any other object. If you want to see these associations, then use a Navigator model.

If you associate a business rule to a specific activity, rather than the Workflow model in which it is placed, then every time you place that activity in another model, the association is a characteristic. In the following diagram, we can see a hierarchical Rule model with the highest level acting as a classification system:

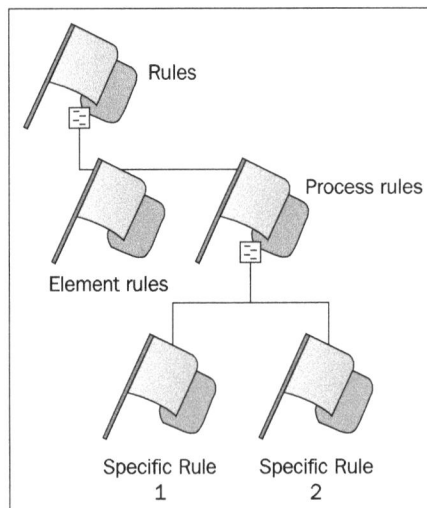

Computer system

A computer system is software that automatically performs work. It receives data as inputs, stores and manipulates it, and then provides useful outputs for the process. Software resides on, and depends on, physical equipment and gear. However, for the purposes of this discussion, the two elements are quite distinct. The primary object used to model systems is the system object.

Naming convention

There is no change for the default naming convention.

Permitted objects

The following objects may be used:

- System

  And:

- Component
- Database
- Interface
- Store
- User Interface

Permitted models

The following models may be used:

- Business Class (subject)
- Business Interaction (participant)
- Communication (subject or participant)
- Deployment (subject)
- Navigator (subject or participant)
- Storyboard (subject)
- System (subject or participant)
- System Interaction (subject or participant)
- Use Case (participant)
- Workflow (swim lane)

Relationships

The System Interaction model shows the relationships between systems (computer applications), databases, networks, the *who* objects (market and organization), and the *where* objects (location, facility, and equipment).

Comments

Many processes use computer systems (applications) instead of actors (people performing roles). If a computer system fails, people do part of the process manually or the process may need to stop. Thus, computer systems are *automated workers* and actors are *manual workers*.

ProVision® is distinct from a **configuration management database (CMDB)**. A CMDB stores information on individual pieces of gear. In other words, a CMDB is about the physical world. ProVision® is about the logical world.

The following figure shows a System Interaction model. The HR System communicates with the Authentication System, providing real time information about who is permitted access to the Corporate data. The two systems are housed in the IT Facility.

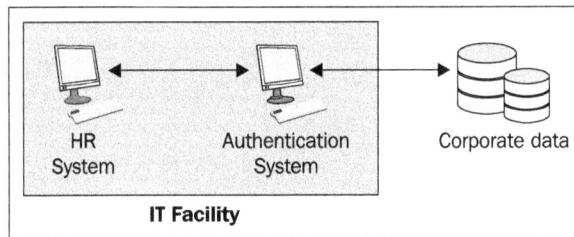

Data

Data is structured information used by the business in processes. A process consumes data; it creates, reads, updates, or deletes data. The primary object used to model data is the business class.

Naming convention

There is no change for the default naming convention.

Permitted objects

The following objects may be used:

- Business Class

  And:

- Attribute
- Message
- Operation
- Package
- Service
- Service Operation
- State

Permitted models

The following models may be used:

- Business Class (participant)
- Navigator (subject or participant)
- Sequence (participant)
- Statechart (participant)
- Subtype (subject or participant)

Relationships

ProVision® provides several model types for the *information architect*. The Business Class model is used to model classes of data such as customer, invoice, quotation, and warehouse. ProVision® defines a business class as *a class that is used as a template to express a business concept.*

If required, a specific business class can be decomposed using a Subtype model. ProVision® defines a subtype as (this definition is taken from a ProVision® help document):

> *a class, package, or interface whose definition is a refinement of the more general class, package, or interface (its super type). For example, "preferred customer" is a refinement of the more general class "customer." Therefore, "customer" is the super type, and "preferred customer" is the subtype*

Again, referring to the same documentation, a package is a general purpose mechanism for organizing elements into groups.

Package models may contain other packages. Unlike UML, ProVision® uses packages for the purpose of modeling data, only not for any other purpose.

Thus the hierarchy goes from package to business class. There is no logical distinction between a business class and a subtype, so you won't find a subtype object in the inventory. They are both business class objects. In the following screenshot of the object inventory, you cannot tell that **Mobile** is a subtype of **Phone**:

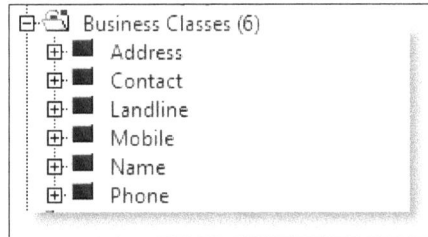

This becomes apparent only if you explore its properties or open the Subtype Model.

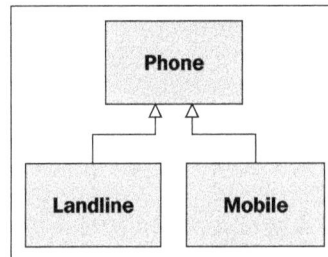

In the object inventory, when a business class is linked to a package, it includes the package name to make it obvious. One consequence is that two business classes can have identical names (provided that they are children of different packages). Another consequence could be a package and business class end up having the same name because they are different object types. (A subtype could not have the same name as its parent because both are business classes.)

In the following example screenshot, the business class **Medical Plan** is an integral part of the **Benefit Plan** package:

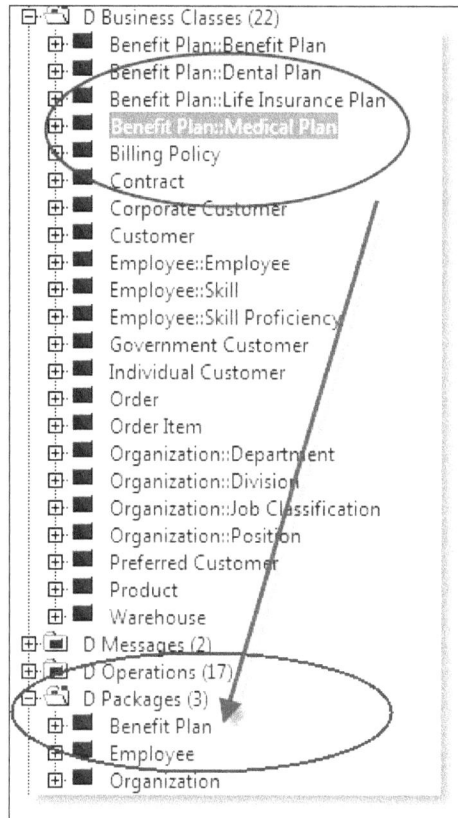

Packages and business classes can be associated with other objects that implement them, such as computer systems.

Comments

Processes require data such as a client's name and address. Data and computer systems are quite distinct. Many older computer systems blur the distinction. As a result, you can manipulate data only through a specific application. This is the same as the problem we find when we hardcode business rules in computer systems.

You can add **attributes** to a business class and these will display and interpret. These attributes are objects in themselves. You will find them in the object inventory. However, attributes are always linked to their parent object.

Similarly, you can show the **operations** that a business class participates in, these will also show up in the object inventory.

You can also show the **states** that a business class may move through, and parts of a business class (package, business, or subtype).

Event

An event is something that can trigger the start of, or stop, a process, or a specific step within a process. Events can be classified into three types — response, threshold, or time (as discussed in *Chapter 2, Making a Business Case*).

Naming convention

There is no change in the naming convention.

Permitted objects

The only permitted object is Event.

Permitted models

The following models may be used:

- Communication (participant)
- Event (subject or participant)
- Navigator (subject or participant)
- Operation (participant)
- Sequence (participant)
- Statechart (participant)
- Storyboard (participant)
- System Interaction (participant)
- Use Case (subject or participant)
- Workflow (participant)

Relationships

ProVision® lets you create parent–child Event models. You can also add events on the links between objects as appropriate.

When an event is included on a link, is displayed within quotation marks to distinguish it from any receivable that may be passed from one object to another. If the model type you choose supports two-way links (for example a Communication model), then events can start at either end.

Comments

Events tell a process when to start, stop, or change course. For example, one type is a time trigger. In the example, *IF it is the end of the month THEN run the debtors printout, end of the month* (isTrue) is the event that triggers the action *run the debtors printout*. You combine all the other elements to produce a process. An event fires up, or is triggered by a process or activity.

By capturing all the events, you can get an overview of all processes without the need to show what takes place within a process. For example, a process may start with Monthly Report Requested and end with Monthly Report Emailed. If you know these two events, you understand the point of the process without needing to know how it works. The process is a black box.

ProVision® does not make a distinction between an event that starts a process and one that takes place within it. Enterprise Designer proposes that it is generally good enough to capture the initiating events of a process. For example, if you look at any workflow, there is usually one initiating event and a receivable at the conclusion. Although there may be exception processes, the main flow or *happy path* is what counts.

If you manage these contextual events, you can treat the workflow as a black box triggered by an event that produces a receivable. In this context, how it does it is irrelevant.

As you create Event models, you will start to see that different products and services have similar starting events. This creates opportunities to standardize and reuse the same event to trigger multiple processes.

If you don't manage events then you lose control of a key component of your processes.

The following diagram shows an Event model:

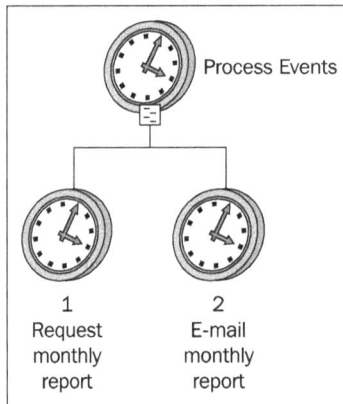

Facility

ProVision® provides three objects to describe where activities take place. These *where* objects are in a hierarchy from location, to facility, to equipment.

Naming convention

Enterprise Designer renames the equipment object to **gear**, in order to fit with its naming convention.

Permitted objects

The following objects may be used:

- Equipment
- Facility
- Location

Permitted models

The following models may be used:

- Communication (subject or participant)
- Location (subject or participant)
- Navigator (subject or participant)

- System Interaction (subject or participant)
- Workflow (swim lane)

Relationships

ProVision® provides the Location model, which you can use to model hierarchical relationships from location to facility to gear (equipment).

For Communication and System Interaction models, you may wish to re-style the object of your choosing to a rectangle or an ellipse. You can then show *placement* by dragging other objects onto the *where* object, as in the illustration in the next section.

The relationship between the objects is interpreted using the interpreter.

Comments

Elements need virtual or physical facilities. In the case of actors, the facility might be an office. In the case of computer systems, the location may be a piece of computer gear. For events, business rules, and data, the facilities may be physical such as a document, or virtual such as a computer system.

Why would you want to use *where* objects in swim lanes? There is a valid case to use them for business continuity. All ProVision® models support the concept of layers, which allows objects to be shown or hosted on different layers. Thus, you could have one layer that would show the normal activities and the locations where they take place. Another layer could show the alternate location if the main location failed.

In the following diagram, we can see that the organization is based in the USA and has two sites. The research center has genome sequencers at its site in New York.

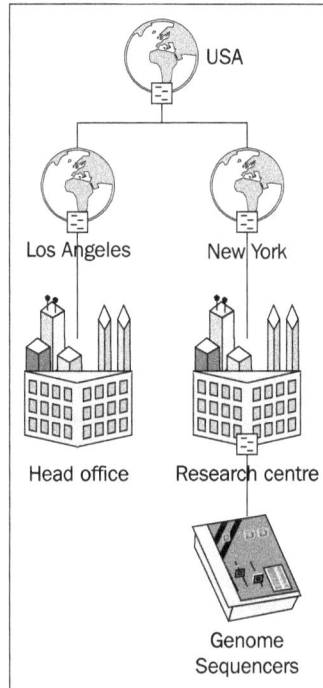

Gear

Equipment used when conducting a process. Examples include computer equipment such as servers and routers, furniture, and office equipment.

Naming convention

Enterprise Designer renames the equipment object to **gear**, in order to fit with its naming convention.

Permitted objects

The following object may be used:

* Equipment

Permitted models

The following models may be used:

- Communication (subject or participant)
- Deployment (subject or participant)
- Location (subject or participant)
- Navigator (subject or participant)
- Platform (subject or participant)
- System Interaction (subject or participant)
- Workflow (swim lane)

Relationships

Open Text Metastorm provides the Location model to show the relationships between locations, facilities, and gear. Because it is a hierarchical model, you can't link equipment directly to locations.

> If you want to get a complete list of associations, go to the free resources at www.enterprisedesigner.com and download the Excel spreadsheet of the framework.

Comments

Many processes need gear, such as equipment or furniture. If the process uses computer systems, then it will need computer gear for the systems to work. If the process uses people, then it may need office furniture and equipment.

You can re-style *where* objects to be shapes by right-clicking on the object. If you want to retain the styling when you use the same object in another model, you can also set that.

You can't use hierarchical models to place objects on top of each other. However, as we have previously seen, non-hierarchical models such as the Navigator model can be used for this purpose.

There are three related terms—networks, platforms, and technology.

Open Text Metastorm defines a **network** as an integrated system of hardware and software used to communicate data throughout an enterprise. Components of a typical network might include a server, PCs, a database management system, a printer, operating system software, among other entities.

So a network combines computer systems and gear. If you need to model a network, first model the computer systems and gear, then combine them together using a System Interaction model with the network as the subject.

Open Text Metastorm defines technology as a capability incorporated within or installed upon a piece of equipment (gear definition taken from the ProVision® help file). A combination of these capabilities (technologies) provides a viable environment for the operation of systems or system components. These technologies provide an essential set of capabilities that the system components can employ (for example, communication, persistence, and so on). Typically, this essential environment is available across all of the pieces of equipment where a system component is expected to be installed. Technology decisions are also made during the design of systems or system components. A set of technologies is chosen to make up the technical architecture that serves as the target for system design. Once these system components are developed, they are installed upon the nodes that support the technical capabilities designed within the components.

Most people think of technology as hardware. But for ProVision®, technology is not gear but what the gear enables the organization to do. It really is a technical capability. Technology models are hierarchical, and the only legal objects are technologies and links to child technologies.

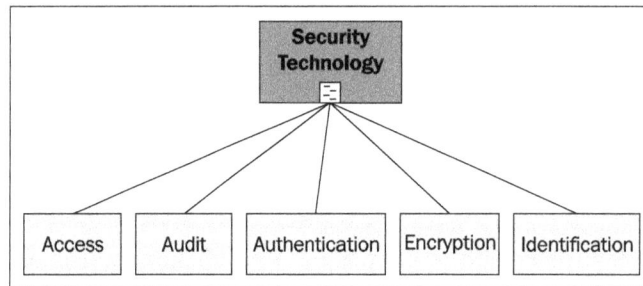

Finally, Open Text Metastorm defines a **platform** as a set of related technologies that provide the ability to execute system components (again, definition taken from the help file). Platforms can be nested in the model to depict the composition higher-level platforms.

So, just as a network combines computer systems and gear (equipment), you can see a platform is a combination of technologies. Putting it another way, you can combine various technologies to make one or more platforms, as one technology could be used to support multiple platforms.

Use the hierarchical platform modeler and make the subject a platform. You can then add platforms and technologies. In the following example, Security Technology has been placed on top of the Security Platform. The various sub-technologies have been placed on top of Security Technology. When you place objects on top of each other in a model, ProVision ® understands the relationship and updates the interpretation accordingly.

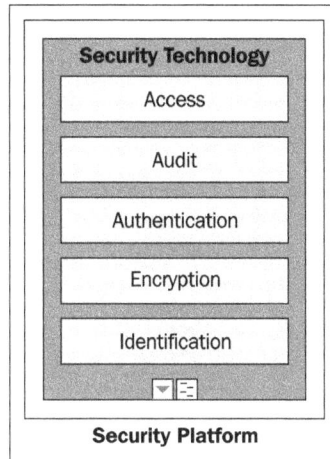

Ten processes H–Q

In the Enterprise Designer framework, processes are classified into 10 types labeled H-Q. It is not always necessary to deploy all 10. However, if one is missing, naturally this will be a candidate for process improvement. The question arises, "Is this process category missing because it is not required, or because its importance was underestimated?". For example, if a business decides to offer a product or service for free, then there will be no need to deploy a collect process (K).

If the company simply forgets to deploy a collect process, then the company will not be paid. If you think that this is not possible, then think again. I was once working as a consultant to a major, publicly listed company, which deployed a new product and forgot to hook up the collect process. Only when the manager complained that he had not been paid a bonus was the error discovered.

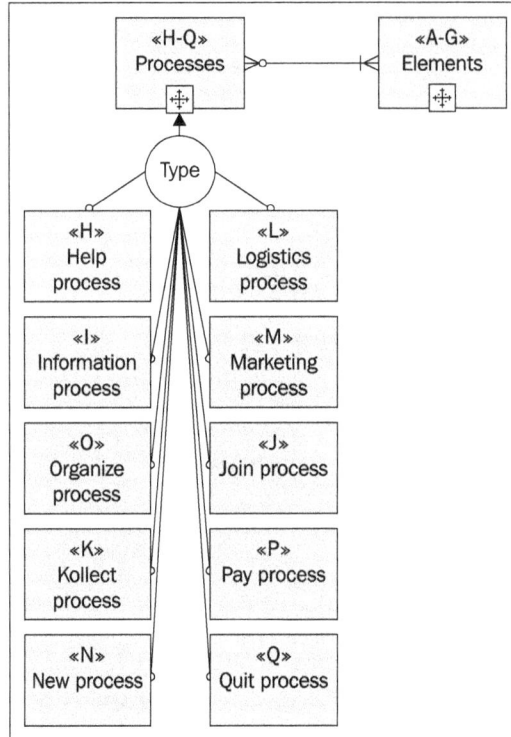

Process

See below under each of the 10 process categories.

Naming convention

There is no change in the naming conventions.

Permitted objects

The following objects may be used:

- Activity
- Process (limited use)

Permitted models

- Communication (subject or participant)
- Navigator (subject or participant)
- System Interaction (subject or participant)
- Workflow (as subject and objects in a swim lane)
- Process (subject or participant)
- Use Case (subject or participant)
- Sequence (subject)
- Storyboard (subject)
- Business Class (subject)

Relationships

While ProVision® provides a process object, the activity object offers more power and flexibility. Thus we use the activity object to model both processes and activities. We need one process object to connect activities to business domains as a direct relationship is not permitted.

Comments

The following definitions and clarifications are provided for the 10 process categories.

- **H – Help**: As the client takes delivery of the product or service, they may have questions. Clients may need a help process to solve problems.
- **I – Inform**: Inform processes provide information on how a service is running. Inform processes provide information but not interpretation. In other words, the output from an inform process is meant to be objective information, not hype.
- **J – Join**: The join processes assemble the components provided by the organize processes. The output from the join processes is then fed to the logistics processes.
- **K – Collect**: The organization needs a mechanism for a client to pay for products and services. This is the role of the collect processes.
- **L – Logistics**: Once you complete the join processes, you can deliver the product or service to the client. The logistics processes do this. This is the point where the organization and the client meet.

- **M – Market**: Marketing processes take the output from inform processes, interpret, and present it. Marketing processes, in the modern parlance, do the job of adding spin.

- **N – New**: The new processes define the way we make or amend a contract with a client. A service-level agreement is an example of how we describe that relationship.

- **O – Organize**: To provide a product service, you must first source or obtain the components. The organize processes do this. The outputs from the organize processes then flow into the join processes.

- **P – Pay**: The organization needs a mechanism to pay bills. This is the role of the pay processes. Consider if you need the same process for paying staff as well as bills.

- **Q – Quit**: Special processes apply when the organization or the client want to end the relationship. Very few organizations understand the importance of these processes. In large organizations people leave all the time. Does your organization have a process to find out why? Consider a process by which your staff can tell you the real reason why they are walking out the door. This is valuable information. What are the processes for returning products or obtaining refunds?

Receivables and services

Enterprise Designer models component parts as *receivables,* and final products and services delivered to the customer as *services.*

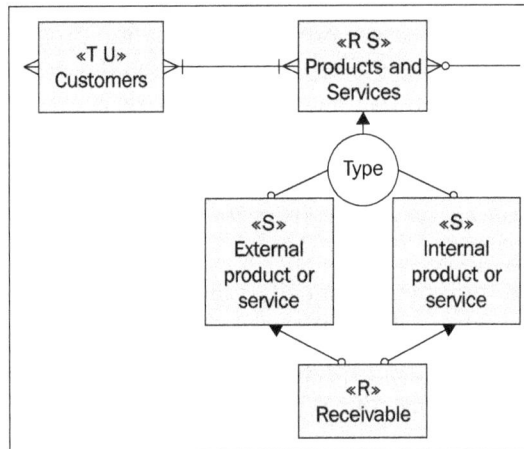

R – Receivable

Receivables are the outputs from any activity.

Naming convention

Enterprise Designer renames the deliverable object as receivable to fit with its naming convention.

Permitted objects

The following object may be used:

- Deliverable

Permitted models

The following models may be used:

- Business Class (subject)
- Communication (link)
- Deliverable (subject and object)
- Navigator (subject or participant)
- System Interaction (link)
- Use Case (link)
- Workflow (link)

Relationships

Receivables can appear on workflow links as outputs from a given activity, which then become the inputs for the next activity in the workflow.

Comments

As shown in the following diagram, the final deliverable from a sequence of activities is associated with its counterpart product. Why not just use the Business Domain object to represent both components and final products? ProVision® does not permit this. Conversely, why not just use the deliverable object to represent components and completed products? ProVision® does not permit deliverables to be used as the subject of high-level models such as Strategy.

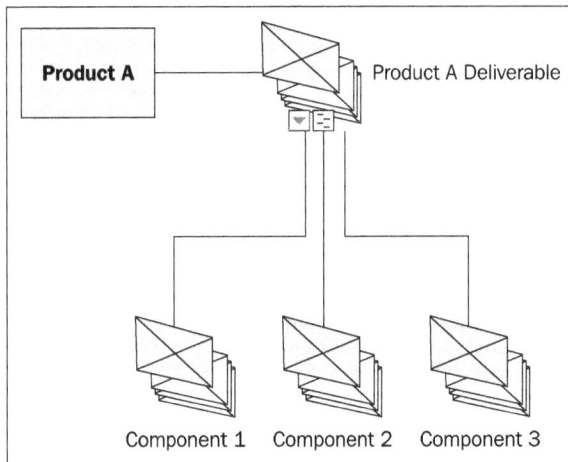

S—Service or product

A service or product is the output received by the customer. Enterprise Designer uses the business domain object to model products and services.

Naming convention

Enterprise Designer renames the business domain object as product to fit with its naming convention.

Permitted objects

- Business Domain

Permitted models

- Business Class (subject)
- Business Interaction (subject)
- Communication (subject or participant)
- Navigator (subject or participant)
- Process (subject or object)
- Strategy (subject)
- Use Case (subject or participant)

Relationships

The starting point for a high-level business architecture is a Client Services model. This is a Navigator model that shows which client groups get which products and services. Communication links are used to demonstrate these relationships. This model is used to set the context for all other models, as it demonstrates, from a customer's point of view, why the organization exists.

The Business Interaction model takes a product or service as its subject and then is used to describe the key players and interactions. The Strategy model describes how changes to the product can be achieved.

Comments

The most common way to model an organization is inside out, reflecting the perspective of the organization. The product is considered the end point. In an outside in approach, the product is the starting point. From the customer's perspective, it is the reason why they engage with the organization. Every product or service, whether delivered to an internal or external customer, can now be understood as a matrix of 10 processes by seven elements.

Customers and clients

In ProVision®, internal customers are modeled as *organization* objects, while external customers are modeled as *markets*. The hierarchy of objects goes from market to organization, to role or person. There are associated markets and organizations, such as suppliers and partners that form part of the value chain.

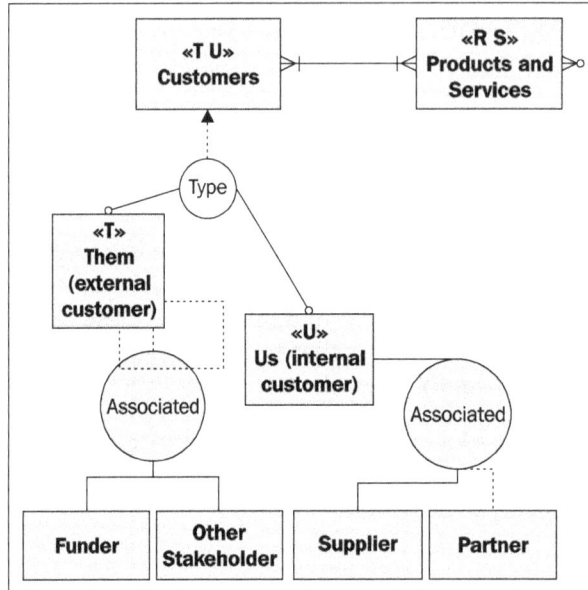

Markets

A customer is someone who pays for a product or service and may optionally use it. We use the market object in ProVision® to represent customers, unless identifying a specific individual customer, in which case we use the organization object.

The role of payer and user often splits. Our view of where the role splits is that, in the long term, the person who pays for the products and services are the more important. However, in the short term the user may bring influence to bear.

Organizations

The organization object is mainly used to represent parts of the business, but can also be used to model individual organizations outside the business such as regulators, competitors, and suppliers. In this case, specific organizations are modeled as children of markets.

Naming convention

Enterprise Designer prefixes the market object with the letter T, and the organization object with the letter U, to fit with its naming convention.

Permitted objects

- Market
- Organization

Permitted models

The following models may be used:

- Business Interaction (participant)
- Communication (subject or participant)
- Deployment Model (subject for organization)
- Navigator (subject or participant)
- Organization (subject or participant)
- System Interaction (participant)
- Use Case (participant)
- Workflow (swim lane)

Relationships

Use the market object when there is no need to distinguish a particular organization.

Comments

An organization's present reality is represented by the products and services it offers to customers. They might not be interested in what you might have offered last year or plan to offer next year.

This holds true for internal and external customers. It is common for one part of an organization, such as the Accounts department, to provide internal services.

Five goals V–Z

A **goal** is an intended measurable future state of the business.

- A strategy is the means to achieve a goal
- A tactic is a component of a strategy

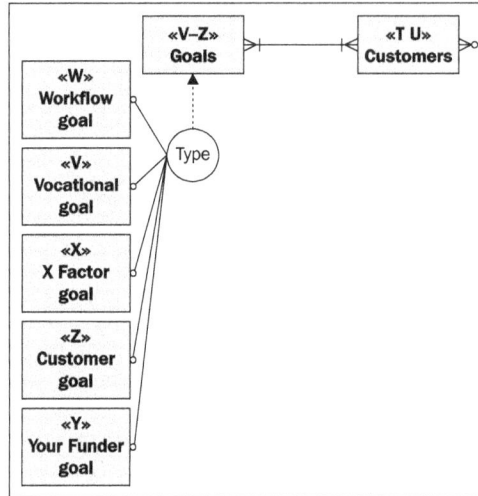

Goals

See below under each of the five goal categories.

Naming convention

There is no specific naming convention.

Permitted objects

The following objects may be used:

- Goals
- Measures

Permitted models

The following models may be used:

- Goal (subject or participant)
- Strategy (subject or participant)
- Navigator (subject or participant)

Relationships

Additional objects and models can be used to describe impacts, influences, opportunities, problems, projects, and requirements. These hierarchical models can then be linked to the overarching Strategy model, if required.

Comments

In the Enterprise Designer framework, the content represents the strategy by which we achieve the context set by the preceding layer. In other words:

- The only way to activate processes is to put in place elements
- The only way to deliver products and services to customers and clients is through processes
- The only way to achieve a goal is to deliver products and services to customers and clients

While goals must be measurable, the less measures the better. You can classify any goal into one or more of the five types described next.

- **V – Vocational:**

  The first group recognizes the importance of people in the organization. How are we developing? What are we doing to retain our staff? How do we make it a great place to work? People who love their jobs call it their vocation. In the future, staff will not want to be a part of an organization that continues to pollute the planet. The finest staff will migrate to organizations that use best practice. Organizations will have to adapt to retain talent. Although the people performing roles are just one of seven elements, they are the most important. We are human, after all.

- **W – Workflow:**

  The next group focuses on business needs. How can we improve the way we do things round here? This is the realm of business analysis and business process improvement. In the future, we will start to measure the carbon impacts of processes. We will start to reconfigure elements to make our processes carbon neutral.

- **X – X Factor**:

  While the other four goals are common to all enterprises, the X factor goals are unique to an organization. They are the goals that distinguish one organization from the other — their X factor. What does our organization need to have to make it different from every other? How can we foster this unique quality? This distinctive quality will form the basis of the company's position. A position is a succinct statement, ideally a single word or short phrase that describes what the company is famous for. Understanding the position is critical to an organization's success. The position precedes any marketing effort and should be the underlying theme.

  The X factor can be the intellectual capital or know-how of the organization. By distinguishing between an organization's capability and what it actually provides, new streams of business can be formed. An Australian company that had expertise in the installation of electricity meters was limited in how much it could grow. After working with a business coach, they realized that they could leverage that know-how to install water and gas meters. While the company thought of itself as being part of the electricity supply value chain, it never considered bidding for water or gas meter work. Once it understood that its X factor was the ability to install meters of any sort, then it was able to establish new revenue streams.

  A UK company that removed asbestos from old buildings wanted to expand its business. After working with a business coach, they realized that their unique expertise was in understanding how to safely remove dangerous materials from a site. With this understanding, they were able to reposition themselves and offer comprehensive services of which asbestos removal was just one.

- **Y – Your Funder**:

  This group of goals satisfies the financial needs of the funders. What do the people investing expect in return? If the organization is public, then the funders will be the agency that controls the funds such as a state treasury. If the organization is private, then the funders will be the shareholders. This group of goals also satisfies the needs of regulators who play a quasi-funder role.

- **Z – Customer**:

  The most important are goals that support clients. It is the last letter of the alphabet to reflect that this is where all the other components are leading. It is easy inside a large organization to forget the golden rule.

Comparing level 1 and level 2 frameworks

In this section, we now look at **Enterprise Designer** and **ArchiMate**, to understand their relative uses.

As discussed, Enterprise Designer is a framework of frameworks. It defines a set of 26 primitive components arranged into three layers called past, present, and future. The past is represented by the processes and elements used to configure processes. The present is represented by the customers, and the products and services that they receive. The future is represented by the goals of the organization. Enterprise Designer is also a methodology. The sequence in which you build models, the amount of detail you provide at each level, and the importance you attach to different aspects of the business are all defined.

A strength of Enterprise Designer is its simplicity. The framework can be understood by anyone in the business and it can be applied to any type of business, including government and not for profit. As it is simple, it acts as a lingua franca. Different specialists within the business can meet and communicate across organizational boundaries using Enterprise Designer, and then add detail and richness with specialist frameworks, in their own areas of responsibility. This section analyzes the similarities and differences between the components of the Enterprise Designer and ArchiMate frameworks using the ArchiMate definitions. The purpose is not to suggest that one or the other is better. By clarifying the differences, it is hoped that organizations that intend to use both can understand how to get the most from each.

In the introduction to the ArchiMate standard, the authors state (refer to `www.archimate.org`):

> *The primary reason for developing an enterprise architecture is to support the business by providing the fundamental technology and process structure for an IT strategy.*

Enterprise Designer takes a different approach. Using the same language we would say: *The primary reason for developing an enterprise design is to enable the business to make better decisions now.* Note that this statement is IT agnostic and thus is applicable to businesses that have no IT function.

ArchiMate framework

In this section, we examine the ArchiMate objects and show the relationship with their Enterprise Designer counterparts.

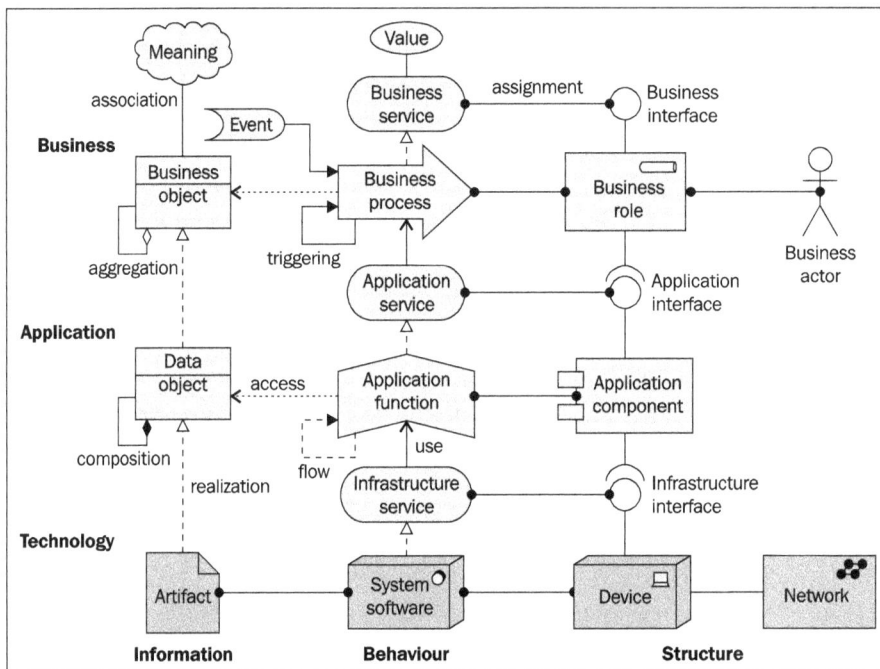

[The diagram is taken from www.archimate.org.]

ArchiMate uses a 3 x 3 grid to organize objects. Objects appear in three layers — Business, Application, and Technology, and are arranged into three columns — Information, Behavior, and Structure.

The Business layer offers products and services to external customers. These products and services are realized in the organization by business processes performed by business actors and roles.

The Application layer supports the Business layer with application services that are realized by (software) application components.

The Technology layer offers infrastructural services (for example, processing, storage, and communication services) needed to run applications, realized by computer and communication hardware and system software.

ArchiMate and Enterprise Designer objects comparison

This section covers the ArchiMate objects used to represent the Business layer. The icons and definitions are drawn from the ArchiMate standard. For each object, I will provide the equivalent Enterprise Designer object for comparison. This way, you can see the differences between the two frameworks.

Business actor

An organizational entity that is capable of performing behavior.

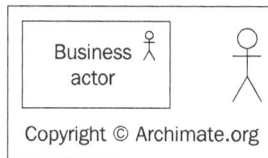

Enterprise Designer

Elements T and U represent external (Them) and internal (Us) organizational entities, respectively.

Business role

A named, specific behavior of a business actor, participating in a particular context.

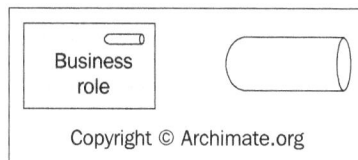

Enterprise Designer

Element **A** (Actor) represents a person performing a role.

Business collaboration

A temporary, configuration of two or more business roles, resulting in specific collective behavior in a particular context.

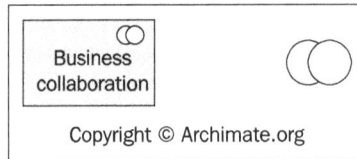

Enterprise Designer

Enterprise Designer does not include composites (two or more primitive objects combined together to form another object with different characteristics). This is because the modeler is expected to make these composites from the primitives.

Business interface

Declares how a business role can connect with its environment.

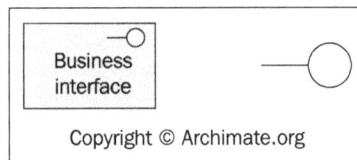

Enterprise Designer

Enterprise designer does not include relationships or interfaces. This is because the modeler is expected to define these relationships or make use of predefined relationships when using a modeling application.

Business object

A unit of information that has relevance from a business perspective.

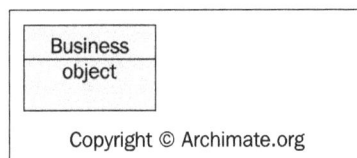

Enterprise Designer

Element **D** represents data that is created, read, updated, and deleted by an application or actors in a business process. The equivalent of a business object is the business class.

Business Process

A unit of internal behavior, or collection of causally-related units of internal behavior, intended to produce a defined set of products and services.

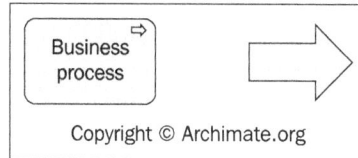

Copyright © Archimate.org

Enterprise Designer

Elements **H–Q** represent the complete set of possible process classifications. These elements have been described previously in this chapter.

Business function

A unit of internal behavior that groups behavior according to things such as required skills, knowledge, resources, and so on, and is performed by a single role within the organization.

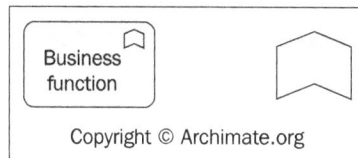

Copyright © Archimate.org

Enterprise Designer

Element **S** can be used to represent both internal and external services. An example of an internal service is the payroll and accounts payable functions. Instead of each manager of an external service having to manage a Process **P**, this is managed as a central service, which all external service managers can draw upon.

Business interaction

A unit of behavior performed as a collaboration of two or more business roles.

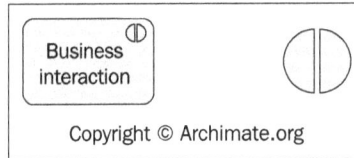

Copyright © Archimate.org

Enterprise Designer

Enterprise Designer does not include relationships or interfaces. This is because the modeler is expected to define these relationships or make use of predefined relationships when using a modeling application.

Business event

Something that happens, either internally or externally, and influences behavior.

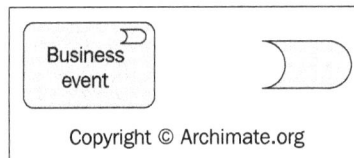

Copyright © Archimate.org

Enterprise Designer

Element **E** represents business events. Events can start an instance of a business process. Events can be of any of three kinds — time, threshold, or trigger.

Business service

An externally visible unit of functionality that is meaningful to the environment and is provided by a business role.

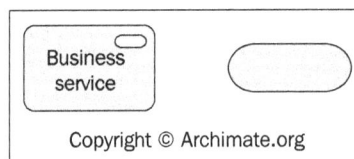

Copyright © Archimate.org

Enterprise Designer

Element **S** represents external products and services.

Representation

The perceptible form of the information conveyed by a business object.

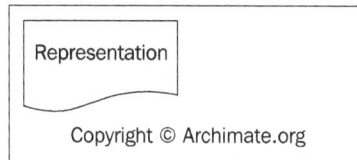
Representation
Copyright © Archimate.org

Enterprise Designer

Enterprise Designer does not include properties or attributes. This is because the modeler is expected to define these characteristics, or make use of predefined relationships, when using a modeling application.

Meaning

The knowledge or expertise present in the representation of a business object, given a particular context.

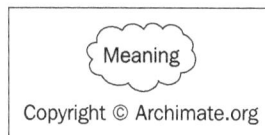
Meaning
Copyright © Archimate.org

Enterprise Designer

Enterprise Designer does not include properties or attributes. This is because the modeler is expected to define these characteristics, or make use of predefined relationships, when using a modeling application.

Value

This is something that makes a party appreciate a service or product, possibly in relation to provide it, but more typically to acquire it.

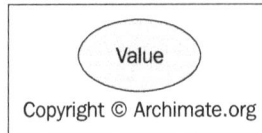

Copyright © Archimate.org

Enterprise Designer

Enterprise Designer does not include properties or attributes. This is because the modeler is expected to define these characteristics, or make use of predefined relationships, when using a modeling application.

Product

A coherent collection of services, accompanied by a contract/set of agreements, and offered as a whole to the customers, either internal or external.

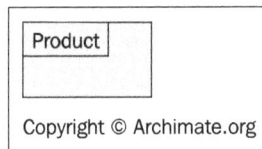

Copyright © Archimate.org

Enterprise Designer

Element **S** (service and product) represents both products and services. Element **R** (receivable) represents sub-components of products and services that are the outputs of specific processes. A set of receivables makes it possible for a business to deliver a product or service. Some of these receivables (such as the payment of salaries) are invisible to the customer but are still essential.

Contract

A formal or informal specification of agreement that specifies the rights and obligations associated with a product.

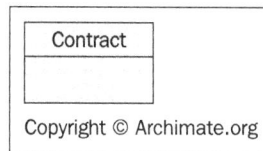

Enterprise Designer

Enterprise Designer does not include properties or attributes. This is because the modeler is expected to define these characteristics, or make use of predefined relationships, when using a modeling application. In Enterprise Designer, a contract would be a receivable produced in an instance of a new process.

What Enterprise Designer has that ArchiMate doesn't

- A non-IT, business-centric focus
- Explicit internal and external customer objects
- Classification of all processes into 10 types
- Goal objects and classification of all goals into five types
- Explicit business rule and facility objects, and classification of all elements that configure processes into seven types
- Wider definition of gear objects to include non-IT gear

What ArchiMate has that Enterprise Designer doesn't

Explicit definitions of business layer object behavior and attributes, including:

- Business collaboration
- Business interface
- Meaning
- Value
- Contract
- Richer detail of element C (Computer systems) as summarized later
- Richer detail of element G (Gear) as summarized later in relation to the Gear used by element C

Conclusion

ArchiMate complements Enterprise Designer by adding explicit composite objects, attributes, properties, and relationships. ArchiMate's emphasis on IT strategy makes it a suitable extension where the focus of the work is in the application and technology layer. It extends elements C and G.

The following table demonstrates the differences between the two frameworks and how they can complement each other:

ArchiMate object(s)	Enterprise Designer classification
Application collaboration, component, and function	Computer system
Application interaction, interface, and service	Computer system
Artifact	Receivable (deliverable)
Business actor	Market (Them) and Staff (Us)
Business collaboration	Staff (Us)
Business event	Event
Business function, interaction, or interface	Not defined
Business object	Data
Business process	H–Q processes
Business role	Actor
Business service	Service
Communication path	Not defined
Contract	Not defined
Data object	Data
Device	Gear
Infrastructure, interface, and service	Not defined
Meaning	Not defined
Network, Node	Gear
Product	Service
Representation	Not defined
Value	Not defined
Not defined	B – Business rule or standard
Not defined	F – Facility
Not defined	G – Non-technical gear
Not defined	V,W,X,Y, and Z – Goals

Comparing level 1 and level 3 frameworks

In this section, we compare Enterprise Designer with eTOM, and understand how Enterprise Designer can complement eTOM to fill in the gaps.

eTOM (enhanced Telecom Operations Map)

According to the Telemanagement forum (`www.tmforum.org`):

> *The eTOM Business Process Framework is a reference framework for categorizing all the business activities used by an enterprise involved in delivering on-line Information, Communications and Entertainment services. This is done through definition of each area of business activity, in the form of process components or process elements that can be decomposed to expose progressive detail. These process elements can then be positioned within a model to show organizational, functional and other relationships, and can be combined within process flows that trace activity paths through the business.*

eTOM defines 401 **process elements** arranged in a hierarchy. If you were to sit down with a blank sheet of paper and define all the business functions required to manage a large complex business, then this could be the complete inventory that you would want to use as a starting point. Individual businesses would select from this inventory to meet their needs. Because it is a standard, the architect knows that they are aligning their business with others in their industry.

eTOM arranges the business into three broad areas—Strategy Infrastructure and Product (SIP), Operations, and Enterprise Management.

There are three aspects of the Enterprise Designer framework that are of particular interest when applied to eTOM:

- The recognition that some business functions are services as distinct from processes

- The classification of all processes into 10 categories

- The importance of modeling receivables (outputs/deliverables) as well as the processes that produce them

Is it a service or a process?

The first thing that becomes apparent when the Enterprise Designer framework is overlaid on eTOM is the absence of a distinction between product, service, and process. To eTOM, everything is a business function, just at different levels of granularity.

For example, eTOM provides the following business functions:

- 1.1.3.7.5 Administer Workforce
- 1.2.1.3.1 Define Product Capability Requirements
- 1.1.2.1.2 Enable Service Configuration and Activation

All have a five digit number, indicating that they are at the same level in the business function hierarchy.

Seen through the lens of Enterprise Designer, these three business functions are representative of an **internal operational service**, **an internal transformational service**, and an **operational process**. They are thus completely different.

Consistent framework

eTOM has different levels of detail depending where you are in the framework. As discussed, Enterprise Designer provides a consistent framework to identify if a business function is a process or a service — a distinction that eTOM does not make. If it is a process, then you can model further levels of detail using the 10 process categories.

How can classifying processes help us? For example, *Customer Relationship Management* breaks down into fourteen business functions, of which one is *Customer Interface Management* and the other is *Bill Inquiry Handling*.

These are not processes as such, but are internal services offered by one part of the business to the whole business. Each of these services has processes defined by eTOM. For example, *Customer Interface Management* has four child business processes, *Bill Inquiry Handling* has six child processes, and *CRM Support and Readiness* has fifteen.

At the other end of the spectrum, *Knowledge and Research Management* breaks down into three processes, none of which has any further decomposition. However, eTOM doesn't tell us about the process of *Technology Scanning*.

Thus, when an organization extends eTOM, there is no consistent way to do so. This means that everyone using the framework to model a service may come up with a different answer. The most common question on eTOM chat forums is "How do I?".

Deliverable models

eTOM does not define the outputs of the business functions. They are implicit in the process descriptions but not explicit. Enterprise Designer has a complete set of objects and models that define what the purpose of each function is.

Enterprise Designer calls the outputs or deliverables of business functions *receivables*. For every business function there is now an equivalent receivable (deliverable) object. Just as there is a hierarchy of business functions that decompose down into processes, so there is now a companion hierarchical receivable model.

Summary

The purpose of a business framework is to define the relationships between key business concepts so that everyone in the organization shares a high-level common language.

Different frameworks serve different purposes and can complement each other. In this chapter we have described the components of the Enterprise Designer framework and compared them with ArchiMate. We discovered that the two frameworks complement each other.

We then looked at the relationship between Enterprise Designer and eTOM, and saw how to resolve gaps and inconsistencies.

A framework is a classification system. In the next chapter, we examine methodologies used to populate frameworks.

4

Adopting a Methodology

Once a framework has been agreed then the next step is to define a methodology.

This chapter shows:

- A methodology to build your models using five projects to start building the repository
- A consultant's view case study

What is a methodology

Which parts of the organization must be modeled? What is the correct sequence? To what level of detail should the modeler go? There has to be a trade-off between too much detail and too little. These are the issues that a methodology is designed to solve. A methodology is a process. Therefore it is repeatable, consistent, and can be learned.

The logical methodology is to start with the goals of the organization, then work down to identify the products and services that support those goals, and finally examine the processes and elements that deliver those products and services. However, we do not recommend this approach unless there is very strong and unified support for modeling at a senior management level. The reason is that the achievement of goals is political and different factions will compete to push their own agendas.

In some organizations the order is reversed, with initiatives that model aspects of specific processes, where there is buy-in for a modeling approach. The hope is that these initiatives extend out and become prototypes for modeling the whole business. As we discussed earlier, the champions of this approach usually do not have the authority to do this.

Therefore, the approach we take is to start in the middle. Model the products and services, customers, and clients first. From there you can move up and down the framework.

In *Chapter 1*, *Designing a Strategy* we outlined five projects that can build a comprehensive model of the business. Each project is complete and thus adds value in itself. After the first project, you may wish to change the sequence of the other projects, to suit your needs.

Project #1 captures the complete list of products and services of the company.

Project #2 develops Workflow models for critical processes.

Project #3 develops System Interaction models of the systems that underpin the critical processes identified in Project #2.

Project #4 develops a Business Class model of the information that is created, read, updated, and deleted in the critical processes identified in Project #2.

Project #5 develops an Organization model of the business units and positions that participate in the critical processes. Other critical element models can be added as appropriate.

In this chapter we will model an organization called Starberry Accounting. This organization provides compliance accounting and independent financial advice to IT companies.

This is a fictitious example and any resemblance to real organizations is coincidental.

Enterprise Designer members can download the complete Starberry ProVision® model from www.enterprisedesigner.com/starberry. Registration is free.

They are strong in three markets — high-tech hardware, media, and games. Starberry has 150 employees and is one of the larger local firms in this industry. The company has a head office and three branch offices throughout the State. Starberry wants to model their organization as part of a strategic review. They want to understand how to leverage their existing client base and move beyond their current services to provide strategic planning, mentoring, and coaching. They need to understand the gaps in team capability to provide these new services. They also need to understand how their existing processes, data, and systems will be impacted.

Project #1—building the high-level model

Project #1 captures the complete list of products and services of the company.

In the Enterprise Designer framework the first principle is that, 'all organizations exist for one purpose only, to deliver products and services to customers in order to achieve goals'. This principle encourages what some people call outside in thinking. Instead of modeling the organization from the inside looking out, our philosophy is that everything needs to be understood from the customer's point of view. It is therefore unsurprising that the first model that we build describes who the customers are.

This sequence of models can be built in two weeks. Given that the world is now changing so fast, having a speedy way to get the key information is essential. During this two week process you will build six models as follows:

- Customer model (what it is, how to build it)

- Product and Service model (what it is, how to build it)

- Critical Customer Product model (identifying criticality and aligning with corporate business continuity plans using layers)

Preparation

1. Create a new repository (**File | New | Repository**) for example, **Sample**.

2. Create a new notebook called **Starberry** (**File | New | Notebook**).

3. Install the Enterprise Designer modeling language (see instructions in End Note).

4. Open the `Starberry` notebook (double-click the relevant Notebook icon).

   Recommended and optional:

5. Change preferences (*Shift + F11*) and check all indicators.

6. Change preferences (*Shift + F11*) and check all **Model | Links** options.

7. Change preferences (*Shift + F11*) and in **Inventory** check **Model**, **Nested Model**, and **Objects**. Uncheck all other options for the time being.

8. Select the **View | Toolbars** menu and check all nine options.

Customer model

Building the Customer model is easy. The key information is highlighted next.

Starberry provides compliance accounting and independent financial advice to IT companies. They are strong in three markets—**hightech hardware**, **media**, and **games**.

Steps

The steps for building the Customer model are given next:

1. Select **Model Inventory**.
2. Select **ATU Organization Model** and double-click to create a new model.
3. Select **T Market** and create a new Market object called **Starberry Customers**.
4. The model will open.
5. **Power add** the following Market objects: **High tech hardware**, **Media**, and **Games**.
6. Draw links from the three child objects to the parent.
7. Add descriptions for each Market.

Tips

The easiest way to add an object on a model is to draw a square with your mouse on a blank area of the model. The **Power add** option will then display.

If you create an object using the wrong type, delete it using the *DEL* key. For example, if you use an organization object type instead of a market, it is not possible to change the object type easily.

The link selector is available on the Model palette. Click it and the mouse will change shape from the default arrow icon. Drag the link selector from the child to the parent object and release.

Use the optional **Auto layout** icon to layout the model alphabetically.

Use the optional **Link Style** icon to change the shape of the links.

Select **Starberry Customers** and right-click **Style | Shape | Right** radio button to display the object name to the right of the object so that it is easier to read.

To add a description, double-click the object and fill in the description field.

The finished model looks like the following diagram. In this view of the model, the interpretation appears in a separate window. The interpretation is synchronized with the model, so that changes to the model instantly update the interpretation. To access the interpretation use the shortcut *Ctrl + I*. This is a toggle. Pressing it repeatedly will change the position of the interpretation window.

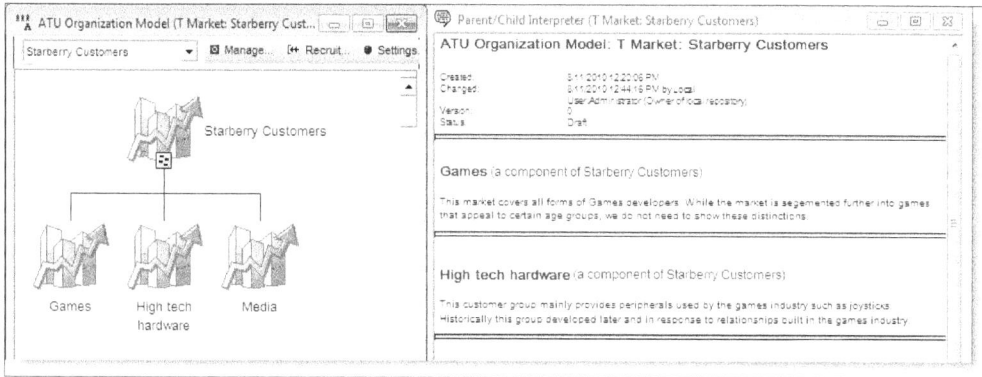

Product and Service model

Building the Service model introduces the concept of layers, one layer for current and the other for future services. The key information is highlighted below.

Starberry provides compliance accounting and independent financial advice to IT companies. They want to understand how to leverage their existing client base and move beyond their current services to provide **strategic planning**, **mentoring**, and **coaching**.

Steps

1. Select **Model Inventory**.

2. Select **S Service Process Model** and double-click on it to create a new model.

3. Select **S Product** and create a new **Product object** called **Starberry Services**.

4. The model will open.

5. **Power add** the following Product objects: compliance accounting, independent financial advice, strategic planning, mentoring, and coaching.

6. Draw links from the five child objects to the parent.

7. Add descriptions for each service.

8. Create two layers for existing and new services.

9. Add compliance accounting and independent financial services in the current services layer, and the other services in the 'to be' layer.

Tips

If you make an error on an object name, just double-click it and correct it.

To add a layer click **Manage Layers | Add** and enter the new layer name.

The layer name will now appear in the drop-down list of layers and, by default, contains all the objects of the base layer. Select **Recruit** and unclick the objects that should not appear.

By default, objects that are not part of the current layer are ghosted. Ghosted means that you see their outline but they are grayed out, as in the example below. You can hide them completely through the Settings menu.

The finished model looks like the following diagram. In this example the 'To be' layer is shown and the current services are ghosted.

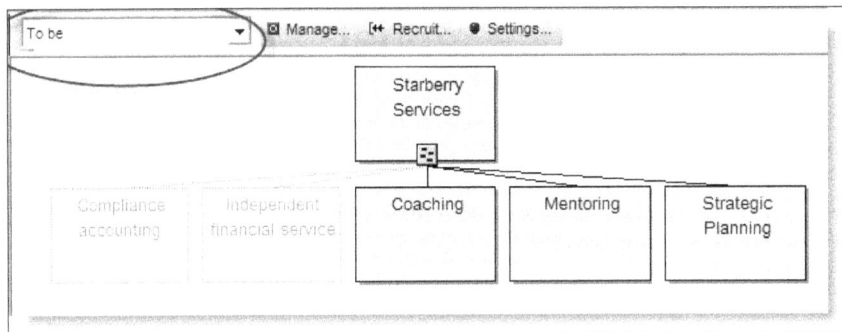

Remember that you can always click the shortcut *Ctrl + I* to see the interpretation. Ghosted objects will not appear in the relevant layer.

ProVision's layer feature is one of the easiest to use and is very powerful. You can create different views of the same model. When making presentations you can jump from one to another in seconds using the drop-down menu as shown in the following diagram.

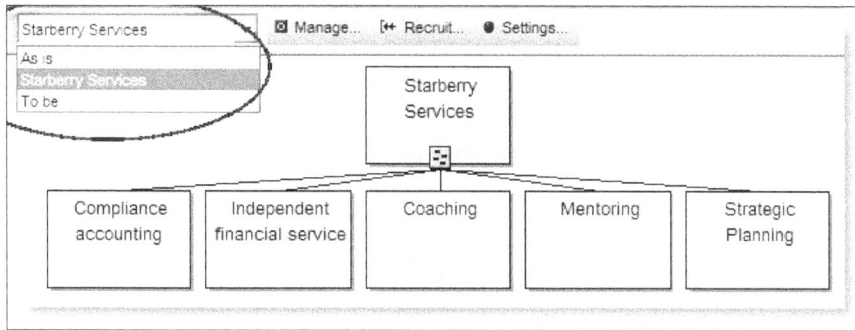

Critical Customer Product model

Now that we have built the Customer and Product models, we can combine them together to create a Navigator model.

Starberry provides compliance accounting and independent financial advice to IT companies. They are strong in three markets—**high-tech hardware**, **media**, and **games.** They want to understand how to leverage their existing client base and move beyond their current services to provide **strategic planning**, **mentoring**, and **coaching**.

The Organization model does not permit us to add Service objects. It is optimized to describe markets, organizations, and their component positions. The Navigator model overcomes these limitations, allowing us to add pretty much any object or relationship.

Steps

1. Select **Model Inventory**.
2. Select **0-Z Navigator Model** and double-click to create a new model.
3. Select **0-Z Topic** and create a new **Topic** object called **Starberry Customer Services.**
4. The model will open.
5. Add the following objects:
    ° The T Market object called **Starberry Customers**.
    ° The S Product object called **Starberry Services**.
6. Use the compass icon to display the child objects.
7. Exclude the parents to simplify the model.

8. Tidy up the position of the objects using the drawing menu to align them.

9. Draw communication links to show which customers get which services.

10. Create layers to show the phasing of the new services.

11. Add emphasis with drawing objects.

Tips

The compass icon will show related objects and models. Select the related objects to display them.

To exclude an object right-click it and select **Exclude**. This does not break the relationship. It just removes the object to make the model simpler.

Use a drawing object, such as a rectangle, to emphasize an aspect of the model. Right-click the object and choose **Draw** | **Send** to place it behind the modeling object you wish to draw attention to. Change the drawing object's style to suit.

Exclude or add drawing objects to the relevant layer.

The finished model looks like the diagram below. The company has decided that the critical customer group is the media companies. They generate the most business and have the greatest growth potential.

They have decided to roll out the new services of Coaching, Mentoring, and Strategic Planning to the Media customers first.

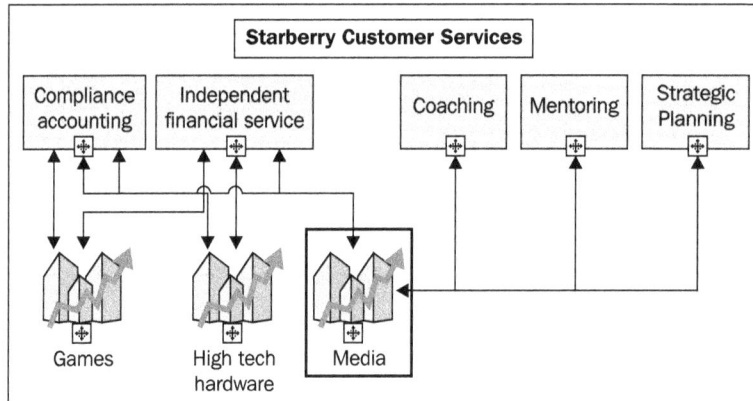

Please note that the Navigator model does not have as rich interpretation as the other model types. The information stored on the property tabs of objects may not show up. This is one of the down sides of using a Navigator model.

Here is the same Navigator model at phase two, where all customer groups get the new services. In this layer, the media customer group does not have the rectangle emphasis and all customer groups have links with the new services; hence there are now three links per service.

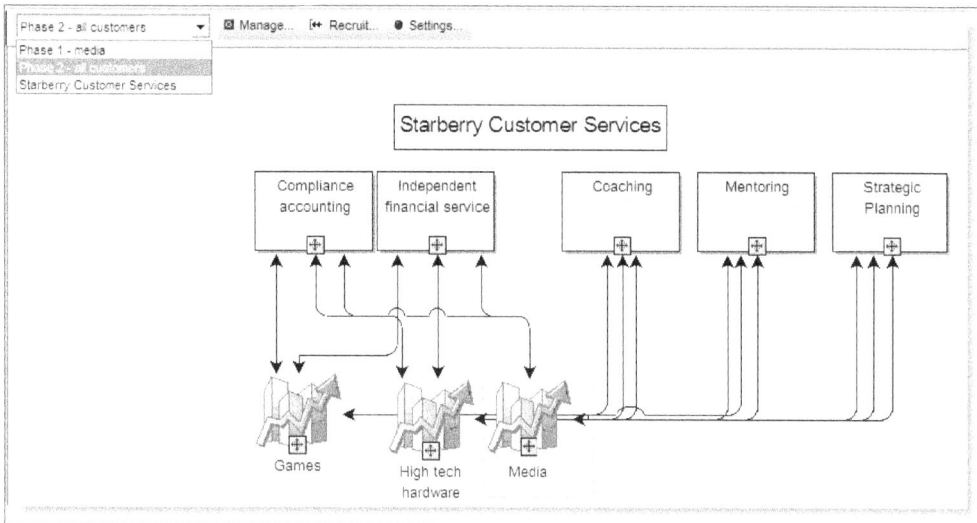

Project #2—building workflow models

Project #2 develops Workflow models for critical processes.

The result of Project #1 is that we now have a context for all further modeling work. We will only build workflow models for processes that are critical. The definition of critical is now agreed and it is a definition that is set at the business level.

While the new services may be important, today there are only two, compliance accounting, and independent financial services. Of the two, the business decides that compliance accounting is the most critical. The reason is that it has to be completed according to deadlines. Financial advice is important to customers but they can tolerate delays. A delay in compliance accounting could cause financial penalties.

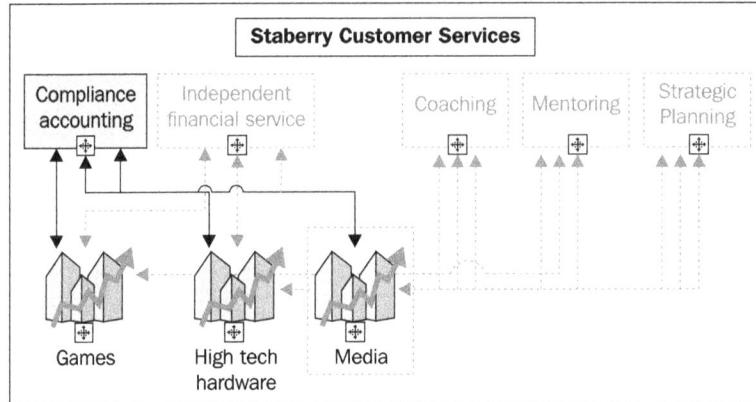

Critical Process model

The Critical Process model examines the ten types of process and determines which of them are critical. The main service this model provides is the preparation of annual Tax Audits. The following table is used to identify which processes are critical and thus require greater modeling effort.

You can find out if a process is critical or not by asking the following question. "If this process stopped for any reason, could we still deliver the product or service on time with some simple workarounds?" The following table shows the ten types of process examined through a critical filter. At a glance, we can now see which processes are critical and hence require further analysis.

ID	Category	Name	Critical?
H	Help	Process by which Starberry explains legal requirements and processes to clients who want or have a Tax Audit prepared.	No
I	Inform	Process by which Starberry monitors the progress of Tax Audits both individually and aggregated.	No
J	Join	Process by which Starberry combines information together to form draft Tax Audits for client review.	Yes
K	Kollect	Process by which Starberry gets paid by clients for conducting audit.	No
L	Logistics	Process by which Starberry delivers the final audit to the Tax Office.	Yes
M	Market	Process by which Starberry tells potential clients that it offers Tax Audits.	No
N	New	Process by which Starberry takes on new clients requiring Tax Audits.	No
O	Organize	Process by which Starberry collects information required for preparing audits.	Yes
P	Pay	Process by which Starberry pays the team, contractors, and bills related to the preparation of Tax Audits.	No
Q	Quit	Process by which Starberry terminates preparation of Tax Audit services for specific clients (either party might initiate).	No

In the previous example, all ten processes are required to provide a professional service. However, Starberry could make do if some of them were not operating due to system failure, ill health, or other factor.

Why is that? While there are ten processes that deliver a product or service, they operate in different time frames and are de-coupled. For example, you may need to pay bills and market, but marketing is not directly dependent on bill payment. You might have a strategy to market once a year, whereas bills may be paid monthly.

Just as Starberry tried to answer the question about critical services from the customer's perspective, so it is that it uses the same logic at this lower level. If Starberry does not collect payment for a Tax Audit, due to some computer glitch, it can still continue to produce and deliver the Tax Audit to the Tax Office on time. In our review, only three of the ten processes have been classified as critical. Therefore, we can give the other seven less attention.

When describing a process there are two views, static and dynamic, that can be expressed in Process and Workflow models, respectively. We might make process models for all ten but only do Workflow models for the three critical processes.

ProVision® ensures that both models remain synchronized. If we add a new step in a Workflow model, it automatically updates the companion Process model.

> If you delete a Workflow model it deletes the companion Process model links. (The objects remain in the model but you will have to reconnect them.)

Steps

1. Select **Model Inventory.**

2. Select **Service Process** Model and double-click to create a new model.

3. Select **Product** object and create a new S Product object called **Tax Audit**.

4. The model will open.

5. Add the following objects: An S2 Process object called **Tax Audit processes** and a HQ Activity object also called **Tax Audit processes**.

6. Draw a link from the process to the product to make it a child object.

7. Draw a link from the activity to the process object to make it a child object.

8. Right-click the activity object and select **Component Models | Service Process** model.

9. **Power add** the ten categories of the process and make them children of the **Tax Audit processes** activity.

10. Double-click into each child object and add the relevant stereotype letter.

11. Sort the objects alphabetically.

12. Add layers for critical and non-critical processes.

Tips

We use activity objects as quasi-process objects because they have more detail, flexibility, and can be simulated if required. However activity objects can't be linked directly to products. The process object is used as a linker.

You will want to change the process names to something more meaningful to your organization. Before you do that, double-click into each object and add its classification letter as a stereotype. That way, when you rename the object you will recall its type.

The following image shows the Tax Audit processes as activity objects. Each has been given a stereotype letter.

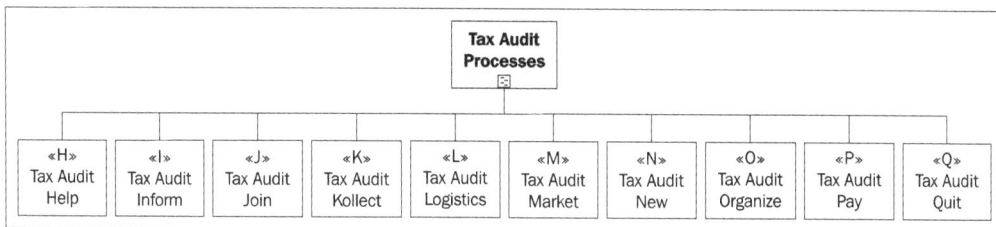

Now a layer has been added to the model shown below and the three critical processes have been added. The other processes have been hidden.

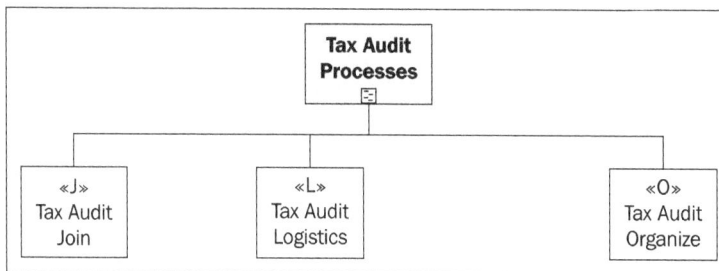

Now the object names are changed to reflect Starberry's language. The three processes have been numbered using **Tools | Renumber** so that when they are sorted they appear in a logical sequence.

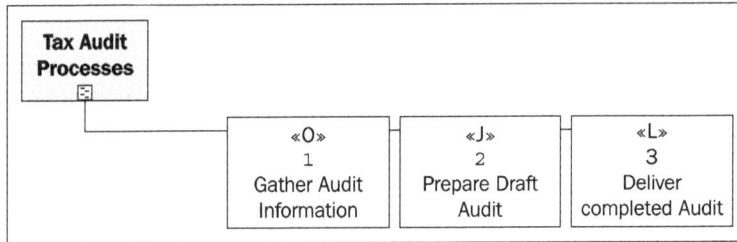

In this example, the non-critical processes have been hidden after the sort by changing the layer preferences from the default ghosting option.

Process models do not tell us who performs the process, the sequence in which the work gets done, the hand offs from one role to another, or what decision points occur. Yet, for the non-critical processes, the information we have gathered is sufficient. It can be added to at a later date if required.

For the critical processes we can right-click and create **Component | Service Process** models where we add more details of the steps followed, as in the following example. As you can see Process models are hierarchical and, in this example, only contain activities.

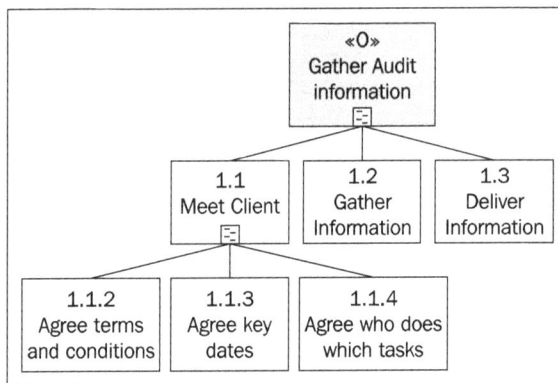

Workflow model

For our three critical processes we will want to create Workflow models. Here is one example.

Steps

1. Select the activity **Gather Audit Information**.
2. Right-click and select **Component Models | HQ Workflow Model (create)**.

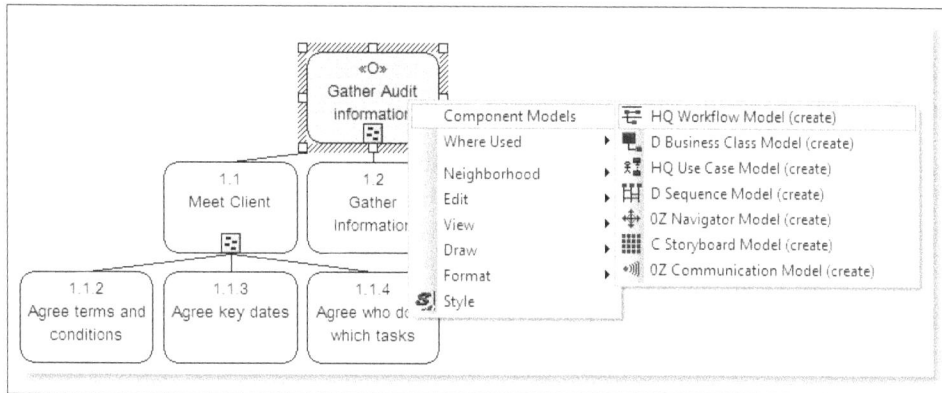

3. The model will open and all the activities created will be waiting to be used.
4. Add the following swim lanes: **Customer**, (**Market**), **Auditor (Role)**, **CRM (System)**.
5. Drag **Meet Client** activity to the **Auditor** swim lane.
6. Drag **Gather Information** and **Deliver Information** activities to the **Customer** swim lane.
7. Add a **Source (start)** and **Sink (end)** icon to the **Customer** swim lane.
8. Add a decision box called **Complete** to the **Auditor** swim lane.
9. Change the percentages so that 90% of the time the answer is yes.
10. Link all the objects together.

Tips

To add a swim lane, click the square swim lane icon and drop it onto an empty area of the model.

The source and sink tool is the same. You decide when you drop it onto the model.

To add a name and change the percentages of a decision box double-click on it to see the detail.

When you link a decision box, the first option is assumed to be yes and the second no.

Notice that the Meet Client activity has children that don't display in the Workflow model. You can make a nested Workflow model that examines this in greater detail.

Notice that if you number the activity objects, that the numbering automatically appears in the workflow. However, if you use the same activity in another model, the numbering will change to reflect that context. As this causes confusion, I avoid using numbering or hardcode a number into the object name.

Develop the habit of working backwards. What is the last step in the process? From a customer's point of view this is the most important one.

Your model now looks like the image shown below. The CRM swim lane has not been used yet.

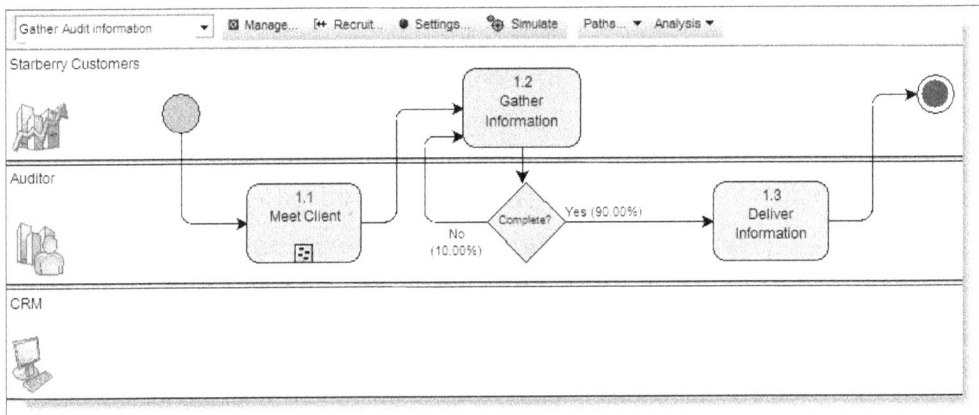

In the process of building the model, we realized that we wanted to show how the manual steps interact with the automated steps taken by the CRM. We will add some high-level activities and workflows to reflect this relationship.

Steps

1. Create two new activities in the Workflow called **Update Client Details** and **Update Client History**.
2. Drop them onto the CRM swim lane.
3. Draw links between **Meet Client** and **Update Client Details** in both directions.
4. Draw links between Deliver Information and Update Client History in both directions.

Your model should now look like this:

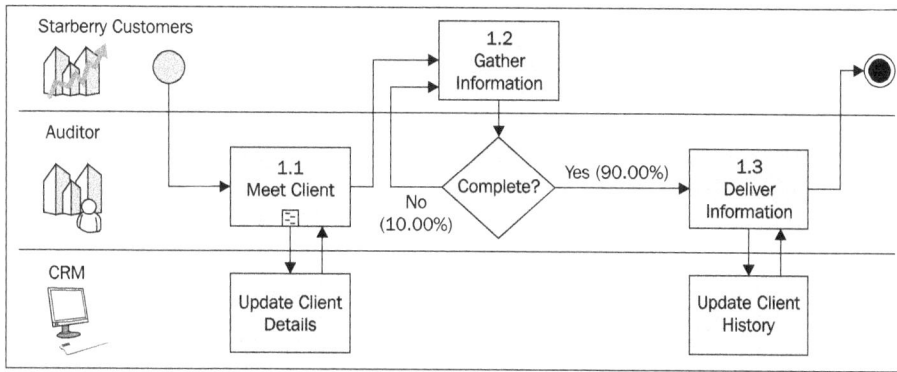

Tips

The links are in both directions as the CRM system is providing information to the Auditor and the Auditor is updating the information. Strictly speaking, activity 1.1 Meet Client has two incoming workflows, therefore would be initiated twice. It also has two outgoing workflows to be activated only when the activity is complete, so this is when Update Client Details will be initiated, along with Gather Information. A human looking at the model will understand what is meant. If the model was being used to simulate the process, the simulation engine would interpret it literally and you would get different results to what you might expect. To resolve this, you would have to split 1.1 Meet Client into two activities. We have not done so here in order to keep the story as simple as possible.

Remember that a workflow at all levels of detail other than the lowest is a story (at the lowest level it is an algorithm). Ensure that the story is simple and makes sense to someone looking at it.

Review your Process model and tidy it up. It will display the new activities you just created. Note that the CRM activities don't have numbering. You will have to add numbering if you think it is necessary.

Project #3 – building System Interaction models

Project #3 develops System Interaction models of the systems that underpin the critical processes identified in Project #2.

The history of the twentieth century is defined by automation. Gradually much work moved from being carried out manually to automatically. Thinking and doing have become separate. More and more repetitive work is done by machines, with analysis and interpretation being done by humans.

We have examined System models earlier on. They are hierarchical models. Workflows are one way to represent the meeting point of systems and processes, System Interaction models show another view and focus on the interface between hardware, software, and location.

We make a distinction between the hardware used and the software that is deployed on the hardware.

The IT department really doesn't need to know too much about the process. All they need to know is which processes a system is involved in. The business doesn't need to understand the complexities of systems and their relationship to platforms, networks, and servers. All they need to know is that a specific system is involved in a specific process.

One way to resolve this is to create two notebooks, one for the IT department and the other for the business. In the business notebook the CRM system appears as a swim lane, but there is no detail behind it. In the IT notebook the CRM system has all the relationships necessary for an IT-centric view of the world. The process is just a placeholder. There is no detail. In this way, the business can happily make changes and add detail, without cluttering up the IT view of the world. Similarly, the IT view is not going to confuse the business with lots of technical detail.

While you can keep all the objects in the one notebook, this approach simplifies the check-in and check-out procedures between the two parts of the business.

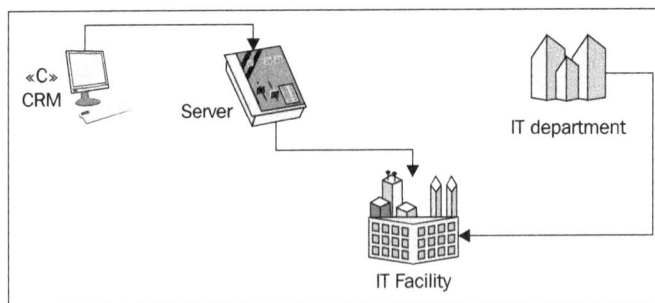

In the previous image we see that the CRM system is running on a server in the IT Facility. The IT department happens to be located in the same place.

In the image below we add another system. The relationship is a system interaction, that is the two systems are talking to each other. The double-headed arrow demonstrates this. In addition we see the event New Client that triggers the relationship.

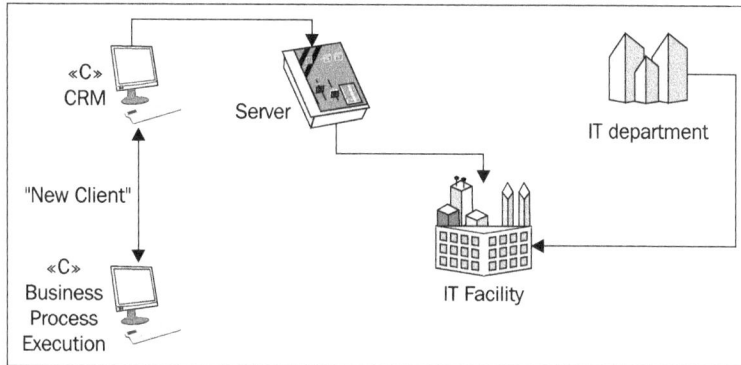

If the image is not clear enough, we can examine the interpretation.

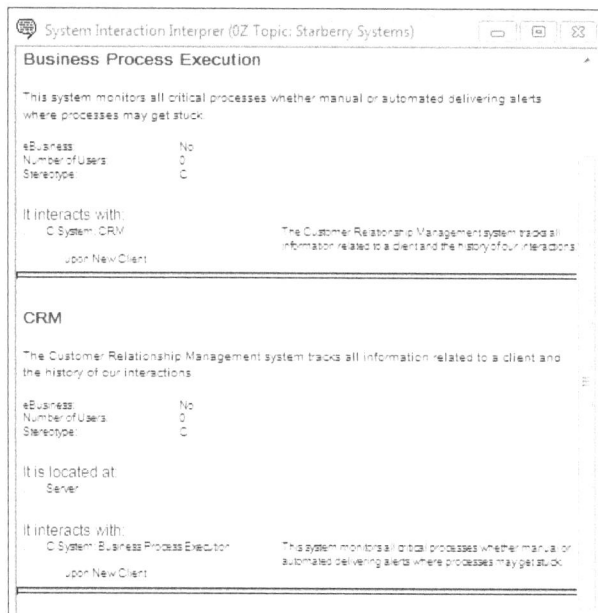

Project #4—building Business Class models

Project #4 develops a Business Class model of the information that is created, read, updated, and deleted in the critical processes identified in Project #2.

ProVision® enables you to understand data at rest and in motion. For data at rest, the most common object to use is the business class, with further detail being added using attributes.

> *ProVision® defines a business class as "a class that is used as a template to express a business concept".*
>
> *If required, a specific business class can be subtyped using a Subtype model. ProVision® defines a subtype as "a class, package, or interface whose definition is a refinement of the more general class, package, or interface (its super type). For example, "preferred customer" is a refinement of the more general class "customer." Therefore, "customer" is the super type, and "preferred customer" is the subtype."*
>
> *A package is a container, or as ProVision® defines it, "a general purpose mechanism for organizing elements into groups." Package models may contain other packages. Unlike UML, ProVision® only uses packages for business classes.*
>
> *Thus the hierarchy goes from package, to business class to subtype. There is no logical distinction between a business class and a subtype. They are both business class objects.*

Enterprise Designer Workbook, by Bill Aronson, published by Lulu 2008. *Together, these three kinds of model, describe data at rest.*

During the Meet Client step, we need to capture or update information about the client. A Data model ensures that how this information is captured is consistent. In this way, different systems can work with the same information. For example, one system might bill customers, while another is used to gather information about a client history. If the way that this information is stored is different, then it becomes harder, expensive, or even impossible, for the two systems to share and exchange data.

The Data model shows three business classes for name, address, and contact. Each has attributes that describe the business class in more detail. The interpretation helps us understand the relationship between the three business classes.

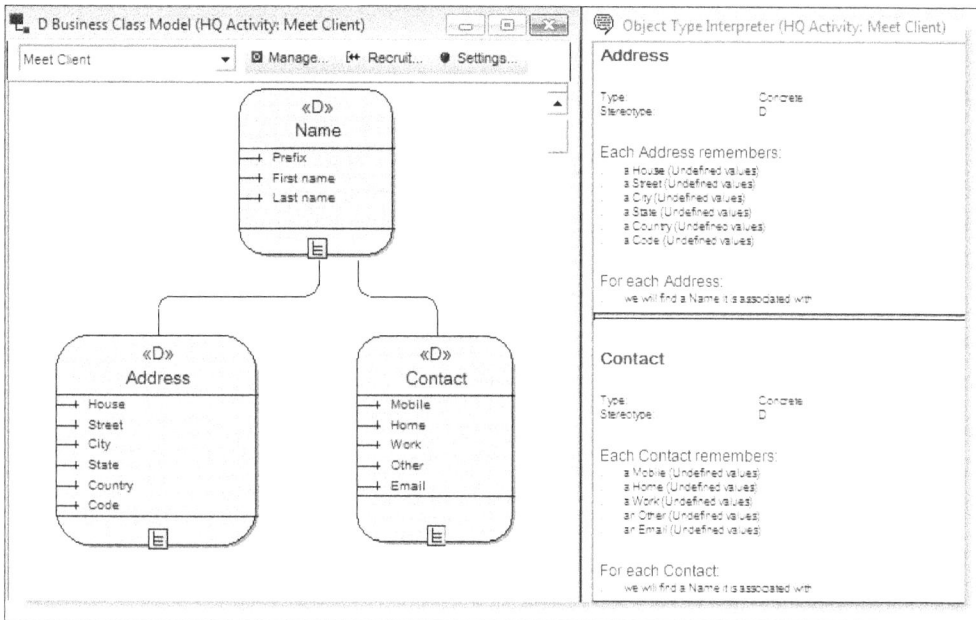

Information architects may also want to use three additional models to model data in motion–Operation, Sequence, and State Chart.

Project #5—building Organization models

Project #5 develops an Organization model of the business units and positions that participate in the critical processes. Other critical element models can be added as appropriate.

We have already seen that we can make models of actors and their business units using an Organization model. Actors also show up as swim lanes in Workflow models. The Business Interaction model shows us the high-level relationships between markets and organizations, either to deliver a product or service, or, one level down, looking at a specific process. Fairly quickly the same actors will show up in a number of different models.

How can we understand all of these relationships? If you want to plot an actor against one specific object then an Association Grid is a good option. Alternatively, a Navigation model is a better alternative if you want to trace indirect relationships that involve multiple object types.

In the following example we use the Association Grid wizard to discover all of the decisions that the Auditor performs. The result shows us that the Auditor role performs the *Complete* decision. As the model develops, the number of decisions that the Auditor might perform will grow. How is this useful? You can use this information to identify other positions that could perform the same role. One reason might be to transfer the role to a less skilled role, thus saving money. Another reason might be to understand who could perform the same role in a business continuity event. If your focus is on customer experience, then you might be doing this to reduce bottlenecks.

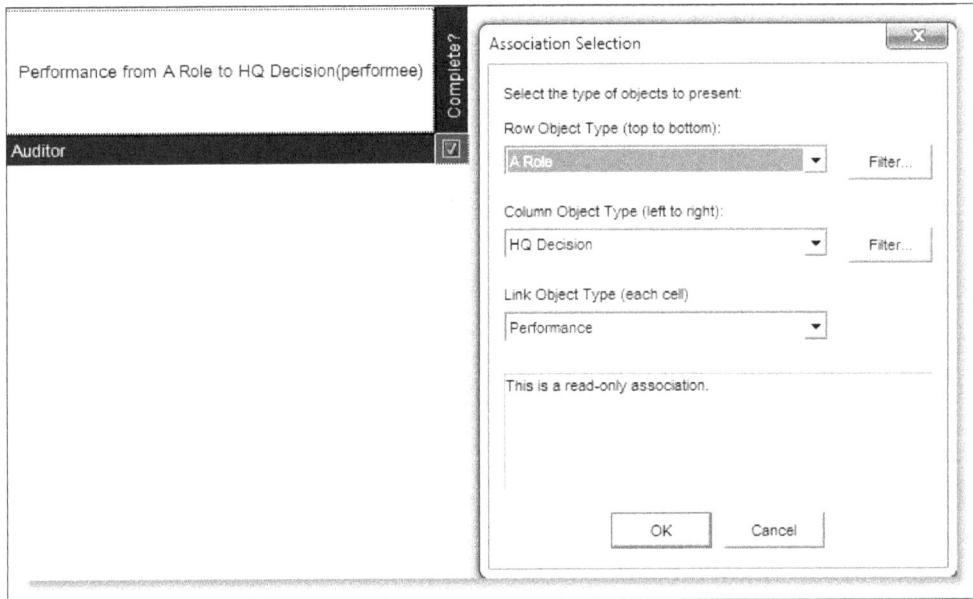

Other critical elements

We have identified ten processes, but not all are critical. This means that we don't have to make ten Workflow models.

For the three processes that are critical, we know that there are seven elements that make them run, namely actors, business rules, computer systems, data, events, facilities, and gear.

Which of the seven are critical? This will vary from process to process. Only model any of the seven elements if by doing so you can now make better decisions. We have suggested that you will often want to model actors, computer systems, and data.

How would you combine them? You can use a Navigator Model to show all or some of the seven elements associated with a specific process, as the example below shows:

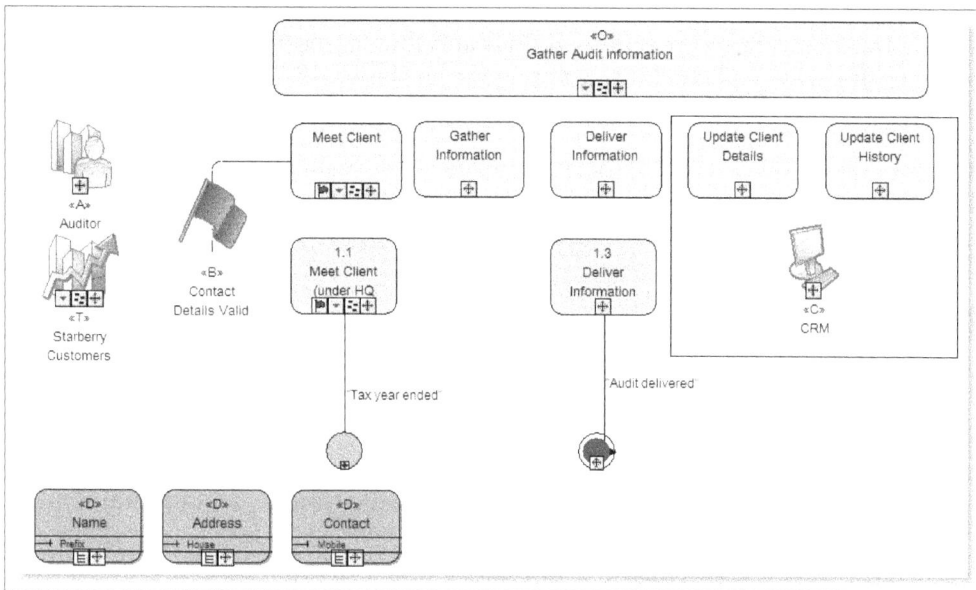

The model shows:

- The actors (**Auditor** and **Starberry Customers**)
- The key activities that are being performed
- A business rule (**Contact Details Valid**)
- A computer system (**CRM**)
- Three data objects that get captured during **Meet Client** (**Name**, **Address**, and **Contact**)
- Two events (**Tax year ended** and **Audit delivered**)

The model doesn't show facilities or gear, because (in this example) neither is considered critical to understanding the process. Let's look at how we would go about extending our understanding by building Business Rule and Event models.

Business Rule models

We have discussed how you can create Business Rule and Standard models earlier. These are hierarchical models. You can also work the other way round, first attaching business rules to specific activities and then gathering them into Rule models. In this way, you can look at how you can standardize business rules across multiple processes.

In the example below we will associate a business rule called Contact Details Valid with the Meet Client activity. Once done, if we use the Meet Client activity in another process then the Contact Details Valid rule will automatically apply.

Steps

1. Double-click the activity **Meet Client**.

2. Select the **Associations** tab.

3. Double-click **Rules** (**Adherence**) object.

4. In the **Power Add** dialog box, add the new rule **Contact Details Valid** and click **OK**.

5. Check the **Contact Details Valid** object and click **OK**.

Tips

If the rule exists, you will not need to create it. Just select it from the list.

If the rule indicator is switched on, the flag icon will display.

You can make associations from anywhere the object displays, such as a Process model, a Workflow model, or the Object Inventory.

Add some description to the object, which will appear in the Interpretation and make it easier for users to understand what it is intended for.

The following screenshot highlights the interpretation of the business rule:

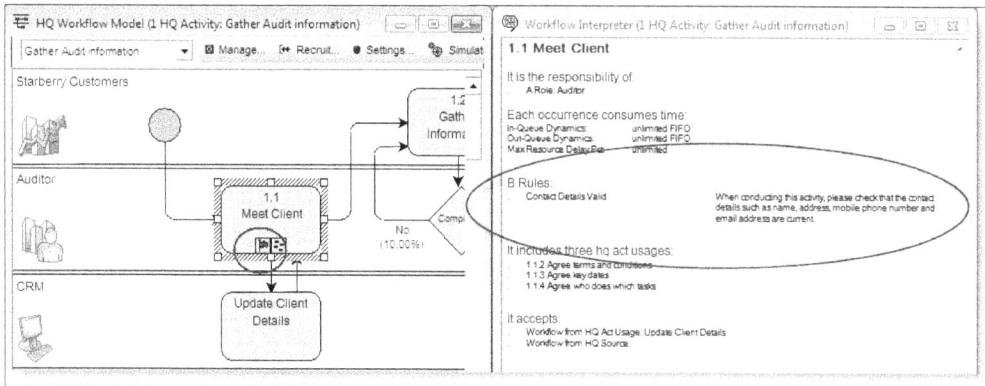

Event models

Events trigger a process, or a specific activity within a process. In Workflow models, an event doesn't appear as an association of an activity, but attached to the workflow that connects it to the next step. Earlier, we looked at Event models, which are hierarchical and only contain Event objects.

Events are displayed in double quotation marks to distinguish them from deliverables that can also be displayed on workflows.

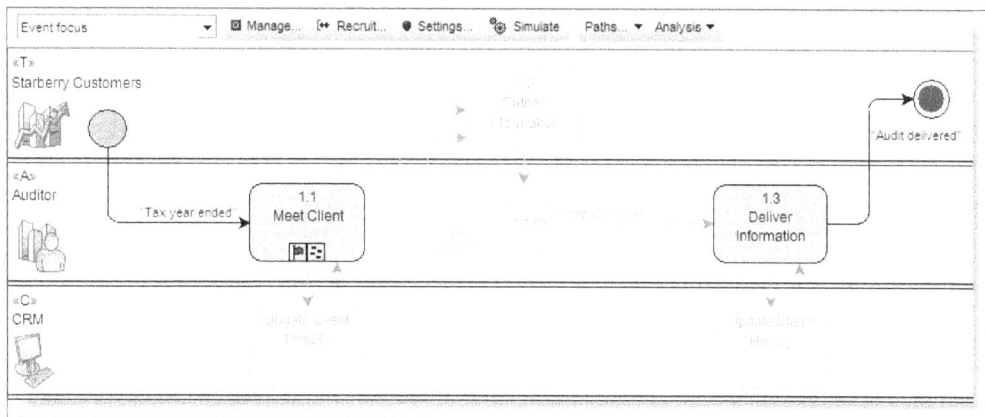

You can add events to workflows in a Workflow model if it will add clarity. In the model below we have created a layer to draw attention to the first and last steps in the process. We can see that the event that starts the process off is "Tax year ended" and the event that completes the process is "Audit delivered".

Why would you want to focus on events? Some people in the business do not need to understand the exact process. This can be a black box. All that they need to know is what starts the process and what ends it.

Case study—the consultant's view

iOctane is a business process transformation company. They are a leading company in using ProVision® in Australia and New Zealand. I caught up with Gordon Lescinsky who has been using ProVision® for many years.

BA: What kind of work are you doing?

GL: We have been working with large companies by Australian standards. They have been automated for some time. If they work on one process, they work on a hundred. We have been working on projects where every single process has been affected because some system that underlies everything has been changed. It might have been put in for the first time, but most likely it has been changed. The context is 'big process project' where many processes are affected, not necessarily improved, but touched in some way.

BA: There are two extremes of context deploying ProVision®. At one end are the people responsible for creating a whole enterprise repository. At the other end are the people responsible for one project or program. Which have you found to be more successful?

GL: As you say, there are people who are in charge of modeling the whole enterprise but won't do all the modeling work in detail. For example, enterprise architects want to map the whole business but the map that they make stays within the architecture department. They would like to show it to the business but the business has other models. They may not be as full or as detailed but the architect's model is never considered to be authoritative. Then there are the people running projects who know that the only way they will get approval to buy ProVision® is to help them with their project.

But they have this dream that their model will become something more. They dream that when their project is done, that there will be another phase where there model will have other uses and start to guide enterprise decisions. If it could be used on the next project, that would be gratifying for them. That is what they are aiming for. So they accommodate that within the project. They want the models to be very good so that they will have another life. Sometimes it is the project owners who want that and the business analysts, who are making the actual models, couldn't care less.

BA: They have a dream, and create a platform which could lead to enterprise-wide decision making being informed. That is the theory. In practice have you seen it happen?

GL: We have seen it happen, and it is a struggle. These projects can be huge, in terms of timescale. Projects that were meant to take one year might still be going after three. Sometimes they never end but just transition. So in some cases, it is hard to say. I think there are some cases where it has happened on a small scale, where the models have been used again. It will be in those places where the individual, who started the whole thing off, is still around. They have the same level of responsibility or even more. It is really individuals who keep the model alive, not the model just sitting there, being available.

BA: What about at the other end, where it is being used for enterprise architecture?

GL: I have come to the conclusion that the people who want to start off doing enterprise architecture should be doing a project anyway, because the project approach is the way to go. If you are an enterprise architect who just builds a model, there is a huge risk that you will be one of those enterprise architects whose team gets taken away from you. These teams do a huge amount of work but it never gets used.

The model has to demonstrate a return on the investment. We have enterprise architect projects now. The ones which are part of a project have a reason for everything that they do. The ones that don't are not tied into the business enough. They don't have guidance on how to focus their effort. They can't get it right because they actually don't know what they are doing or why they are doing it.

BA: So, when you say a project, do you mean a business project of a significant size?

GL: Yes.

BA: So the enterprise architect is working at the frontend to make it more effective?

GL: Yes. Now a big project is not necessarily better than a small project. Ideally we would like to have small projects, improving one process at a time. Sometimes we are trapped. For example, a new CRM is going to cost a million dollars and impact multiple processes. All the processes have to be moved and the project is going to take over a year.

It would be good if we could select a project that took three months. We would like to select those processes which will impact the customer and just work on those. If there is a way to do that, we would rather do so. So a series of small enterprise architecture projects would be ideal, because the architects would learn and so would the business. Each project would be a new learning. If it is a huge project, there is less opportunity to learn. They might do a hundred processes and only learn one thing. If they had done them one at a time they might have learned a hundred things. If you make a mistake on a large project you might make it a hundred times.

So, for me, the context is learning. The project leads to learning. The learning turns into an enterprise architecture capability.

BA: One of the challenges in large organizations is that many businesses have Visio embedded. It is sitting on everyone's desktop. Is it difficult for business people to see the need for a central modeling repository? What are some of the messages that you use, when talking to the business, to explain the benefits?

GL: The main thing between the difference between modeling and drawing (or diagramming) is that modeling is now seen as something you can't live without. It is a capability that you have to have. If you have a lot of processes, there is no other way. So we don't have to sell the benefits of modeling anymore. Mostly we are talking to people comparing modeling tools.

BA: So what would you say are the reasons for using ProVision® over one of the similar competing products?

GL: The main reason that sways people that we work with is that it is easy to use. It works the way that they expected a business modeling tool should work. They know that they are making a commitment to a platform, so that is important.

BA: ProVision® is part of the Open Text Metastorm suite, and thus it makes moving to business process execution an easier route, down the track. Does that make a difference? Do they get excited about that?

GL: It's not high on the list. The business leaders who make decisions like this usually take things one at a time. So they look at what the business can handle now. They leave decisions for the future to the future. I think that is as it should be.

BA: Apart from ease of use, is there anything else that makes it stand out?

GL: It is used all over the world, so there is wide experience and support. Some of the other products see modeling as a technical thing that only technical people do. That is the ease of use point seen in a different way. There is a list of requirements that people expect. One of them is web-based access. Another is the ability to check in and checkout objects. Those things are all there. When comparing products in the market it comes down to features.

Either you like the people who are selling the product, or it comes down to features. Often it comes down to a feeling. You try several products and you decide on the overall impression.

BA: Can we talk about governance. What is your view about who needs to be involved?

GL: The way that we look at it now is that the stakeholders need to be involved. It needs to be engaged involvement. It is the people in the process who will make the change. As modelers we help. We don't do the transformation. At best, we enable it. If the people, say, in the sales process, didn't really want to change, then it wouldn't happen. If we force change, then it isn't really an improvement. But, if we get the salespeople together to look at the sales process, then they do the transformation work and we do the enabling work.

A project needs to figure out how to get the business to do the thought work, to take ownership, to care about it. If the project is big, you need people to do modeling. You need an expert ProVision® user. They go to the stakeholder workshops and capture the information. They may not do everything in the workshops but they are not inventing the model. They are capturing what they saw and heard.

So two groups of people need to be involved, the business and the enablers. Who needs to be involved from the business? It depends on the project.

BA: So to summarize, the modeler is an enabler, in the background. They may not necessarily work on big projects; in fact smaller projects are better, as they gradually build capability. They don't invent models, but capture and express the information of the stakeholders.

GL: Yes, this is the iOctane approach. The ideal is that the business does its own process. The gathering of the information is done by the business. The understanding is reached by the business. You don't have people sitting in workshops pretending that they understand, or only commenting on the one or two things that they do understand. They are fully engaged. Everybody should be able to comment and have input. The modeler gets to learn. The business analyst should not be the first person to see and understand the process. We want the business to increase its self knowledge. The business analysis is there to serve. I would like to see enterprise architects being part of the business. They are experts, yes, but they need to see themselves as part of the transformation team. The main game is not the model. The main game is understanding the processes and redesigning them.

BA: So if you have an enterprise architecture team, who understand frameworks and methodology, who understand process, ideally where should they be sitting? Who should they report to?

GL: It's a very good question. You can have a Program Management Office. However, just because you form one, it doesn't necessarily mean it will be any good. It is important to do one project, then another, then another, to build up capability. They need the opportunity to learn.

Large organizations could have centers of excellence. They have to be continually going out doing the servant role, doing the enabling role on all of these projects, which could include running the projects. The transformation work has to be done by the business. The knowledge will always be in the business. What they are learning is how to enable. What knowledge do they have of the business? All those things that they are doing, doesn't mean that they know how a sale happens or how to develop a new product.

So someone who is good at abstract thinking will work in those projects. I can see that they would want to be more than just an enabler and find a place in the business. The natural place in the business would be in enterprise architecture. Let's say an organization uses Oracle. They can't do any change without it touching the Oracle setup. So they have to understand Oracle. They have expertise that is not just frameworks. They know the systems, how things are put together and how much they cost. You would want that person to represent the business.

BA: Can you give an example of a recent success story?

GL: We have recently been working with a large organization on an enterprise architecture project. It had a business case. It had to happen. The scope was a bit vague and ambitious. They had a huge project which required them to create an architecture from scratch. There was no way they could have done that project without the models. The documentation is key.

The people who built the architecture are not the ones who will have to live with it. The audience is a certain group of people in the future who will need to be able to look online to discover information. It started small and it was iterative. I decided that it should be that way. I could have used the TOGAF framework, which has four parts to it. But how do you go about populating it? You have to start somewhere. The starting point was one particular type of model.

They had these scenarios where there were a whole lot of business processes which were automated. You can see on one model how a process started, which systems were involved, and where they ended up. They were very important models because they were completely automated. There weren't any people who you could ask about how they work, except the architects. They were important because, if one of them failed, then money wouldn't get to the bank at the end of the day or bills would go to the wrong people.

They called these models Integration workflows. Sometimes they called them Interface workflows. They would forget the name. They weren't standard workflows. They were something that they had invented. This group of models had to be done by a certain date. That isn't enterprise architecture necessarily. But it is enterprise architecture if you see EA as a service.

The methodology for doing that is the same as good software development. You go to the users and ask them how they are going to use the models. You ask them what they need to do with the model. So you create use cases. For example, you are going to go to the portal, navigate the hierarchy, find the model you want and open it.

In order to deliver, you need standards. You need standards so the models are consistent. So you make prototypes and test to see how hard they are to use. The navigation might work but the models are too hard to create because the users are new to ProVision® and they are being asked to do some fiddly stuff. So then we changed the specification, made them, and delivered.

None of this was perfect. We didn't always deliver on time. However it was a software development methodology and that was good. Now for enterprise architecture purposes we have chosen one type of model to go live with on the portal. That is great. That is perfect. There was a real, live audience that needed those models. They were already using the Visio versions so going live just meant sending out an email saying, "don't look at the Visio models, go and look in Knowledge Exchange®".

Now, because there was a real audience, you could tell if the models had been done properly. If they are done properly then the customers will be happy, and if not they complain. There were no complaints and if you looked at the logs you could see there was plenty of activity. That is brilliant.

Then we moved onto our next model type. The basic approach is a winner. You have to do it that way.

BA: Do you use the Project Inventory to simplify the navigation?

GL: Yes, we created a Navigator Model which was pretty ugly but acted as a Home Page with links off to other models. Then the chief architect replaced that with a TOGAF image from which you could drill down. Right now there are only two links that are populated and the rest is empty. Then we added user-specific entry points. So now there is an Application Architecture entry point and a Technology Architecture entry point.

The philosophy is that nothing gets added unless there is a customer. There was a data architect who was invited to add some models. He looked at it and said that there was nothing that he wanted to add. It has to be that way. There is no point in forcing people to add information if they think that their tools are better and if there is no audience waiting. So now there is no Data Architecture entry point. There may be in the future.

BA: What about going the other way? What about ProVision® becoming a slave repository, rather than the master? The data architect, in this example, has an external repository.

GL: That is completely on the cards. What we have is an Enterprise Architecture practice, not a ProVision® practice. So we could just change the use case for data architects. But one thing we discovered is that it is an incredible amount of work. When I was there, I was able to add to the repository quickly. When I left, that capability was gone. So it has to be simple. The more models you have, the greater the maintenance work.

Summary

In this chapter, we understood what a methodology is and have looked at five projects that will build the basis of your central repository using a fictional business called Starberry Accounting. We now know how to model their Tax Audit process in sufficient detail to make better decisions.

Who should do this work? As Gordon Lescinsky says:

> *The ideal is that the business does its own process. The gathering of the information is done by the business. The understanding is reached by the business. You don't have people sitting in workshops pretending that they understand, or only commenting on the one or two things that they do understand. They are fully engaged.*

The role of the modeler is to facilitate and support.

5

Implementing Effective Governance

This chapter describes how to design a governance structure that will support modeling activities, that is the creation and maintenance of models. The governance of the organization is out of scope of this discussion. We are only interested in the candidate topics for inclusion in the central repository.

Too often modeling is seen as a technical function and is conducted in a vacuum. Getting the governance right is a key to successful strategy. By ensuring that all key stakeholders are involved, the models will reflect the higher needs of the business. In this chapter we discuss four topics around governance:

- Who needs to be involved?
- Agile Management
- How to model a governance structure?
- What to do if there is no governance?

What is governance

What is governance? Governance is a set of policies, procedures, and processes that ensures that work is done effectively. It defines roles and grants authority to implement the policies, procedures, and processes. Governance is an operational management activity as distinct from leadership which creates and communicates a vision.

If there is no vision that there is a need for a central repository, there can be no effective governance. The reason is that leadership comes before management. Where leadership hands off to management, there governance begins.

Modeling an organization is often done by business analysts located in an IT department. They have only a limited relationship with the key decision-makers inside the business. Sometimes the modelers are assigned to different departments. This results in different frameworks, methodologies, and toolsets being adopted. Instead of one central repository of knowledge the business has many, resulting in duplication of effort and fragmentation. Successful modeling at the enterprise level is impossible without an effective governance structure.

Who needs to be involved

In an ideal world, senior management would understand that one of their most important assets is the knowledge of the organization itself. They would be fully committed to the creation of a central repository, ensure that there were sufficient resources to maintain it, and support the development of effective processes. Every major decision would be informed by the content of the central repository. Every project would obtain information from and contribute to the central repository.

Most of us do not live in such a world yet.

Motorola change process

Motorola knows a thing or two about the process. Here is their humorous analysis of what really happens:

- Assign a manager
- Set a goal that is bigger and better
- Define the direct outcomes
- Determine the measures
- Dissect the problem
- Redesign the machine
- Implement the adaptation
- Test the results
- Assign blame

In this chapter, I will suggest how a governance structure might look, once the vision has been implemented. I will then move on to show you what you might do in the absence of that structure and give you techniques that will enable you to manage up more effectively.

Agile Management

One of the best governance structures for modeling can be derived from Agile or XP programming. So what is Agile and how did it develop?

When software development began, it copied the project management methodology of engineers. The problem is that their context, however, is completely different. If you are building a bridge, it makes sense to plan the design in great detail, so that when you actually start the work you know exactly what to do and can build it in the least possible time. As much as possible, the thinking is done up front. It's much cheaper to spend a couple of years thinking about the project, than have a lot of equipment on-site, people milling around with nothing to do, while you figure out the next step.

This approach is called the waterfall. Everything cascades down from the previous step, separate streams of work coming together to create a great river.

When the **waterfall approach** was applied to software development about 70% of projects failed. We covered up these failures by looking at the outputs and checking to see if they were delivered. If they were, we said that the project was successful. Most of the software development in large command and control organizations, such as the government, is still done in this way and the 70% failure rate continues to this day. Included in that percentage are the zombie projects, the living dead. They have delivered all or most of the outputs but nobody uses them, thus there is no useful outcome.

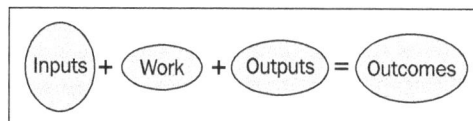

That being the case, why haven't more organizations adopted Agile? It comes down to control. As one Agile proponent, www.ccpace.com, explains:

Traditional management theory assumes that:

- *Rigid procedures are needed to regulate change*
- *Hierarchical organizational structures are means of establishing order*
- *Increased control results in increased order*
- *Organizations must be rigid, static hierarchies*

- *Employees are interchangeable "parts" in the organizational "machine"*
- *Problems are solved primarily through reductionist task breakdown and allocation*
- *Projects and risks are adequately predictable to be managed through complex up-front planning*

Within this context, it is small wonder that the new methodologies appear informal to the point of being chaotic, egalitarian to the point of actively fostering insubordination, and directionless in their approach to problem solving. We believe that the slow adoption of agile methodologies stems mainly from this misalignment between the fundamental assumptions of traditional management and those of the new agile development methodologies. As such, we believe there is a significant need for a change in assumptions and a new management framework when working with agile methodologies.

For more on this topic read http://www.ccpace.com/Resources/ documents/AgileProjectManagement.pdf.

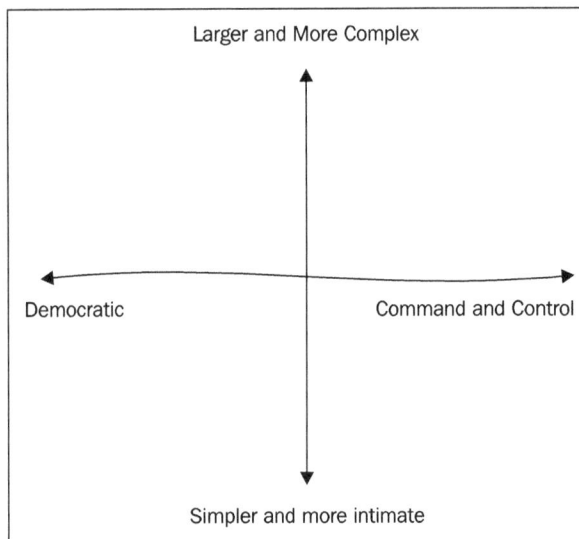

Without doubt, it is easier to implement an Agile Management structure within a smaller, more democratic, organization as it will fit within the overall culture. However, there is no reason why Agile Management can't be used even in a command and control structure. You are not trying to change the overall structure, just to "carve out" autonomous areas within the structure where Agile is used. You are simply asserting that when it comes to governing the maintenance of the repository, this is the way things get done.

Let's look at how Agile concepts can be used to implement modeling governance.

Governance and leadership

In order to implement a governance structure you first need leadership. Leading is a role quite distinct from managing. Leaders coach, manage the team's energy and hold the vision. Managers consult, train, mentor, and facilitate. Only when a manager starts to coach, do they start to move into a leadership role.

A leader's actions and behavior create leadership.

Leadership comprises three things—**vision**, **confidence**, and **communication**. Vision provides clarity about where we are going. Confidence inspires and motivates the whole team that we can get there. Communication ensures that everyone understands the vision, strategy, and the importance of their role, so that the vision is achieved in the most effective way and the least possible time.

> The Aboriginal people of Australia have been around for about 40,000 years, which makes our civilization look puny by comparison. They know a thing or two about leadership and governance.
>
> *In our Aboriginal way we learned to listen from our earliest days. We could not live good or useful lives unless we listened. This was the normal way for us to learn – not by asking questions. We learned by watching and listening, waiting and then acting. Our people have passed this way of listening for over 40,000 years. My people are not threatened by silence. They are completely at home with it.*
>
> Miriam-Rose Ungunmerr-Baumann
> An Aboriginal Elder from Daly River, quoted by Peter d'Plesse in *Leadership in Australia*, Esperance Press, 2007

People who have all three qualities are rare. To resolve this, two or more people can collaborate to create a leadership team. One may have a clear vision but be hopeless at communication. Another may have lots of self-confidence and a great ability to listen and explain. Separately they are not leaders. The visionary may sit in their room dreaming up ideas that nobody else can understand.

They may be seen as a recluse and a difficult person to get along with. The communicator may be seen as being very affable and enjoyable company, but doesn't have the depth to inspire others. Alone each will be known, not for their strengths, but for their weaknesses. Together they can do extraordinary things.

Leadership has nothing to do with role or responsibility. Leadership can occur anywhere in an organization. A person becomes a leader when they care enough about an issue to step up. They remain a leader when they convince others.

[See www.margaretwheatley.com for more on this approach to leadership.]

Measurement

The easiest way to monitor success is to look at if the project comes in on time or on budget. These factors are very clear and easy to measure. Unfortunately they measure the wrong side of the equation. You can have a million dollar project that achieves very little and a $100K project that achieves an enormous amount. The fact that the $1M project might have come in under budget is irrelevant in terms of its impact.

The only way to judge the success of a project is by looking at the desired outcomes and determining whether these were achieved. The challenge is that outcomes are much harder to determine and can take months or years to show up. By that time, the team has moved on, and nobody takes responsibility for checking if the outcomes were achieved.

There is no reason why Agile can't be applied to the governance structure of modeling. Here are some of the principles that you can apply.

Do the minimum

To prevent the modeling team going off track, do discrete chunks of work, each of which is no longer than two weeks from start to finish. The idea is not to do the maximum but the minimum. This is very counter-intuitive. Surely the more detail you can provide, the better?

At the end of the two weeks you have a model which has been created to enable your business to make a specific decision, just better than if the model did not exist. A working useful model is the key measure of success.

When you present the model, either it will serve its purpose, or it won't. Your audience can't tell you before what they really want, because they generally don't know, or can't explain it in a way that you will understand.

If your model is a mistake, then you have lost two weeks of work, but learned a lot.

The client is part of the team

Ideally, you will have a representative of the client sitting in your office and building the models with you. If that is not possible, then they need to sit in on the initial planning meeting, the meeting at the end of the first week, and the final meeting when the model is presented. The team is not building for the client, but with the client.

Have daily stand-up meetings

Start the day with a 15 minute meeting in which everyone participates. Each person shares one thing in a minute or so. There is a sense of urgency. The idea is for everyone to know what everyone is up to and how they are feeling. Team leaders can take any issues they discover off line. By making the meeting a stand-up meeting, that is where you physically stand up in a circle, nobody gets comfortable and the meeting doesn't get drawn out. The absence of furniture means that there is no hierarchy. The context of stand up meetings is energy. You get a quick snapshot of the mood and whether the team is excited or stuck.

Keep it simple

The simplest model is the best. It is the easiest to build, the easiest to explain, and the easiest to modify.

Trust the team

Choose people who are self-motivated, passionate about delivering benefit for the client, and able to live in an environment of constant change. Allow them to self-organize and then trust them.

Work in pairs

Every model is built by two people. One models, while the other looks over their shoulder, offering suggestions and corrections. The pair are equals and will switch places on a regular basis. Pairing creates community and delivers better quality results faster.

Modeling a governance structure with ProVision®

We said earlier that 'governance is a set of policies, procedures, and processes that ensures that work is done effectively'. Let's look at how we can use ProVision® to model these.

Policies and procedures

All organizations have policies and procedures. In some organizations they are written down. In others, they are not documented because the organization is too small to warrant them. Often, nobody has the time to create and maintain procedure manuals. If you don't know something, just ask someone who does.

As an organization grows, the argument for documenting policies and procedures gets stronger. Again, we must look at the context. Why document? We see two contexts and they lead to very different conclusions.

The first context is *compliance*. The purpose of the documentation is to demonstrate that you have effective and consistent policies and procedures. The more documentation, the more compliant you are. If there is a failure, then you can point to the documentation and say that the reason for the failure was that the policy was not followed or it was the wrong policy.

So the higher context is *reputation*. You know that something will go wrong at some time and you want to ensure that this does not damage your reputation.

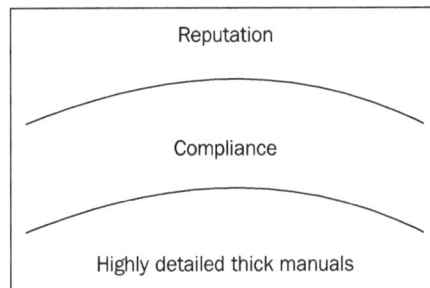

```
Reputation

Compliance

Highly detailed thick manuals
```

Unsurprisingly, these manuals don't get read, because it was never their purpose that staff would actually do so! They were created, so that they could be pointed to. Some writers even include what are known as *submarines*. These are pieces of text that are complete nonsense and are in plain view. If they don't get spotted by readers, the author knows that nobody actually read the text. Let's see what happens if we change the context to that of smaller organizations. The reason that small organizations don't document their policies and procedures is that if you need to know something, you can just ask. What happens to policies and procedures when we keep in large organizations the same context of *understanding as in small ones*?

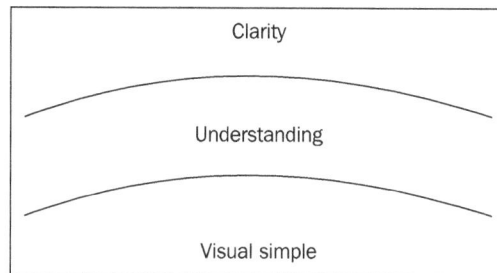

```
┌─────────────────────────────────────┐
│              Clarity                │
│                                     │
│           Understanding             │
│                                     │
│            Visual simple            │
└─────────────────────────────────────┘
```

When someone looks at the policies and procedures, they are visual and simple to understand. If they need more detail, they can drill down to find it. Everything that they need to know is in one place. They don't need to hunt for it. The higher context is to create *clarity*. They know what is expected of them and they understand the overall context of what they are doing.

How can we use ProVision® to support this context?

To create understanding:

- There is no need to put everything into the central repository
- There is no need to replace existing data sources, we can leverage them
- We can use the visuals to represent processes, workflows, and relationships in the context of organizational goals, rules, and standards

No need for everything

In this context, the central repository becomes a portal. When Tom Schnackenberg won the Americas Cup in 1995 he used the context word *faster*. While he was open to all suggestions from the team, his only consideration was: "Does it make the boat go faster?"

When someone from the team came up with a good idea, he would ask them that question. If the answer was 'no' then it didn't matter how good it was. As it transpired, Black Magic NZL 32 proved very fast and far too strong for the defender, Young America.

Our context word is *understanding*. Does this model increase understanding? It is the client who will use the repository. While it is nice that it increases our understanding that is just a side benefit.

So unless it increases their understanding it doesn't go in. Making the client a part of the team is a way to ensure that the customer's voice is heard in time.

Linking to other sources

There are a number of ways in which we can link to information in other places. In the following example, an activity object has two associations, one of which is an Artifact. This kind of object enables the modeler to link to an external document, website or intranet page, or email address. If you create a link to a web page on the intranet then that can become the point of truth. As it is a hyperlink, it will show the most current information. Provided the information is current, then you have just eliminated a maintenance task.

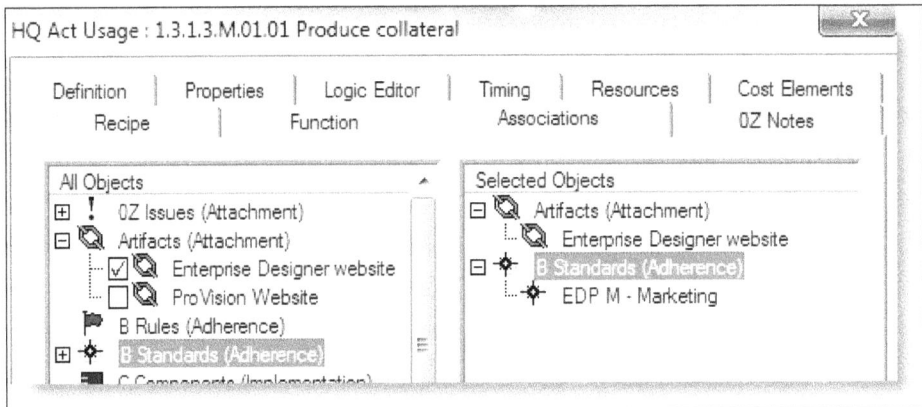

If you need to import or export information frequently to another system then ProVision® is compliant with several standards, including XML. You can import and export information from the Repository using the various wizards available. The **CIF (Common Interchange Format)** is an XML dump, which includes all of the information about the presentation of the objects (color, style, and font) as well as the content.

It is also possible to automate import and export by writing a piece of code that will extract information from one system and place it in the other. If you are interested in doing this then I recommend you ask Open Text Metastorm to put you in touch with your nearest consultant with that expertise.

If you just need to import or export content (objects and their relationships) into a spreadsheet then we recommend the **Translator** option. Anyone with a reasonable knowledge of Excel can do this.

Visualize information

The Enterprise edition of ProVision® includes the Navigator model. You can create a **Navigator model** on the fly, just by right-clicking an object.

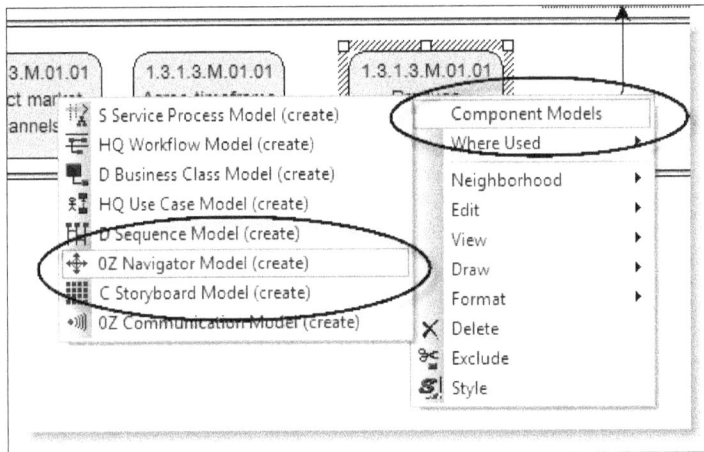

You can then select which objects in the repository to display on the model. Objects that are not selected, or objects in the model that have even been excluded, are still in the repository there and all their associations are still valid. In the following example, we have traced relationships beyond the first level. Now we can see that the activity *Produce collateral* is part of a specific model called *Market benefits,* and implemented by a specific role named *Market internally.* The compass icon tells us that there are more relationships that we have chosen not to display, to keep the model simple.

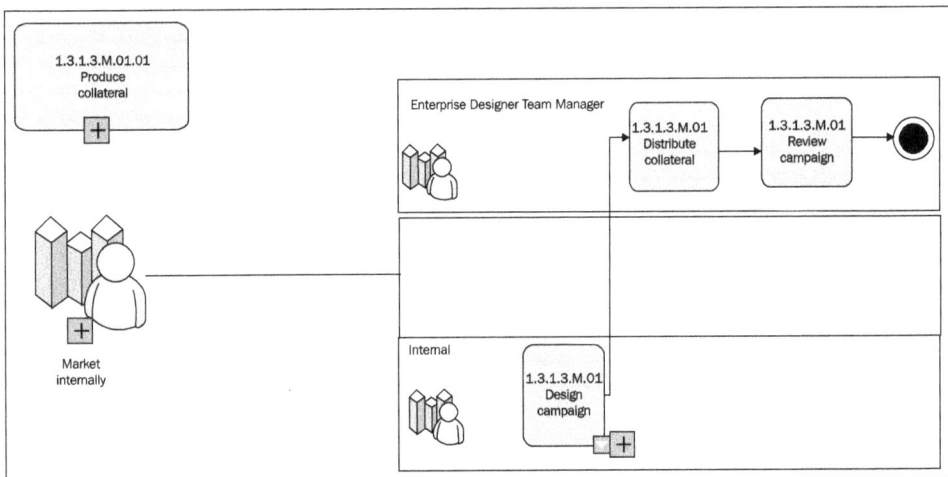

Processes

The process of governance can be described using the 10 Enterprise Designer process types:

- H = How will we *help* users that need to use the central repository?

- I = How will we *inform* or monitor the use of the central repository?

- J = How will we *join* or assemble the information to produce the models?

- K = How will we *collect* payment for the information required?

- L = What is the *logistics* process for presenting the models to the client?

- M = How will we *market* the service?

- N = How will we select *new* areas to model?

- O = How will we *organize* or procure the information?

- P = How will we *pay* for the service?

- Q = How will we *quit* or retire the models that are no longer useful?

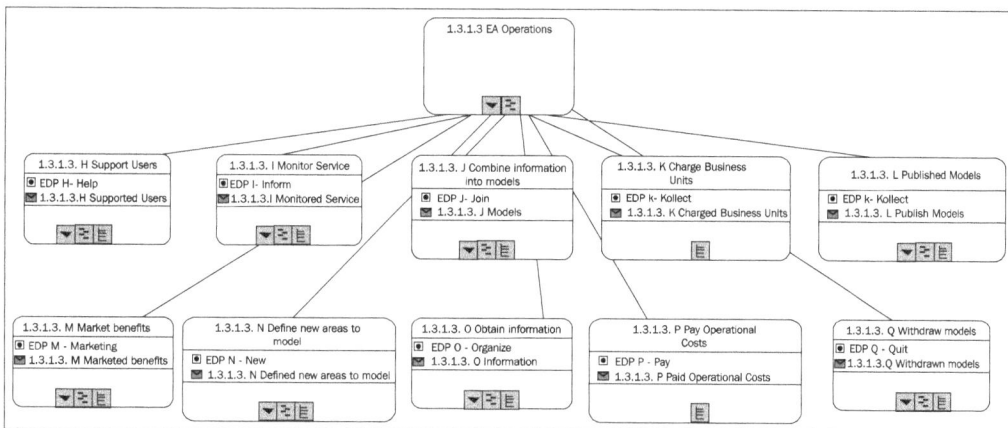

The preceding model is a process model using the eTOM framework. eTOM allocates the code number and name 1.3.1.3 EA Operations and leaves the modeler to determine what the process will look like. The Enterprise Designer Institute has developed a comprehensive governance model that takes eTOM deeper.

For example, here are the activities under EA operations. Notice that the *Monitor Service* and *Market benefits* activities appear twice. This is because they have been aliased in the workflow. The same activity is done by two different swim lanes, first by the Enterprise Designer Team and then by Strategic and Enterprise Planning. You can't create alias objects in a Process model. If you create an alias in a Workflow model, then it will automatically appear in the companion Process model.

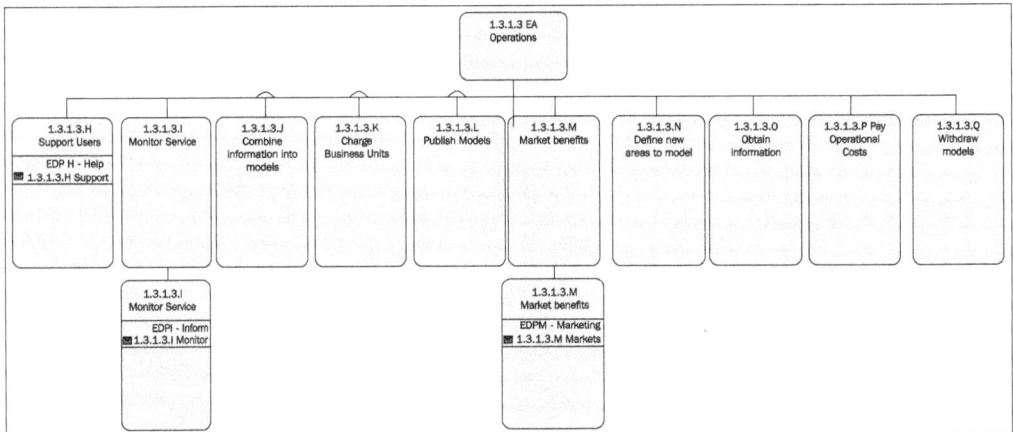

Here is the same model represented as the workflow. In fact, there are three different workflows going on. The work done by the Accounts Department is unrelated to the Enterprise Designer Team. Strategic and Enterprise Planning is operating on a different time cycle to the Enterprise Designer Team. At this high level, we could have used a Communication model instead. However, we chose to use a Workflow model so that we can show the detailed workflows as nested models. The small icon in the top-left corner is a map of eTOM with the relevant area highlighted. Now you can see the alias objects. You can obtain a copy of these models through www.enterprisedesigner.com.

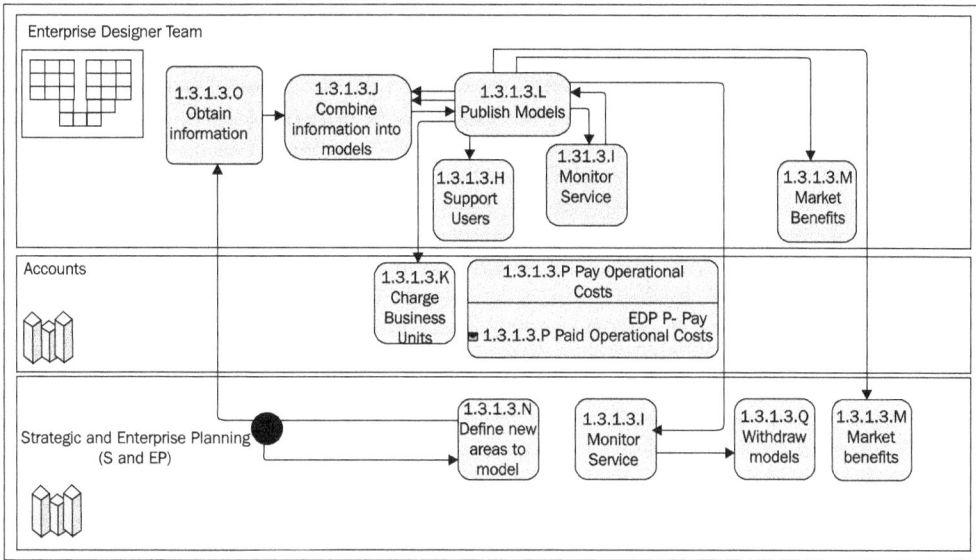

Because of ProVision's design you can create nested models, each of which has more depth and less breadth.

Here is the model for the Marketing process, showing three levels. The numbering scheme is inherited from eTOM.

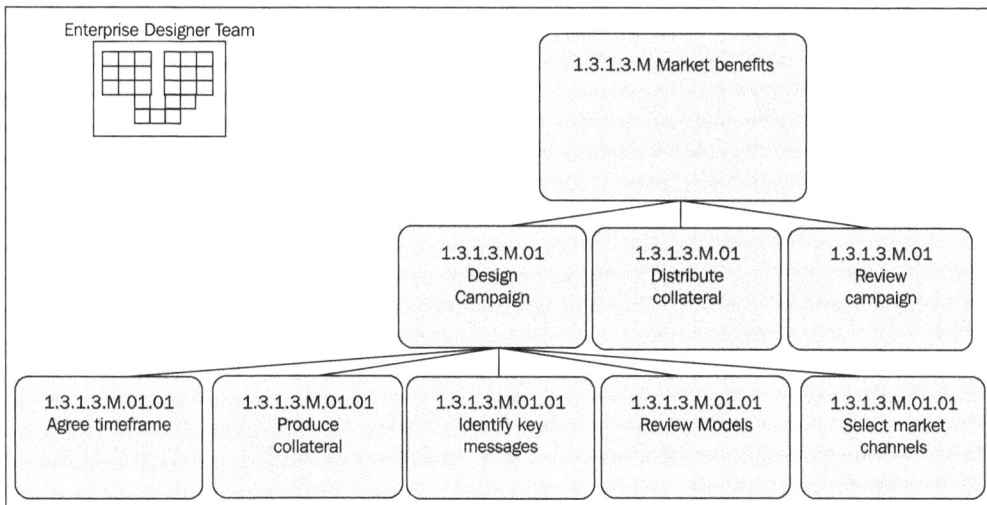

Here is the same level 2 process seen as a workflow. The process model above tells us that there are sub-models under each of the three objects. In this example, the nested model indicators have been switched off, to keep the model simple. With the indicators switched on we would see that there is a nested model under the **Design Campaign** activity.

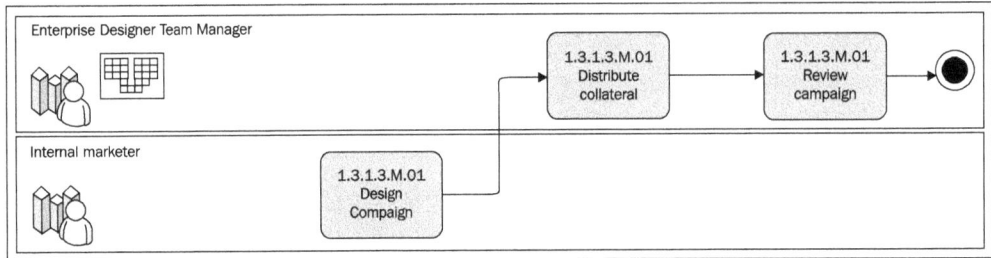

When capturing information about a process we want to understand the emotional, as well as the rational, aspects. How can we express this using a model?

There are a number of ways, depending on how you might want to use the information. For example, it may be sufficient just to color code objects where there are emotional issues. In the example below, a convention is used. Gray boxes are the default. White boxes denote there is an emotional issue. It may be that the staff find the *Review Campaign* activity difficult, or customer complaints peak inside that activity.

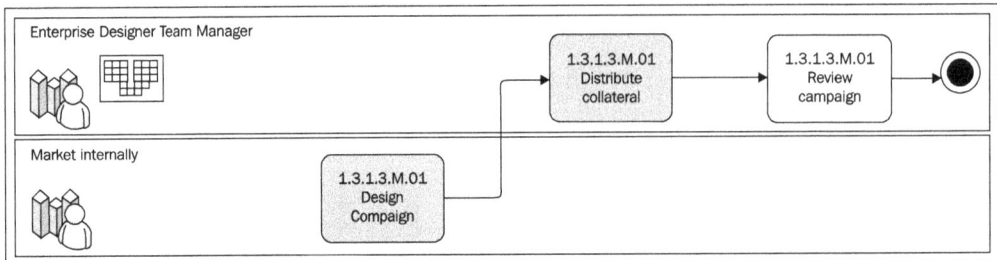

If you use the *Appreciative Inquiry* approach, described in *Chapter 7, Obtaining Buy-in* later, the color coding could highlight all the steps that work particularly well! Be aware that color coding has some limitations. It gets lost in black and white printouts and you cannot filter or layer by color.

In the following example we see that **Review Campaign** is best practice. To do this, we created an opportunity object called **Best practice** and associated it with this activity. To emphasize the relationship we told ProVision® to display it on the layout. This layout option is currently available only in Workflow models. To switch the layout on, right-click the activity and choose **Format | Layout**.

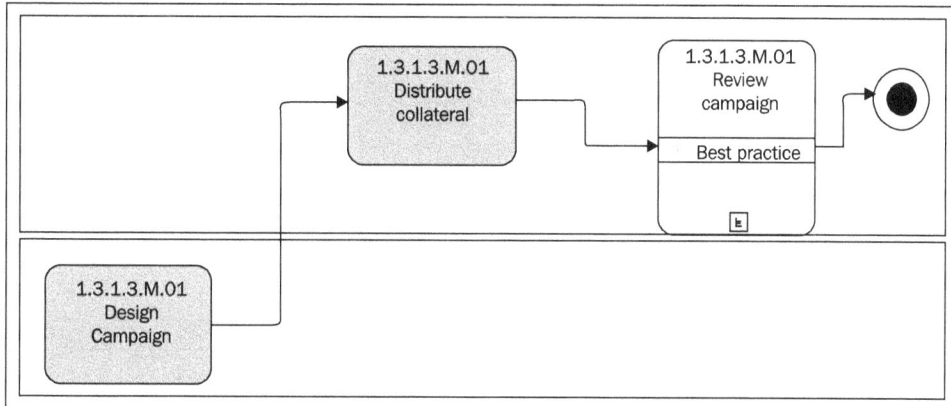

There are a number of other objects available that could be used for this purpose. If you want to highlight things that don't work, then you might prefer to use the problem or issue object instead of opportunities. Of the two, the issue object is the more flexible as it can be associated with a wider range of objects.

Now, in our example, we can associate the business activities that we consider best practice and represent them on an association grid. This is a great way to gather the information and display it one sheet.

One limitation of an association grid is that you can only display one type of association at a time. You can get round this by creating a Navigator model. In the following example, we see the two activities and other areas of the business that are also considered best practice but are not activity objects.

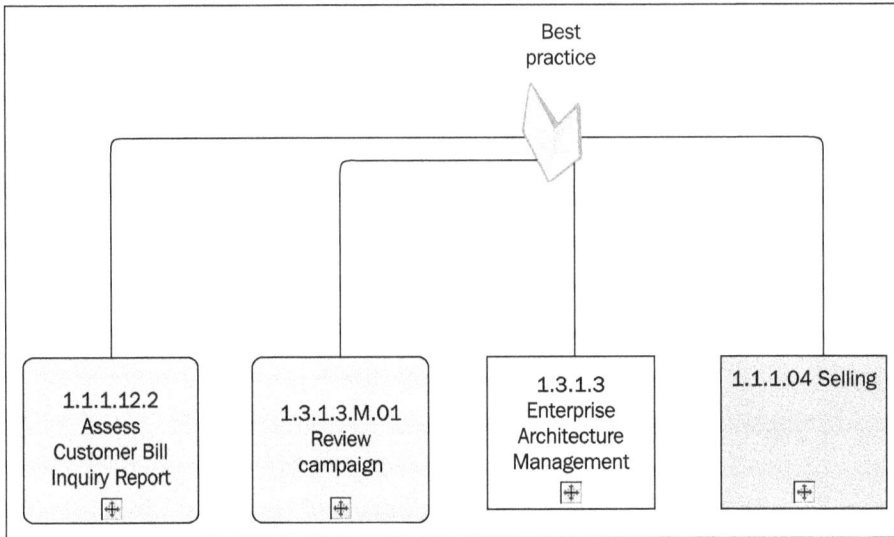

What if there is no governance

Your organization may not have yet reached the point where there is a maturity of understanding that there is a need to model a business. Without that understanding, there can be no conversation around governance. So what do you do if faced with that situation? You have no choice but to learn how to sell an idea.

This technique has been developed by Shirlaws. You can use it in any situation where you need to communicate an idea. So it doesn't matter if there is governance or not. I will introduce the idea, but there is not sufficient room in this book to explain it in great detail. If you see merit, then go and connect with your nearest Shirlaws coach, to get the full understanding. All I can say is that before I learned it, I was effective about 20% of the time. Now that percentage has probably increased to 60%.

Four steps

The way most people try to communicate an idea follows four steps:

1. Take some time to build rapport. (How are you doing today?)

2. Outline why the sky will fall in if the desired solution is not adopted. (Our expansion plans can't continue at this rate. The companies that we buy have wildly incompatible systems. It is taking us months to get a handle on what we need to do to integrate them.)

3. Present the solution. (Let's start collecting the key information in a central repository. It will be far easier to manage and maintain, and we reduce any single person dependencies.)

4. Lock in an agreement. (I need you to approve this budget proposal that goes to the Program Management Committee next month. As you sit on that Committee I want your agreement to champion the proposal when it comes up on the agenda).

Many people with an IT background have never been taught the art of selling and have very little interest in becoming a salesperson. However, to be successful, you have to learn to communicate your ideas in such a way that others get inspired and take action. People with a sales background will know that these four steps are known in the sales world as relax, disturb, relieve, and close. First you relax the person who you are trying to make a case to. Then, once you have gained their trust, you disturb them with the issue. Once you have got them thoroughly worried, you relieve them with the solution to the issue and finally close the deal.

How much time do you spend in these four steps? In the 1970s the thinking was that the first step was the least important. You might represent the importance of each step in the diagram shown below:

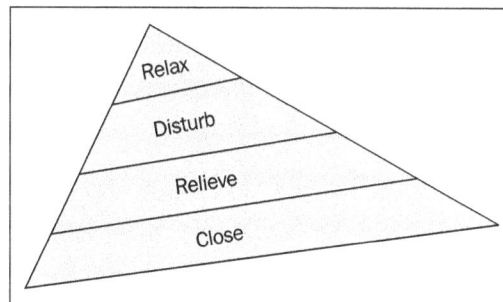

When a detailed analysis was done, it was discovered that for every ten prospects, the salesperson might get three people sufficiently interested to meet. Of those three people, one might buy.

These ratios are not hard and fast. Skilled salespeople can improve the odds. Still, it is a depressing statistic. For every 10 conversations, only one is going anywhere.

In the 1980s they came up with a brilliant new concept.

Why not turn the pyramid upside down! Let's really get to know the potential customer, so that we don't need to spend much time in the close. In fact, if we do it right, they will just say, "where do I sign?"

Unfortunately, when the analysis was done, the ratio hadn't changed. For every 10 prospects, only one sale was made.

So if you want to sell the idea of a central repository to your boss and your co-workers using this four step approach, you are not likely to succeed.

This is the issue that the Shirlaws six step process is designed to solve. It works, if you are prepared to focus on building relationships rather than making sales. We all know when we are being sold to and our defenses go up immediately. However, if you change the context of the conversation from *make a sale at any cost* to *cultivate a relationship and see what happens*, a curious thing occurs. You start selling more and it is easy.

Six step process

Step 1 -	Agenda		Think
		Global Specific SCI	
Step 2 -	Position		Think
		SCI	
Step 3 -	Find	Facts Feelings SCI	Think Feel
Step 4 -	Present		Feel
		Pause	Know
Step 5 -	Summary	SCI	Think
Step 6 -	Open		

(SCI stands for **summarize**, **confirm**, and **introduce**.) So what's different?

Agenda

Expectations

Agenda

SCI

- What are your expectations of...
- What are your expectations of today?
- What are you hoping to...
- What are your expectations of how we will work together?

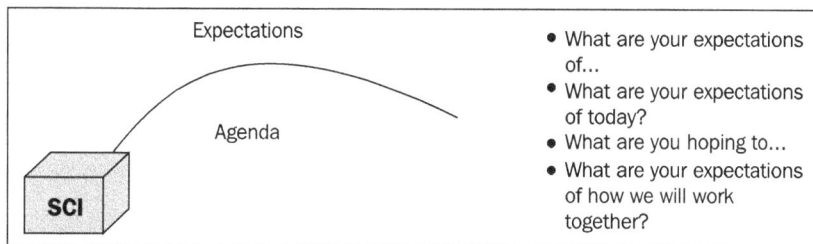

First of all, when you communicate with another person, it is essential to understand their agenda, not yours. What are the issues that they want to solve? This part of the conversation starts by looking at what their overall objective is and then how you can best use your time in this meeting.

"I am really frustrated by how slow it is to integrate, when we acquire companies." That's a global agenda.

After further questioning they say, "What I really want to know today, is what you can do to help me with this issue we have right now with our latest acquisition." That's a more specific agenda.

SCI stands for summarize, confirm and introduce. Unlike the sales pyramid, you don't go to the next step until you are sure that the current step is fully covered. A salesperson wants to close the deal and can brush aside objections. When understanding the other person's agenda, it doesn't matter if the whole meeting is taken up in discovering what the real issue is. So, the metaphor of the pyramid doesn't help. Every conversation is different and you can't allocate different amounts of time in advance to the various steps.

So, you **summarize** the conversation so far and you **confirm** that you have clearly understood what they need, before you **introduce** the next step.

Often people don't know what their specific agenda is. They aren't used to others listening so don't have much practice in explaining. Allowing lots of time and space enables the real issue to emerge.

Eventually they say, "What I really need to understand is whether we should ditch their systems or if there is anything worth salvaging?"

Position

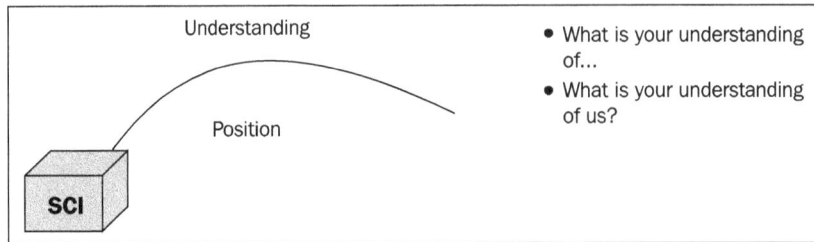

Once you have understood what they need then you are able to see what, if anything, you can do to assist them. This is not to be confused with the solution. Your position is how you are known.

You might say, "We are experts in identifying the key information required to integrate. We help you to make better decisions now. We can help you decide whether to scrap or integrate".

Again you use SCI to ensure that they fully understand what your position is before introducing the next step.

Fact find/feel find

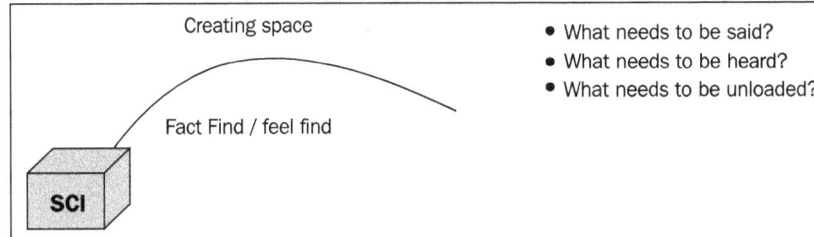

Now that you know what their issue is you can start getting the facts that you need. At a certain point, the feelings associated with the facts can start to emerge. You will notice a change in the mood. Their language will change from rational to emotional. They will start to tell stories. It is as important to understand the feelings around an issue as the facts.

Present

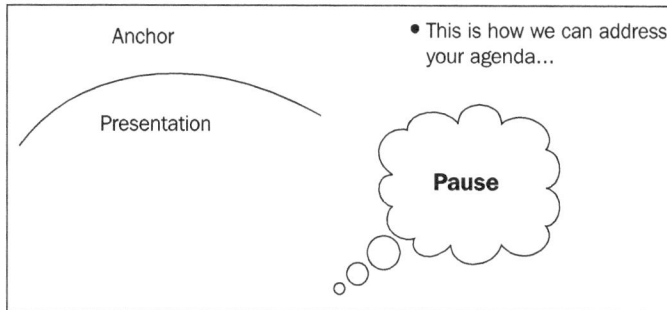

We are halfway through the process and we still haven't tried to sell them anything.

You might be the first person that they had to deal with in a professional capacity who has not come in with their own agenda, intent on selling something to them, irrespective of whether you can be of any help. Most people find this very refreshing.

Now that you know what they need, are in possession of the facts, and are aware of their feelings, you are able to present a solution. It may be that you can't help but know someone else who can. When building an authentic relationship with a work colleague, be willing to walk. If you can't help, don't try. In this way, next time they need something and you can help they will know that you can be trusted.

You might say, "The reason why you are not getting the information you need quickly is that it is scattered and very hard to pull together. This is a very common issue. Fortunately, there is a new breed of tools on the market that we can use. I have determined that ProVision® is the one which has the best business focus. It's designed to solve the problem that you face and has been used in our industry, both here and abroad. It is generally considered to be the most user-friendly. Two of my team are already familiar with the solution because they have used it in other companies. This issue is only going to get worse. The sooner we start using the right tools, the sooner you can start getting the information you need, when you need it."

Pause

At the end of the presentation, stop. Allow them time to mull over what you have said. This means there will be a period of silence. However tempting, avoid breaking the silence. This is the most delicate moment in the whole conversation. They are processing the conversation. If you disturb their time to reflect, then you will have to go back to square one.

Eventually they will say one of two things. "Thank you, but I don't think this is the right time", or some other polite way of saying no. Otherwise they will say something like, "So what do we do next?"

If they say no then move on and make your case to someone else. There will be other opportunities, other doors.

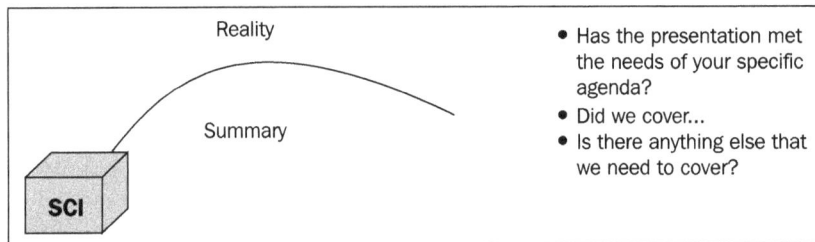

If they say yes, then you can summarize everything said so far. In the process of doing that, another deeper layer may open up. They may tell you things that they forgot, or were not prepared to tell you earlier.

You might say, "The senior management team intends to continue growing by acquisition. The number of acquisitions will remain at one or two a year for the next few years. The process of integration is not keeping pace. Right now you don't feel you have the information to decide whether to integrate or scrap the systems of the most recent acquisition. You are frustrated that you can't easily get the answer that you need. Our team can build a central repository and populate it rapidly with the key information. We are able to do this because we have a framework and methodology. However we need to deploy a central repository, as the tools we have right now can't support you."

Open

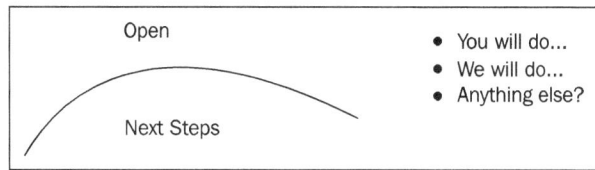

Finally, when building a relationship, the last step is not to close a deal but to open a relationship. In this step both parties may state what they intend to do next, to start building the relationship.

You might say, "I will approach Open Text Metastorm and get a 30 day evaluation copy and populate it with the key information you need for the current acquisition. You will have that by 1st June. You will arrange for me to present to the Board at the next meeting, so we can show you the results. You will make the case for us to get funding for an initial five licenses and Knowledge Exchange®. I will get you the costings on that by the end of this week. Is there anything else I didn't mention?"

When we make decisions we can make them in a thinking, feeling or knowing space. Some people are naturally thinkers. It shows up in their language which tends to be rational and logical. Others are feelers. They sense if something feels right or not. Leaders are often knowers. They make decisions from their gut. The six step process combines all three. When the discussion begins it is in a thinking, logical, and rational space. However if it stays there, you are unlikely to get to any decision. By moving the conversation in the 'find' step from the facts to feelings, you are able to add a second dimension to the discussion.

When they take the moment to decide, it is in the knowing space. If you disturb them, they will go back to the thinking space. It is a continuous cycle, so thinking is the next step. Once they have decided, you want to circle back to the thinking space to agree on the next steps. That's very different from reversing direction and thinking more about what decision to make.

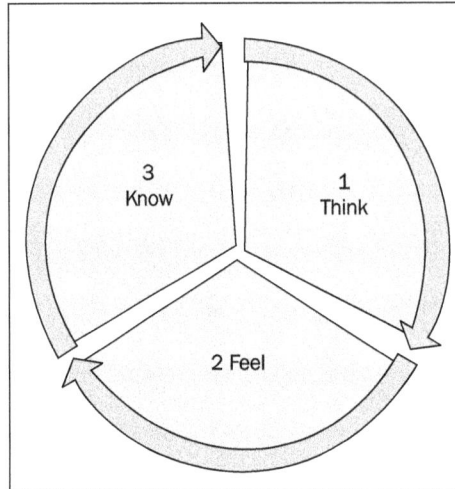

Summary

In this chapter we have learned some of the principles of Agile Management to run the governance of the central repository. We have also been introduced to the Shirlaws methodology of communicating ideas effectively. We saw that decision-making combines head, heart, and gut and we need to use all three to manage up. We saw some ProVision® models using the Enterprise Designer framework, and we learned that we can get the original models from the Enterprise Designer website.

In the next chapter, we will complete our explanation of what the toolset does and how it integrates with Knowledge Exchange® to provide a communication and collaboration environment.

6
Understanding the Toolset

This chapter provides a high-level view of the features and functionality of ProVision®. This is the shortest chapter in the book because the purpose is to provide information that can be used to introduce the tool to modelers and explain what it can be used for.

This chapter covers the following two areas:

- A high-level view of ProVision® features and functionality
- Understanding the limitations of the tool

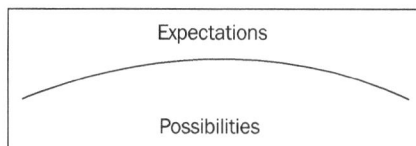

As this is not a technical book, this chapter is also designed to explain to the people developing the strategy what the tool is capable of, so that they have realistic expectations of what is possible and what is not.

> If you wish to understand the technical capabilities and functionality in detail, then please read ProVision® 6.2 Made Easy and ProVision® 6.2 User Guide. The former is a comprehensive technical guide to all of the features, while the latter shows you how to use the toolset to achieve common tasks.

ProVision® features and functionality

The Open Text Metastorm modeling suite consists of:

- **ProVision®**, which is used to model information
- **Knowledge Exchange®**, which is used to store models and objects, created with the help of ProVision, on a central server

If there is only one person who is modeling, there is no need for Knowledge Exchange®. However, as soon as you get a team of modelers, you need a mechanism to share objects and models. This is the problem that Knowledge Exchange® resolves. It uses the same paradigm as software development. When teams of software developers work together on the same code, they check parts out. While checked out, objects are locked. Another user can check out the same objects as read-only. When a modeler checks in the objects, the locks are released.

As models are checked in, Knowledge Exchange® makes a website copy. Thus, users with the appropriate permissions can view the models using Internet Explorer. They do not need a license to do this. Not only can they view the models, they can even make edit changes. There are limitations. You cannot create objects or make relationships. You can comment and add information about an object—for example, you could edit an object's description or properties tab.

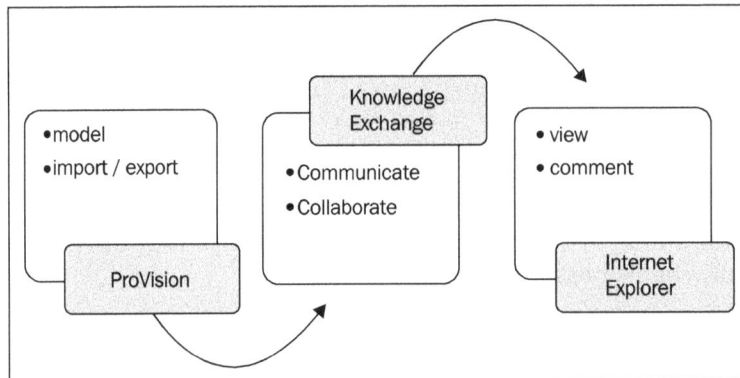

The advantage of this feature is that a modeler can create an object and then request the subject matter expert to add the detail. Next time the modeler checks out the relevant model, the changes will appear for them to review.

Sharing models without Knowledge Exchange®

Some organizations might start off with a few licenses before purchasing Knowledge Exchange®. The ability to create multiuser repositories is built into ProVision®. This functionality pre-dates Knowledge Exchange®. Therefore, the check in and out mechanism is less sophisticated. It is good enough to get you started, but I wouldn't recommend that you see it as a long-term solution.

There are a host of features in Knowledge Exchange® that are not available using a multiuser repository. The security is less sophisticated and it is built on an Access database. With these points in mind, to create a multiuser repository, select the **A multi-user repository that supports object locking, check-in, and check-out** option and follow the wizard.

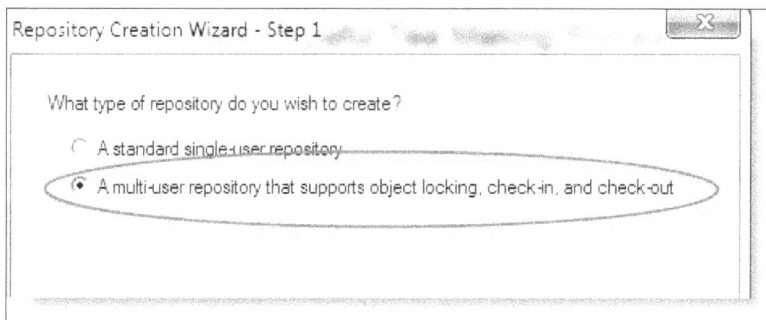

Visio or ProVision

ProVision® is a sophisticated, top of the market, modeling solution. As previously discussed, modeling is not the same as drawing.

Visio is a low-cost business drawing tool. It is closer to Microsoft Paint in architecture, than to ProVision®.Visio lets you paint static business-orientated images. When you create a drawing using Visio, you can't reuse the same object on another drawing. You can copy and paste it, but then you have to remember two places to make edit changes.

Visio doesn't enforce any rules. You can use whatever object you like to make your picture. Consequently, there is no standard and everyone will do things differently. By contrast, ProVision® has a set of objects with predefined properties. You can customize them, to a certain extent, but the idea is that you just need to get started with them and don't have to think too much about that aspect.

With Visio, you just start drawing on a blank sheet. ProVision® is built on a completely different architecture. First, you create a repository and then you create notebooks inside each repository. These notebooks contain stereotypes of models, objects, and relationships. When you create a new object, you have to also choose its type. The new object is stored in the object inventory of the relevant, currently open notebook.

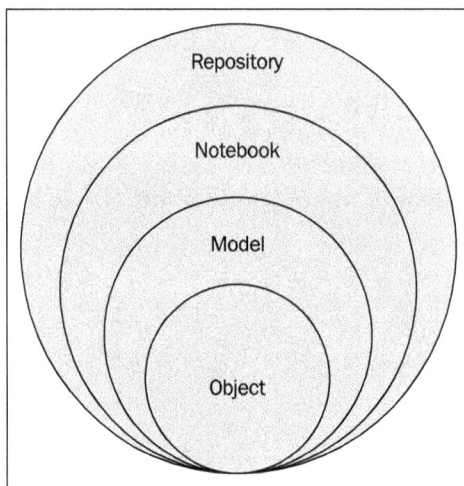

Thereafter, you can place the same object inside multiple models. If you make edit changes to the object on one model, all the other instances are updated. While this might seem slower and more complex than just starting a drawing, much of this complexity is hidden from the modeler. You can create and edit objects on the fly as you build a model. ProVision® takes care of managing the object inventory behind the scenes.

This approach follows the architectural principle of *create once, use many*.

One of the new features of ProVision® is that you can create objects that are stored centrally on the server and can be reused across multiple notebooks. These objects are created in ProVision® but housed in Knowledge Exchange®. In this way, multiple users can reference the objects in their local models, instead of creating them from scratch.

This ability to create centrally hosted templates and reference models is very powerful. For example, if you have a set of objects that represent the organization's facilities, these can be stored centrally. Now, any time that a modeler needs a specific facility, they can just reference it. **Referencing** is like a hyperlink. The object is not sitting on the local computer, which means the administrator can edit that object once and update that across multiple notebooks in multiple repositories.

Multiple organizations can share the same model. So, there is no technical reason why a consulting company could not make templates that their clients then use. For example, a company with expertise in the building industry could develop best practice workflow models. All of their clients could reference these models instead of building and maintaining them independently, even though they are in different parts of the world, and are, in all other respects, completely independent of each other.

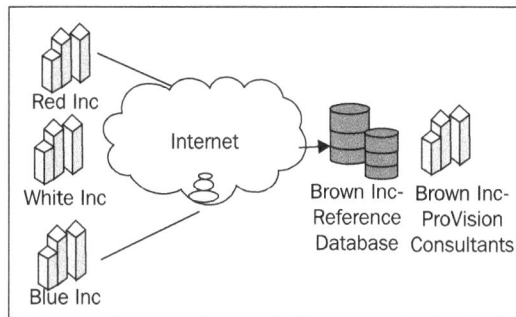

Everything is an object

In ProVision®, everything is an object. Links between objects are also objects. They appear as lines rather than shapes, but they are still objects. Even models themselves are objects. As a result, you can treat a model as an object and place it inside a Navigator model.

Model and grid

Because everything is an object, the same information in the repository can be displayed not only in a model but also in a report or grid format. Thus, it is not even necessary for an object to appear in a model. The relation between two objects may be an association or property that is not even visible on any model.

Pursuit from Goal to Business Process	Acquire Raw Materials	Develop New Product	Fill Order	Forecast Sales	Market Product	Ship Order
C.2 Increase Sales to Existing Customers	☐	☑	☐	☑	☑	☐
P.2.1.1 Decrease Material Handling	☑	☐	☑	☐	☐	☑

In this example, the modeler has created a set of associations between business processes and strategic goals. These might be scattered across multiple models. Using grids, the information can be gathered and edited without the need to open the models or objects. The result can be exported to Excel for further analysis.

Model and interpret

The purpose of modeling is to represent a complex idea in a simple visual format. What do you do with the information that you don't want to display on the model?

Every object has a series of tabs in which you can record more information that is hidden from the viewer. To access this information, the modeler double-clicks the object.

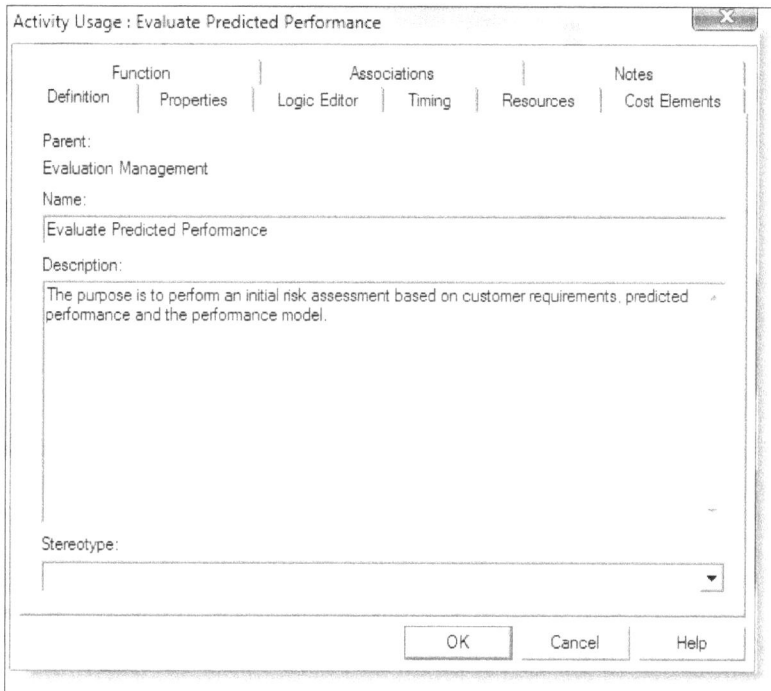

As you build the model, ProVision® gathers all that detail and can display it as interpretation. When you want to publish, you can include the interpretation alongside the models. In other words, your models are self documenting because the model and interpretation are synchronized.

For example, if you change the name of an object or add some description, the interpreter updates at the same time. In the following example, we can see that the screen has been split to show the model and the interpreter side by side. The modeler can work in either window.

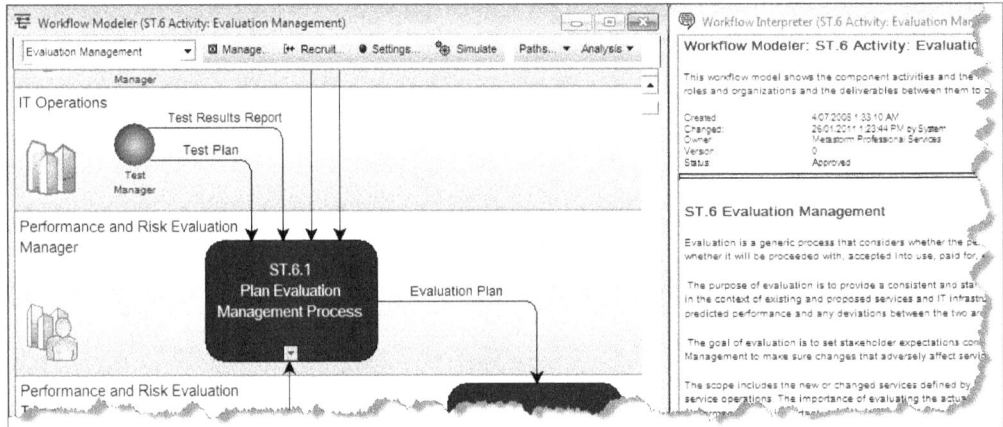

Model and simulate

Workflow models have extra features because they are the heart of ProVision®. Many organizations will never use all of the model types, but the majority will do much of their work in the Workflow and Process models. In addition to being able to visualize a process, you can also simulate how long it takes, what resources are required, and how much it costs.

The result is that you can quickly see where a process has bottlenecks. You can try different scenarios to find the best solution and present this information as a set of charts and tables to the decision makers.

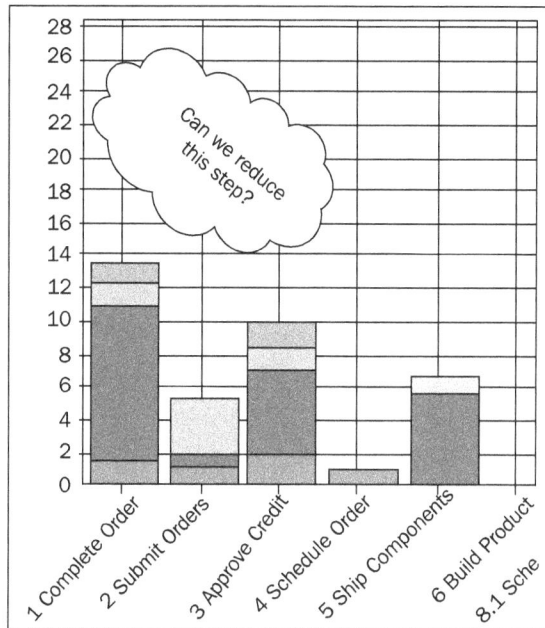

Model and execute

When simulating a process, the result is only as good as the assumptions that you have made. If one of the variables is incorrect, or the model does not reflect reality, then the results can be skewed. What if you could use real data as the basis of your model?

ProVision® is part of the Open Text Metastorm suite. The flagship product is the business process execution engine, Open Text Metastorm BPM. This is the software used to monitor and control a process from end to end. Often, a process is part manual and part automated. Different systems are used. You might have a CRM system that is completely independent of your Accounts Receivable and Payable system. Both contain information about your customers. Some of your systems will have business process execution built in, but only for the time that the process is inside that system. It can't manage the manual steps that take place elsewhere. Nor can it manage the automated steps that other systems perform.

Business process execution sits up in the clouds, looking down on every aspect of the process. Over time, you will replace one system with another, or perhaps automate a manual process. To the business process execution engine, that is all detail. It is very easy to switch from one to the other.

So, if you use business process execution, you gather real-time information about the process. You can then take that information into ProVision® and simulate changes using real data. Much of the guess work is now removed.

Open Text Metastorm are making incremental changes to streamline the relationship between the modeling and execution environment. The vision is to make the round trip seamless—design a process, execute it, gather live data, feed it back into the modeling environment, make improvements, and re-execute in a continuous cycle.

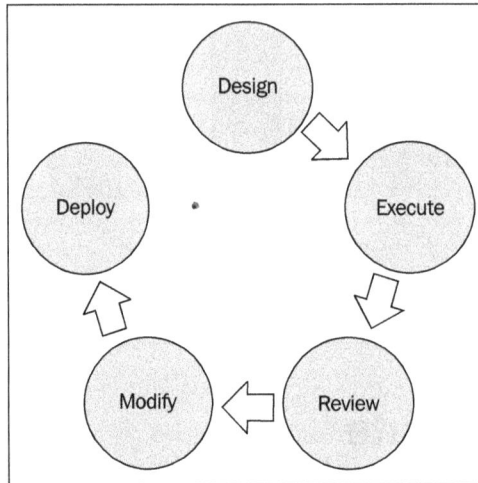

Modeling, not configuration management

I hope that the information provided in the previous sections excites you about the possibilities of what you can do with ProVision®. However, you also need to understand its limitations. In your enthusiasm, you might think that it is possible to do more with the tool than is realistic.

I hope that you have gathered, from previous discussions, that it is neither necessary nor desirable to try and make ProVision® the place where all information about a business is stored.

The reasons are both technical and political. From a technical point of view, other applications can manage information far more effectively. A configuration management database (CMDB) is designed to track the lifecycle of every instance of hardware and software. You might have hundreds of laptops, each of which has a unique serial number. On each laptop there will be software and you need to track which version has been installed for you to manage upgrades. You will also need to know about any differences in hardware, such as how much memory is installed. A CMDB enables you to understand the impacts of a software upgrade across a whole class of computers in a way that would be very difficult otherwise. A CMDB is the right tool to monitor this information and enable you to manage the lifecycle.

In theory, you could create individual objects in a ProVision® notebook to represent each laptop and record the serial numbers, hardware and software details, as part of the description. However, you will find that the features and functionality of the CMDB far outperform ProVision®. It is better to create one object to represent a class of laptops than try to manage and maintain hundreds of instances.

The political reason is that different business units have invested heavily in other applications. If you seek to make ProVision® the single source of all business information, this might be seen as empire building on your part, irrespective of how good your intentions are. It may be better to make another application the master, and ProVision® the slave. That way, they retain control and you publicize their work using ProVision® as a portal.

As long as you keep in mind that ProVision® is a tool to design a business and a portal to gather information, you will get the most from it.

Summary

ProVision® is a high-end, feature-rich, modeling environment that can be used to design and understand your business. It is a relational database that represents information such as models, text, and grids. Information can be imported and exported to other systems easily using industry standards such as XML and Microsoft Excel. A wide variety of publishing formats are supported.

Many ProVision® modelers can collaborate with each other using the server side Knowledge Exchange® to keep track of each object and ensure that only one person can make changes to an object at any one time. Knowledge Exchange® also enables stakeholders to monitor and comment on the models as they are being built. All they need is Internet Explorer and the appropriate permissions.

ProVision® includes basic multiuser features, allowing users to communicate and collaborate with each other, even without Knowledge Exchange®.

The models are self documenting, with the textual interpretation synchronized with the models.

Processes can be simulated to identify opportunities for improvement. Live data can be imported from the companion business process execution engine to improve the accuracy of the simulation.

ProVision® is a design and communication tool. It should not be used to store information about, or attempt to run, every aspect of your business. Other applications are optimized for this purpose and ProVision® can collaborate with them quite happily using industry standards to import and export information.

7
Obtaining Buy-in

Business is emotional. According to Gartner, there is now strong evidence that emotional engagement is four times more important than rational engagement. The purpose of this chapter is to reinforce the message that a successful strategy depends on the buy-in of people across the whole organization. If you have not done so already, read the *Six step process* section in *Chapter 5, Implementing Effective Governance*. It is an essential technique for obtaining a buy-in.

In this chapter, we will explore more techniques that win hearts and minds, and ensure alignment between the commercial and cultural aspects of the business. These include:

- Top 10 tips for process modeling
- Using *Appreciative Inquiry* to engage staff
- Distinguishing between change and transformation
- Understanding the outside-in (customer-centric) approach

While our focus is on implementing strategy, some of the lessons learned here can be applied in many different situations.

Top 10 tips for process modeling

One way of ensuring a buy-in is to use a methodology that is proven to deliver results. Nothing overcomes objections like success. So, here are my top 10 tips for modeling with a bonus tip thrown in for free. I have gathered these tips over the years, and I wish to acknowledge the business analysts and modelers with whom I have worked and who have contributed to a few of the tips.

#1 Identify and engage the process owner

- Unless the process owner is fully committed to process improvement, it will not happen and any attempts will be met with resistance.

- Failure to engage a committed process owner guarantees failure to improve the process in the long term.

The people who understand the process the best are those engaged in it, either as customers, suppliers, or staff who run the process. Getting engagement from everyone who has responsibility is the best way to deliver transformation. The appreciative inquiry method is an innovative way of doing this, by engaging individuals in organizational renewal, change, and focused performance through the discovery of what is good in the organization. This leads to my second top tip.

#2 Talk to the people who deal with errors

- Engage the process staff from the beginning, especially those who fix mistakes. Ensure their participation in the process improvement. They know what is necessary to fix the mistake, so they can help design to prevent mistakes from occurring.

- Managers frequently do not know how work is really done. They may think they do, but in reality the work is often done other ways. Look for informal processes based on relationships and local knowledge, which are often more important and effective than the formal, documented process.

#3 Capture the current "What" in detail but not the "How"

The two most important aspects of a process are what and how. The question of **what** is the information that is required to run the process has its answer as data. Whereas, the question of **how** is value created and enhanced has its answer as a process.

- If the current process is broken, the new process will probably reuse the data but not the process itself. It is only necessary to model the current process at a high level.

- Ask why at least five times to get to the root cause of the process problem.

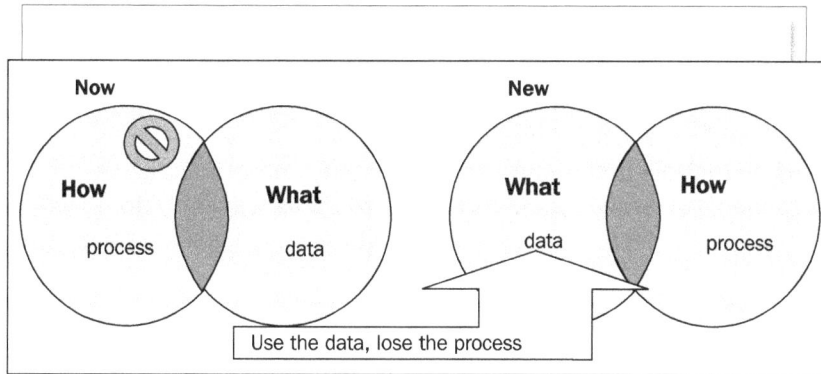

Now | New

How
process

What
data

What
data

How
process

Use the data, lose the process

#4 Reduce moments of truth

- The customer judges a process on the experience when they engage with the organization. For any given transaction, strive to limit the number of contacts with a client. Think of eBay's one-click process for ordering a book. Isn't that preferable than filling out a long form?

- Seek to minimize these moments. Add value to the customer at these moments while reducing effort for them; in short *simplify* any process for your customers.

#5 Reduce handoffs

- Many problems occur at hand-off from one person to another. The fewer the handoffs, the less opportunity there is for delay and miscommunication.

- Where handoffs are essential, you can consider parallel processing rather than sequential.

#6 Eliminate non-essential checking

The workflow in the following diagram shows the tea making process at Café Hopeless. There are three swim lanes, one for the customers, one for the role that makes the tea, and the third for the role that checks whether or not the tea is made properly. While the role that makes tea is normally a noun such as Tea Maker, I prefer to use the verb-noun combination *make tea*. This way, you do not confuse the role with position. Remember that several positions may be able to perform the role *make tea*.

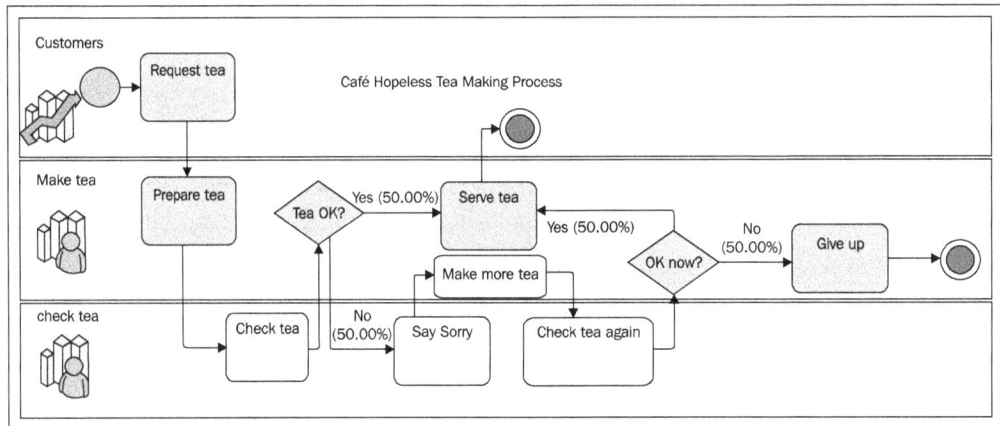

- Checks add no perceived value to a process other than to slow it down. Develop a culture where process participants have the ability to self monitor.

- If you have not done so already, read Steven Covey's book titled *The Speed of Trust*.

At Café Hopeless, the tea making process is so bad that they employ someone to check each cup of tea before it goes to the customer. If you can create a culture where everyone checks their own work, this saves time and eliminates steps that add no value.

At Café Hopeful, the process is much simpler.

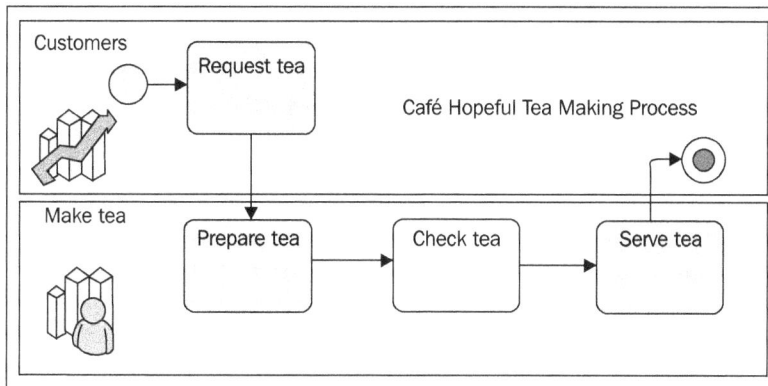

By default, all activities can be allocated a property type. This is a drop-down list. If you select **Value Added** as the type, you can then create a property grid to see all of the activities of that type.

HQ Activity	Qualified Name	Type
1	1.3.1.3.M.01 Design Campaign	Value Added

#7 Focus on high-volume processes

It is preferable to improve a high-volume process than one that occurs less frequently because you will benefit more.

#8 Implement the right process for right now

- The process will change. Don't be concerned about the future. Allow small incremental changes to develop over time.

- Look at the exception processes and try finding what causes them. Then design the process so that the exceptions do not occur in the first place — to put in a single term, simplify!

#9 Use the 10 Enterprise Designer processes

Processes exist to deliver products and services. Ensure that all 10 processes exist and identify which is critical. Even if you don't want to use the Enterprise Designer framework, memorizing the 10 process types will be invaluable. You can look at a service and identify which of the 10 processes need attention. The others can remain out of scope. When having conversations with stakeholders, they may not appreciate the difference between two process types. This will result in scope creep. Here is a brief reminder. Notice how they fall naturally into pairs.

- **Contract (New and Quit)**: Processes that begin and end a contractual relationship.
- **Deliver (Help and Logistics)**: Processes that deliver the product and support it.
- **Explain (Inform and Market)**: Processes that gather and communicate information.
- **Fund (Kollect and Pay)**: Processes that receive and distribute revenue.
- **Get Set (Organize and Join)**: Processes that gather and assemble components.

#10 Don't automate a broken process

- Automation should be considered the last step.

Other than tips #1 and #2, you can use all of the tips in any sequence, but automation is always the last step. You don't want to make a bad process faster.

#11 Bonus tip—model backwards

- When talking to subject matter experts, get them to describe a process backwards. That way, they have to stop and think and are less likely to forget a step. It also encourages them to see a process from the customer's point of view as it starts with them.

Let's look at this in more detail in the context of Appreciative Inquiry.

Using Appreciative Inquiry to engage staff

What is Appreciative Inquiry?

Appreciative Inquiry (AI) is an organizational development process or philosophy that engages individuals within an organizational system in its renewal, change and focused performance. AI is based on the assumption that organizations change in the way they inquire and the claim that an organization that inquires into problems or difficult situations will keep finding more of the same, but an organization that tries to appreciate what is best in itself will find/discover more and more of what is good.

The source of the definition is `http://en.wikipedia.org/wiki/Appreciative_inquiry`.

The only way to create ownership is to involve people in creating the product. This does not mean that everyone *has* to be involved in every aspect, but it does mean that everyone can be involved if they choose. People need a voice. People don't always do what you tell them to do, but what they feel engaged with. Involve them in the aspect of the creation of the work. There is a biological principle at work here: to create health in the human system or any biological system, you create more connections, that is, you bring in more parts of the system.

A fundamental act of leadership is identifying the things that matter to people. If people don't care about it, it doesn't matter how engaged you want people to be, but in reality, they won't be. Are we working on an issue that gets people's attention? Are we working on an issue that they care about?

We have always talked together to think well together. Problem solving techniques have demoted conversation. We have tended to think that conversation is too casual, it doesn't go anywhere, and it's nonlinear and messy.

So we go back to the flipcharts, and to the project planning techniques. But it is important to remember that people discover what they care about only through conversation. They discover shared meaning and they discover each other.

The question we have to ask ourselves is: How often are we confident enough to use conversation as a legitimate problem solving thinking process together, rather than using these very technical processes, which not only bore us, but disengage us, and separate us from one another?

It's also important to notice where your conversations happen. Are they legitimate? Do they happen inside meetings, or do they happen in the parking lots, bathrooms, in the hallways, or on e-mail late at night? Conversations always happen, the question is can we use this process? Can we legitimize it so that we strengthen our relationships, as well as develop much better thinking?

This is a taste of the Appreciative Inquiry approach.

Conversation about Appreciative Inquiry

To understand the approach more, I spoke to Jeremy Scrivens, who is Australia's leading practitioner in Appreciative Inquiry. Jeremy has 30 years of experience as a senior HR professional, manager, and organization development leader. He has either facilitated or has been part of the cultural alignment and stakeholder engagement assignments and projects, in over 50 organizations in the public and private sectors. These organizations include Federal, State, and Local Government, NGOs, and Tier 1, 2, and 3 commercial enterprises.

JS: A few years ago, when I was working with Gate Gourmet, we mapped the process backwards from the time that the passenger eats the food.

BA: Let's talk about that.

JS: The focus was to recognize that every action in a process has to have value for the customer. There are two types of customers. The internal customer is where we are serving each other. In this case, there were 15 different people involved from the time the food was cooked, assembled, and taken out to the aircraft where it was served and consumed. We identified all the different relationships. We also recognized that everyone needed to be aligned to one common purpose, which was that the end user had the best in flight catering experience that they could get. There was this notion of aligning a process to a purpose.

So, the first few questions you can ask around purpose are:

- Who are we?
- What are we passionate about?
- What do we do better than anyone else in the world?
- What is our purpose that we share together?

This leads into the question, "Who is our true customer?" Our customer is the person who uses our shared product or service. So that is what we did to map the as-is and to rebuild it. To do that work, we had to break down the traditional barriers. So we included the Qantas and Ansett flight attendants, as they are obviously part of the process. They didn't see themselves as part of the inflight catering process even though they were the ones who served the food. They are the final individuals involved in the process.

Mapping it backwards was a breakthrough in terms of focusing on line of sight to purpose. The other thing it did was to create this idea of the customer pulling value through, rather than having it pushed onto them.

If you model a process from the start, then you end up with a push conversation. If you reverse it, then you have a pull conversation.

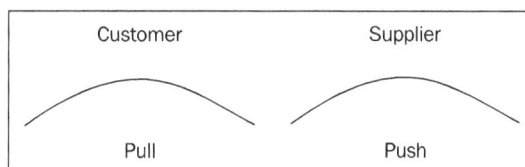

BA: Please explain what you mean about the difference between push and pull.

JS: Push is where, at the start of the process, the supplier says "This is what I am going to make. I am going to do that because I want an outcome for me." So the customer is really serving me, so I get my outcome.

What was happening at the Gate Gourmet process was that the chefs were estimating the amount and types of food that would be needed on the flight. That's OK but they weren't talking to the people who assembled the food, took it out to the aircraft, or served it. Nor were they talking to the customer to know what they wanted or when they wanted it. So what they were doing is batching up large amounts of food to make meals. Rather than making what the customer wanted, they were making what they wanted to make. The result was that the system was pushing food through. The chefs had the attitude, "You guys should be serving me. I am the one who is making the food. Now you have to assemble it. Now you have to eat it." That was the attitude. That was the culture.

When we listened to the stories of when things worked really well, customers had the selection that they wanted and food was prepared at the latest possible time, so that it was fresh. The process started at the last possible moment to get the food to the aircraft on time.

BA: This is very interesting. If I ask you to say the alphabet forwards, you can just rattle it off. If I ask you to say it backwards, you have to stop and think. So, modeling a process backwards is a good technique for discovering steps that might otherwise be missed. But you are looking it at from a completely different perspective.

JS: When I had this insight about nine years ago, it completely transformed the way I looked at it. When you start at the frontend, you focus on the how and the what. As Simon Sinek says, most people know what they do. For example, I produce product ABC with particular features. That's what it is. Buy it off me. Some people know how I do it, the process. Very few people know why. Why are we doing this? Why are we here?

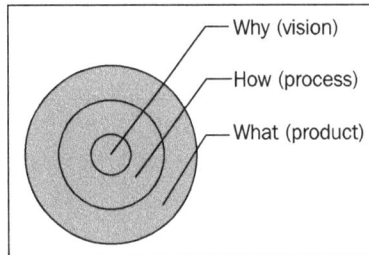

By mapping the process backwards, it goes immediately to the why question. Who are we serving? What does a great experience look like? Every stage of the process, you are now looking at it from the customer's point of view. What is their why? How can we supply that?

If you map forwards, you get a me-centric perspective.

BA: Apple and other companies who take this perspective say that if you ask a customer what they like, they will come back with improvements or embellishments on the existing product or service. They will never come back and tell you that they want a quantum leap up in the quality or offering. That is why, when Steve Jobs designs iPad, he first creates the product and then creates the market for it. In your view, how does the customer know what they want?

JS: They will tell you. Usually it comes down to three things. The first two are around what I call the two As. I want the food to be what I expect. The customer is expecting a certain kind of meal at a certain time. When they get it, their expectation is met. This is accuracy. The second expectation is around availability. When their choice is not available, then customers switch off and get disengaged.

The two As stand for **accuracy** and **availability**. The research from Gallup and others shows that whatever area you are in, asking customers what accuracy and availability means to them and really listening to their answers can give you tremendous insight.

Yes, you can create new and innovative products that the customer may be unaware of, and you can then sell these products to them. However, if your delivery is not accurate and available, you can't create that market. It's the basis of your relationship with a customer. We are interested in what works for the customer, because that is what builds trust.

So that is the first part. If I am a customer and you consistently deliver accuracy and availability, that is, you consistently give me exactly what I want, then I am going to stay with you. It then changes the conversation. Until then the conversation is around trust. Customers are used to being mistreated and so are suspicious. Now that you have proven that you can be trusted, they can enjoy your service, free from that suspicion. You also free up time. Instead of spending time dealing with issues around accuracy and availability, you are also ready to have a different conversation. So the third thing is that conversation is about what you want from us in the future, what is possible. That conversation is far more emotional. It is about meeting customer feelings, not expectations.

"I feel that my life is better by being connected with you." I never knew this nine years ago. When we worked with Gate Gourmet, we didn't just bring in the Ansett and Qantas flight attendants, we also brought in real passengers. We got the drivers, the assembly workers, the chefs, the flight attendants, the customers all in a room together. What we discovered was that, at its best, what you had was alignment around purpose and what people believe in. When you get that alignment, in this case around quality of the meal and a great eating experience, this pulls through the how and the what in terms of the process improvement.

A lot of process improvement is push. Someone outside is telling the people who do the work, these are the values, this is the vision. That is just their opinion. When they engage the people who do the work, and when they engage the customers, the story is different each time. You can't engage people if they see you as a threat. When you have a pull approach, it is far easier and quicker to identify and change those things that need to be changed.

BA: Do you believe that all processes should be modeled backwards?

JS: Yes, but can I qualify that? There is another conversation that is around who are we. Process improvement and process optimization will benefit from having that conversation. So LEAN, Six Sigma, and other quality approaches focus on the how and the what, which is why they end up working on accuracy and availability. Those conversations are tainted by blame. You are designing the system to prevent the bad ball, rather than encouraging the good ball.

Are you designing the system for the one time when things don't work, or for the 99 times when it does? If you have the context of abundance, then you build on what works. So if some people in the room are focused on compliance and others on abundance, then there are two different world views. Having the why conversation up front is a way to bring out these different viewpoints and get alignment. If you do that, then the process goes faster and the result will be optimized.

Traditionally, the conversations have been around what and how. I think we are seeing the emergence of conversations that start with why. I would build that into all process improvement engagements.

BA: I buy why.

JS: Yes. Process optimization is relational. It is about people and relations in a living system.

BA: You talked about Steven Covey's idea of the speed of trust.

JS: Yes. When trust is high, business is fast, and costs are low. On the other hand, when the trust is low, speed is low, and cost is high. You think about that from a process optimization point of view. Are you building a process where you will build trust or distrust?

BA: So how do you move from a process where there are lots of checks and balances put in because you don't trust that it will be done right first time? How do you change that culture? The best, fastest, and cheapest way to do a check is to have the person doing the work to check themselves. How do you get there?

JS: By moving the conversation from a change conversation to a transformation conversation. The best works being done in this field right now are based on Margaret Wheatley's 10 principles. You can Google her name and see short clips. Just briefly though:

- People support what they create. (A mine in South Wales was so dangerous the supervisor refused to go down. Remarkably, without any supervision, productivity went up).

- People act responsibly when they care. (A fundamental act of leadership is identifying the things that matter to people. Do they think that this issue is important?)

- Conversation is the way human beings have always thought. (Conversations always happen. The question is where? In the parking lot or in meetings? Can we use them?)

- To change the conversation, change who is in it. (If the conversation is stuck, invite in new people, people who have different perspectives. This is where diversity comes into play.)

- Expect leaders to come from anywhere. (Transformation creates surprise. What causes someone to step forward as a leader is their interest and their caring for the issue.)

- We focus on what works and it releases our creative energy. (The right question is: "what's possible here and who cares?")

- Wisdom resides within us. (No outside consultant can ever understand an organization as well as you can. Our role as coach is to create the right conditions so that you can do it yourselves.)

- Everything is a failure in the middle (Every breakdown is the doorway to a breakthrough. Failure is essential to success. Breakdown and breakthrough are the two sides of the same coin.)

- Humans can handle anything as long as we're together. (Focus on the relationship, and the quality of the services we offer take care of themselves.)

- Generosity, forgiveness, and love. (What would it really feel like to know that all your colleagues were all really there for you? What would it feel like if, when things go wrong, you know that people aren't going to gossip or spread rumors; they are going to help you learn from your failure, learn from your mistakes, and move on in ever more trusting relationships? What would that feel like?)

If you apply these principles when developing your ProVision® strategy, then you will let the people in the organization select the processes to improve, not the managers.

Organizations always have a challenge in getting people to take responsibility. By engaging people in reflective conversation, you can find out the issues that they care about. Once you do that, they will take responsibility because now it is not a chore but a passion. You keep the energy up by focusing on what works, and not on what doesn't. Let's tell stories about phenomenal service, not about what is broken. When we do that, these stories become models which can be extended.

If you are an airline, let's talk about exceptional arrival experience rather than the lost bag horror story. As Peter Drucker said before he died, "make your weaknesses irrelevant". Look at the language that we currently use. We talk of decomposing a process. That is the language of death. We look for defects. We look for disconnects. We know now from all the psychology that when you do that, people disengage.

This stuff is not soft!

Distinguishing between change and transformation

Transformation is not just another word for change. It is profoundly different.

Any organization is a system. As the leading proponent of Appreciative Inquiry, David Cooperrider, says:

> *The task of organizational leadership is to create an alignment of strengths in ways that make a system's weaknesses irrelevant.*

The characteristics of change are better, faster, and cheaper. The issue is defined. The outputs are known. Change works inside the system. Transformation works on the system. Change always has unintended consequences; if you change one part of the system, it has impacts over the horizon. By contrast, transformation releases energy and invokes surprise.

- The first quality of transformation is its **emotional color**. It always results in surprise. If you are not surprised, then what you are experiencing is not a transformation but just a change. Change has the power to surprise, but only once. Next time you will be bored. Therefore, keep in mind that if transformation creates surprise, change creates disappointment. As one friend has shared: there is no greater disappointment than success, nothing which is more likely to make you suicidal.

  You work hard, you overcome all the obstacles, you sacrifice much, and you achieve the goal. You really do. What you have created is remarkable. It is better, it is faster, and it is cheaper. You get that new car, you design that new product, and you marry the woman of your dreams. The next day you are filled with the feeling that can be summed up in the phrase: "so what?" You are so ashamed of this that you hide it.

  Transformation is not the same. It is not just an improved version of change. There is a discontinuity. Change arises from the mind, while transformation arises from the being. If you have experienced love, you will know that you did not wake up one morning and say, "Today I will fall in love" and it just happened. It is always unexpected. Millions of people will awake today and have no clue that this is their last morning. Death is the ultimate transformation. So if you prefer, then use the word *surprise* instead. Transformation is male, while surprise is its female counterpart.

- The second quality of transformation is that it is **very cheap**. It can even on occasion be free. Why? Because a change in viewpoint requires no physical change. To transform means to see the world differently. Because of the transformation, a company can achieve greater return on investment.

  The three reasons for promoting change are that the solution will be better, faster, and cheaper. Transformation encompasses change and is yet very different. So transformation is better, faster, and cheaper as compared to change! Transformation is better than change because it is an inner change in understanding and therefore can be applied in multiple situations. It is faster and cheaper because it does not require anything to be changed on a physical level. It just requires that bolt of lightning when you *get it*. The paradox is that transformation creates meaningful change.

- The third quality of transformation is **respect**. There is no distinction between the object to be transformed and the people involved. The focus is no longer on the product but on the relating. If you treat what you have to sell as a product, it is inevitable that you treat your customer as a product. You then treat your staff as a product, and ultimately you treat yourself as a product.

  The origin of the word *respect* is Latin and it means to take a second look. We judge each other instantly, forming an instant opinion. Respect happens when the other says or does something that does not fit the view. It causes you to take a second look.

  An organization that has the courage to embark on transformation, cannot treat customers, staff, suppliers, or even competitors, as objects. It will treat them all as they wish to be treated.

  We may even begin to see models where the business unit that manages staff and manages customers is the same.

  One thing is for sure. It will not be called the Human Resources department. As soon as you call people resources, then you have made them into an object, a thing to get a certain result. Why not call them human machines? It would be more authentic. Hy Smith, former marketing head of Universal Pictures, once shared with me how marketing used to be called exploitation. We are more subtle now. The pig has had a facelift, and Botox, as well as the obligatory lipstick.

We know when marketing is done well, the product sells. Coca-Cola sells sugar water and has done for over a century. Every day, week after week, Coca-Cola is advertising, advertising, and advertising. For this is the downside. Once you start marketing, you can never stop. You will have to market for ever. How exhausting is that? Imagine if Coca-Cola decided one day to cease all advertising. No more billboards, no more TV spots, no more product placements in movies. Imagine what would happen to their share price after a year.

Just as whom we are as individuals is created in language, so it is with organizations. If Coca-Cola no longer shouted at us from every conceivable vantage point it would languish and disappear.

- The fourth quality of transformation is **acceptance of what is not**. Transformation cannot be forced. You can neither coerce nor cajole. All the normal techniques of manipulation or brute force will not work. Transformation cannot be done to another because that would imply that there is something wrong with them. It also implies that they are a thing because only things have the static quality that allows them to be changed. Transformation is an invitation.

  Transformation accepts the *what is* part, which is an easy part. More importantly, transformation also accepts *what is not*.

  If you have an agenda that you are going to transform someone else, then all you have done is put a new set of clothes on change. Transformation arises from an authentic relationship.

- The fifth quality of transformation is **self remembering**. When you engage in transformation, the experience is strangely familiar. You are coming back to yourself. It feels true and authentic. How can you know whether something is true if you have not known it all along?

Now that we have distinguished transformation from change, let us look at how the two contexts play out. If your context is change, then everything shows up as a problem. Once you are in problem solving mode, then you will seek solutions. To develop solutions that are repeatable, you will examine the processes that are defective. From there it is only a short hop to look for the weaknesses in the process. Once you identify and correct these weaknesses, the best you can hope for is that you achieve what you set out to do. Because you always had that in mind, when you get there, you will feel disappointment.

When running a workshop where you are looking at defects, notice the energy in the room.

Change is done to people, while transformation is done by people. In a change process, an expert outsider comes in and manages the process. People participating in the process see them as a threat. In a transformation process, if outside help is needed, the role of the outsider is to mentor and facilitate. The transformation is done by the people who own and participate in the process.

We learned from Scrivens that if you set your target as achieving accuracy and availability, all that you have done is meet expectations. Your clients assume that you will deliver accuracy and availability, and will not congratulate you if that is what you provide. If we set our targets high, accuracy and availability come along for the ride.

It is a mistake to think that language just describes reality. It does far more than that. Language creates reality. Use different language and your reality starts to transform in subtle ways.

I am not talking about positive thinking. Positive thinking puts lipstick on the pig, while refusing to acknowledge that it is a pig. Transformational thinking starts by acknowledging that you have created a pig and then asks what you want to change that pig into.

Therefore, in the context of transformation, you open up the realm of possibility. Multiple choices become available and, as you open them up, you move into the world of discovery. Options that you never considered now become available.

To identify what discoveries will support you moving forward, you tell and listen to stories. These stories express what your organization is like at its best. From the stories, you can extract your strengths, your core DNA.

The result is the release of energy. The acid test of transformation is that it engenders surprise. It results in something happening that you had no idea would happen or believed was impossible. It results in laughter. It results in a deep emotional engagement with the organization, whether as a member of staff, a customer, or a supplier.

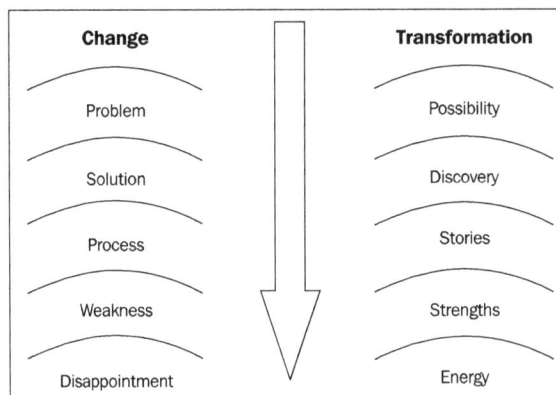

Change	Transformation
Problem	Possibility
Solution	Discovery
Process	Stories
Weakness	Strengths
Disappointment	Energy

Understanding the outside-in (customer-centric) approach

In an inside-out approach, one looks at the world from his/her own perspective. The customer is outside our organization and so we think about them as an external entity. This affects everything we do, and how we make models of the world. When we do process models, they start at the point where the customer knocks on our door. We don't think to model what happened before they contacted us, nor are we concerned with what they do once we deliver the product or service that they want from us. This me-centric view of the world prevents us from seeing the world through their eyes. We may do things that we see as perfectly normal and rational, but our customer might find them offensive. For example, we may batch up several orders for production, making the customer wait. To us, that makes complete sense. To the customer, they may feel that we do not value them or their business. As soon as they find someone who can offer the service on demand, they leave and never come back.

B2Me

The alternative outside-in approach is still not main stream, but this will change over the next decade. One of the innovators in this space is the ClienteerHub. In this interview, I caught up with Ray Brown, the founder of ClienteerHub, to understand the implications for modeling strategy.

RB: I'm Ray Brown. I am Scottish. I came to Australia five years ago. I am a Shirlaws Coach and I am also CEO and founder of ClienteerHub, which is a social learning website for a community of clienteers, who are going to be developing some new processes around customer centricity in businesses.

BA: This word clienteer is not a word with which most people will be familiar with. Why did you think there was a need for this word clienteer and what it means to you?

RB: What we found is business is very siloed, in the way that it works. You have got sales people, marketing people, IT people, accounts, and they are all very necessary. But today, the customer is looking for a unified face to business. The business needs to take the voice of the customer into the business.

What we discovered is that everybody was dabbling in that. Marketing people would do a bit of market research. Accounts people would have dealings with customers. But that never came together in one unified message for the business. What we discovered is that there are a lot of skills required to have those conversations. Who does that in the business? What we thought was, there was a need for a new language around dealing with customers, and the word clienteer seemed an obvious choice. It is a word for a role and an activity. Clienteering is a verb and represents a set of competencies that a clienteer needs.

There has been a lot of thinking over the years around CRM and process improvement. Everybody is trying to figure out how to respond to the customer, but not in a holistic way. Everyone who deals with a customer has a context of hunting more business or new business. What can we get out of the client? The context for a clienteer is completely different.

The context for clienteering is *understanding*. This means being in the customer's space, and not trying to sell them anything or solve any problems, but really to try and understand what they need, where they are going, and how we can create products and services that best align with what they want, not what we want.

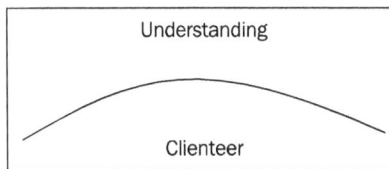

BA: Is the role of the clienteer to act as an interface between the customer and the organization, to communicate what the customer wants to all the departments?

RB: We have been working with our very first clienteer in Melbourne. We have been learning alongside him. He is working in an accounting firm. Some of the questions that you have been asking, they were saying also. For example, "I have a relationship with my clients. Why would you want a clienteer speak to them?" That has been a recurring theme for the past few months.

Where does the clienteer fit in with other people who interface with customers? Delivering the product or service, there is always going to be a transactional component. The opportunity that we have now, and I think it has always been there, is to go to the other end and for the business to have a relationship with the customer. The clienteer manages the relationship, leaving the other person to focus on getting right the delivery of the product or service. Sales and marketing are relatively new disciplines. They have only been around since the industrial revolution. For a hundred thousand years at least, we have traded with one another. The relationship has been separate from the products and services we exchanged. I think that is where we are going back to. The business has a relationship with customers and employees. That is one eco system and the clienteer can work in that space. They are interested in reputation, trust, and understanding. The operational and sales people will facilitate the delivery of the product or service.

BA: So the clienteer fosters a relationship with external customers, independent of the transactional relationship. You are saying that they have this same relationship with staff, that is, internal customers?

RB: Absolutely. People inside the business have a view of how we should treat the customer. It has to do with culture and the golden rule of treating others as they wish to be treated. Staff members want to do that, but sometimes they are constrained by systems and processes that prevent them. These things are very difficult to shift. So the clienteer talks to the customer, who says that they want a process to work in a particular way. The clienteer then talks with staff who, as often as not will say, "Well, I was saying that two years ago, but nobody listened".

We have talked for a number of years about B2C (Business to Customer) and B2B (Business to Business). To me that is a transactional description. You are providing a product or service for a customer or partner. I think that we are going to be interested in B2Me. It's about me; whether I am an employee or a customer, I want to be heard, I want to be taken into consideration, and I want to contribute.

I think, because of the impact of social media, we are going to go back to trading partnerships. We have drifted away from this and, since the industrial revolution, it has all become very transactional and mechanical. A few hundred years ago, there were limited means of communicating mechanically. So you assessed people, their honesty and trustworthiness, face to face. The fact that you were buying spices or cotton was secondary. Trade is the key word. You trade with people, you sell to people, and you market to people. The clienteer role can facilitate that.

BA: You are changing the language from "to" to "with"?

RB: Correct.

BA: In my book titled *Turning up for Life*, I suggested that there are three kinds of business relationship. The first is a transactional relationship, the second is a loving relationship, and the third is a compassionate relationship.

RB: Yes.

BA: It sounds to me that what you are talking about with clienteer is turning that idea of the loving relationship into reality. The clienteer creates the loving relationship.

RB: Yes, the clienteer provides a conduit for a new kind of conversation. Most of the thinking has been done by large corporates who may have hundreds of thousands of customers. How do we communicate with them? But 95 percent of business is made up of smaller businesses that may have less than a thousand customers. So you can actually speak to all of them, or a significant proportion particularly, if you segment them. For example, one segment is customers who have left. Another segment is new employees. What do they value?

Take a company such as Zappos that produces shoes and clothing. You can probably get the same shoes anywhere. The culture is what distinguishes them. The *no questions asked* returns policy is embedded in their ethos. It has nothing to do with the delivery of the product. It is a philosophical position that they have taken. It is attractive to customers and staff. People want to be a part of it. It's about me. I want to be part of that game. I want to play with them. Businesses that get B2Me are going to be ahead of the game.

BA: I love this term B2Me.

RB: It is consistent with clienteer. How do you link the buy-in of the staff with the needs of the customers? Existing silos are not very good, perhaps incapable of doing that holistically. The metrics are around sales, average call time. They are not aligned to the needs of the customer but the needs of the business. The clienteer is able to extract the missing piece. How can people treat each other in a respectful way?

BA: You mentioned that you have the first clienteer working in a business. How did that come about?

RB: In 2008, we set up a business called Client Service Support. I knew that there was something in this story. It was a sub-contract business where we said that we would work through the filing cabinets of past customers, contact them, and feed back to our clients what we found.

That really didn't work for two main reasons. We got the insights. We got the information, but there was nobody inside the business who was listening. They wanted the hot leads. The business sold telephone systems. We would call the old customer and they might say, "Keep in touch with us. We didn't know you supplied the old system, so we went somewhere else". The client didn't twig that this was a big issue.

The second problem was around CRM. We discovered that there was a whole lot of confusion about what CRM was. Is it a technology, or a strategy, or a holistic approach to business? Coincidentally, one of our clients at that stage got the concept of clienteering but he didn't have the support in his company.

Two years on, he now finds himself working in an accounting firm, doing business development, and so he comes back to us. This accounting firm has almost two thousand clients. The sales operation wasn't working. Business development rarely works in accountants and lawyers because it just doesn't feel right. Accountants don't like selling. It does not feel natural.

He said, "I would like to try some of the work that you were doing with us at my old firm". The last six weeks have been absolutely fantastic. With huge resistance from his boss, we managed to get a three month project where he would talk with existing customers, new customers, and customers who had left. We started very scripted and controlled. This is what you say. We quickly found that didn't work. So now we start with a "thank you for your business". Even if they have left, we thank them for their business.

People are shocked by that as an opening line. I don't know about you but I have never been thanked for my business when I have left.

In later stages, the calls have been very open. As soon as they know that you are not selling, as soon as they know that the call is about them and not about you, the B2Me thing, they are absolutely desperate to speak about what you do, how it impacts them, what they value about it. They lose the fear about: "This is just a sales call. You say it is a survey, but it is really a sales call".

We have polluted people's minds so that people don't trust that we want their opinion and that it matters to us. We need to get good at having those conversations. We need to learn how to do that one to one, and on a bigger scale. We now have social media. People want to participate and contribute. We need to find the skills and how to tap into that.

We have spoken before about outside-in. That is a fundamental change. The inside-out approach is to sit in a room and figure out what we think customers want and then build processes to support that. The outside-in approach is that everything starts with the customer; everything starts with successful customer outcomes. If you can't draw a direct line between what you are doing and customer outcomes, then you have to ask yourself, "why are you doing that task or running that process?" I think that the businesses that get the outside-in approach will be ahead of the game. I think that the clienteer will be the role that provides that intelligence. Otherwise, how do you get that information? Lots of businesses do satisfaction surveys, but that really tells you very little. Quite often, people who are satisfied will still leave your business. There is a correlation between being dissatisfied and leaving, but not between being satisfied and staying.

BA: I just came back from Club Med, which I had never been to before. I had expectations about what it was going to be and it was different to those expectations. They sent me a survey, which I completed. It was quite a detailed survey. But there was no opportunity for me to say certain things that I wanted to say, because it didn't fit within the structure of their survey. There were things I thought were important, and they hadn't even put on their survey. So, I filled it in, but I didn't feel there was any communication. They controlled the conversation. They decided the questions and the possible answers. That doesn't do it for me.

RB: And do you expect to get any response from them?

BA: No.

RB: What the customer wants is for their opinion to be sought, to be listened to, and to be acted upon.

BA: It sounds to me that the only way to do this is to listen.

RB: Absolutely. I have been telling managers for the past thirty years that the key skill of a manager, and now I understand that it is the key skill of a supplier, is to listen. Yet we are very poor at it. I have used this game to illustrate the point with my students. I have three medals for you. Make a list of the top listeners you have come across at work and give them these medals.

You could see people struggle to think of three people. Sometimes they would only be able to find one. So then I would open it up and say, "it doesn't have to be at work, it can be at home as well", people would still struggle at times. They would write down their dog [laughter].

Listening skills are very poorly distributed at work. Then, we would have a conversation about the people who they had put on their list. Invariably, they had a positive opinion of them and they were often successful, in their own terms. So, we would make the connection that people who listen are successful. Then, we would make the next connection by asking the question, "Did this person, who is a really good listener, have an influence on you?" They would see the person as a great mentor.

So we see that to influence people, it is not about being eloquent, but it is about listening. This is a massive *ah ha* moment. You don't have to tell people. Ask genuine questions and listen to their answers. That is why it can't be scripted. We reject 19 out of 20 people who want to be business coaches because their questioning and listening skills don't come naturally to them.

I see all of these things as being linked.

BA: So you will have a "Listener of the Year" award. Wouldn't that be great?

RB: Definitely, we need a prize for "Clienteer of the Year". This is a very exciting time. I have been working on this now for almost three years and it has been very frustrating. My thinking wasn't clear. Now, I can explain it better and other people can get it. I think that we have reached the tipping point. I think that people will start to see that, "if I use this language then I get this result". By changing the language, I get a different result.

CRM is a classic example. There is a group on LinkedIn called the CRM experts. We have just had a conversation on who should handle CRM — sales or marketing? There have been about 150 comments, and I would say that at least two-thirds of those people are using the phrase CRM to mean technology. How do you implement it? Who do you buy it from? The other third are saying that it is much more than that. It is a strategy, a philosophical approach to business.

I keep going back to them and saying: "Your market is confused. You are supposed to be the experts but you are calling two things by the same name. To me, you need to treat CRM as a technology because that is what the market thinks it is. The wider philosophy is actually clienteering."

Clienteering means getting meaningful change in a business that is driven by the customer.

BA: If you look at the phrase Customer Relationship Management, it is quite an aggressive phrase.

RB: Yes.

BA: Why don't we call it herding sheep? How can we have a relationship in which you don't have one party? We want to own that relationship.

RB: I think that is right. Now we are hearing of Social CRM, which is CRM with the social media laid on top. I think that some of these people just don't get it. I don't think that they get the revolution that is happening. Customers are saying, "Stop, the world has changed. Stuff that you were doing twenty years ago, not only is not relevant, it is actually counterproductive".

The customer of today is much better informed. They have researched the whole market. If you don't start the sales process really early around reputation, trust, respect, and brand building, and if you don't realize that brand is personal, then you aren't going to get their business.

People buy from people; they have always done it and always will.

BA: With your accounting firm, is it too early to share some of the results that you have been getting?

RB: We use the analogy of the tightrope walker. It looks easy, it looks like fun. Surely anyone can do that. You don't even have to sell anything. In fact you are not allowed to.

However, that hides the fact that it is quite daunting to phone people up. It is quite daunting that you don't know what you are going to hear. We have spent a lot of time supporting our clienteer, both practically and emotionally. For example, we have been helping him with his time management. How should he spend his time and what proportion should be spent on the different activities?

The first thing we got from clients who have left was, "If I had had this call a year ago, I wouldn't have left." A number of people have said that. The people who had left were very open about why they had left. You can make a fair assessment that there must be clients within your current client base who are feeling the same but just hadn't left yet. So that is gold dust.

We found that some of the partners were inaccessible. Clients felt hurried. The accountants do the tax returns online. It is a high volume, low margin product. The customers who left were saying that they wanted more and they would have paid more. "We liked the accountant; we just didn't like the product".

Once we started to speak to existing clients, we found people who didn't know about the range of services. The Accounting firm had a financial planning arm. Some people were very naive about what financial planning was. We had one specific instance of a high-earning individual who had no financial planning at all. As a result of the conversation with the clienteer, he decided to fly from Brisbane to Melbourne to see the financial planner. It came out naturally in the conversation that was what he should be doing.

We had a pharmacist who had his annual accounts prepared. He was about to buy two other pharmacy businesses and he had a number of investment properties. He was not aware that his accountancy practice could handle the whole thing. He actually asked if they could provide advice on the purchase of the businesses and handle the whole portfolio of investment properties.

BA: So, even though the clienteer's job is not to sell, these opportunities are falling out with no pressure or persuasion.

RB: Yes, the questions are being asked. The other upside is the reaction of staff. Quite often, what they are hearing is reinforcing what they thought already but perhaps they didn't have the courage to say.

They might feel that they didn't have the authority to say what they see. In a classic *command and control* structure, they might assume that the boss knows best. Well, perhaps the boss doesn't know best. The staff and the customers certainly do know. It opens up the possibility of empowering staff. This has to be good for the business.

BA: This is a radically different way of doing business development.

RB: Absolutely. As a business coach, I spend a lot of time with accountants, lawyers, and other professional services. They are notoriously bad at what they call business development. A story that I have been telling lately is the manager of a recruitment firm who proudly introduced me to his new business development manager. He showed me his new business card with the title Business Development Manager. I said to him, "If you handed me that card, whose business are you actually developing?" [laughter].

The whole business development thing has to go out the window. What the client will see is that their title is "Let me sell you something Manager".

BA: Someone who is a professional services person doesn't want to be a sales person. If they had wanted to do that, they would have gone and made a career in sales. They are interested in using their skill and expertise to help their clients get the best outcome. Then, if you ask that person to go and do business development, they cringe.

RB: Absolutely. It takes us right back to the conversation with our accounting firm. They are selling a product and that product has to be first class. To do that, there has to be interaction with the client, but that conversation is about the product. Yes, they will have the conversation about "how are the kids", but that is peripheral. The accountant needs to stay focused on getting the product right. He wants to get into the numbers. Quite right. The clienteer conversation does not belong there.

BA: So you said that the senior partner was resistant to the idea initially and yet agreed to the trial. What are you noticing now that you are getting these results?

RB: It is a complete about face. He is a young accountant. He has four accounting firms already, and he has a big vision for a $50m business through acquisition. The phrase he was using two months ago was, "You can't organically grow a business. If you buy a business, you have got to expect to factor in 20% loss, the attrition rate, when the owner leaves."

He has completely turned around. He wants a clienteer in every business that he buys. He wants the clienteer piece to be part of the due diligence. He thinks that the clienteer approach will actually be a point of difference to the seller. The seller, perhaps, has been looking after his clients for 30 years. He is concerned about what will happen to them when his business is acquired.

A group clienteer can reassure him and do a customer centricity audit. If the business being acquired is already customer-centric, then the seller can command a premium. If they are poor at it, then the clienteer can unlock hidden value for the purchaser. We think that we can cut the attrition rate using this approach. I think there is a massive upside.

So the senior partner has gone from being very negative, to being skeptical, to being interested. He is still quite challenged by it. He sometimes asks why the clienteer needs to spend so much time on the phone with a customer. He doesn't quite get that if the customer is prepared to spend time with you, then you have got to listen to them. The diamond might come only 20 minutes into the conversation. It might take that time before the customer says, "there is something I really want to tell you." Then out pops the big gem. It could be any number of things. We can never be on the outside, seeing ourselves the way others see us. We can imagine. But if a customer is prepared to tell us about what we need to do for them to do more business with us, that is invaluable.

BA: So, do you see clienteers as external people who come in and work with the business, or do you see them as employees who take on a new role?

RB: I think it will take a number of forms. I think it will be internal. We tried it with Client Service Support. We didn't have enough product knowledge. We didn't have enough cultural attachment. We were a sub-contractor. So we didn't give them full value. I think we need dedicated time and authority. I think the clienteer needs training. It could be an existing employee who does this role once a week. We don't want to create a hurdle where the CEO feels they have to hire a new person. I think that some of the resourcing that goes into sales and marketing will need to be redirected into clienteering. It will attract a different kind of person.

There will be a need to provide soft support, what we call "training the tightrope walkers". We want them to feel confident and have fun. We want them to be charming on the phone. That doesn't come easily to everyone. We also need to give them the return on investment metrics.

BA: So that they can demonstrate that they aren't just chatting on the phone?

RB: Yes, correct. So the metrics will be around average spend, average life of the client relationship, number of new products that the client takes. Our role is to create what we call "social learning". There are quite a lot of people doing aspects of this already. They are quite alone. So our website will be a place for people to come together—practitioners as well as experts. There are quite a few experts out there with their own tools, books, articles, so we will have all of these things on the site. We think that, over time, the best will float to the top.

It is a bit like LinkedIn meets Wikipedia. You have the discussion and you capture the learning. The other piece will be people doing similar things around the world, coming together with the context of learning. When you learned a computer, you didn't learn it from a book; you learned it from someone else who knew a little more than you did.

BA: You don't want to know how I learned a computer in the 1970s! I used to sneak into the accounting department when nobody was there because they were the only ones who had computers. I used to try and figure out how to use WordStar. Once it jammed up, because I pressed the wrong button; I would leave! In the morning they were always baffled why the computer had got stuck [laughter].

RB: That is the other option, trial and error. You didn't go to a seminar. About 30 years ago, we slipped into this approach that the only way to learn was through seminars and videos. It is helpful, but we learn best with each other. I think that social learning will be the next big thing in social media.

Summary

In this chapter, we have learned about some of the exciting new approaches for transforming the way that organizations are connecting with their staff, customers, and suppliers.

These approaches are all about focusing on the emotional relationships and recognizing organizational processes as being purposeful social systems, that is, living systems, as per Russell Ackoff. The old mechanistic view is giving way to an approach that combines the commercial and the cultural, the rational and the emotional, to create businesses that have relationships *with* rather than *to* the rest of the world.

These approaches will replace the current mechanistic view. There is no possibility that they can co-exist. Let me end this book, appropriately, with a story.

I lived in New Zealand for a year. While there, I went with my daughter on a school trip to Goat Island. The clear waters team with life. We swam with stingrays. Some of the fish were older than me.

This was the first marine reserve in New Zealand and one of the first in the world. When it was proposed, the local fishermen hated the idea. They fought it tooth and nail. The legislation had to be pushed through against huge opposition, but finally in 1971 it happened.

Some people agreed that it was good to have marine reserve, but didn't see why recreational fishing shouldn't be allowed. After all, what harm could be done by taking a few fish?

What they discovered is that although fishes don't have physical boundaries, they mostly stay in one place. So the marine reserve had become an incredibly protected breeding ground. Humans were not interfering. Then the fish would go off and out to sea, and the benefits would spread more widely.

The key is zero fishing, not even recreational fishing, in these sanctuary areas. The fishermen became the greatest advocates once they saw how it benefited them. If they saw a person fishing, they would stop it. They showed leadership because they cared.

We went in a glass bottom boat and the skipper would stop at a particular point and say, "In a moment you will see six fish of a certain type." Lo and behold, there they were. They had lived at that spot for twenty years. It was wonderful and inspiring.

You cannot combine appreciative and negative inquiry. The stain of negativity will pollute the clear waters. If you want a buy-in, then everyone has to be engaged.

References

Agile Project Management

http://www.ccpace.com/Resources/documents/AgileProjectManagement.pdf

Appreciative inquiry

http://en.wikipedia.org/wiki/Appreciative_inquiry

APQC (American Productivity & Quality Center)

http://www.apqc.org/

Archimate images, Archimate, and Enterprise Designer objects compared

These images are licensed under a Creative Commons Attribution 3.0 Netherlands License. For more information go to http://creativecommons.org/licenses/by/3.0/nl. You can also refer to the Telematica Institute website, http://www.telin.nl.

BPMN

http://www.bpmn.org/

BPTrends

http://www.bptrends.com/

Business Rules definition

www.businessrulesgroup.org

Capability Maturity model

The Capability Maturity Model describes the maturity of organizational processes. Five levels of maturity are defined, starting at the initial or chaotic, repeatable, defined, managed, and optimized. For more information go to http://en.wikipedia.org/wiki/Capability_Maturity_Model.

Deloitte's Enterprise Value Map

`http://public.deloitte.com/media/0268/Enterprise_Value_Map_2_0.pdf`

Enterprise Designer framework

`www.EnterpriseDesigner.com`

Enterprise Designer meta-model

The definitions of the 26 elements are based on material first published by Bill Aronson in *Enterprise Designer – building a Conscious Organization*, Lulu 2008.

Enterprise Designer modeling language

Enterprise Designer members can download the Enterprise Designer modeling language from `www.enterprisedesigner.com/starberry`. Membership is free.

eTOM

`http://www.tmforum.org/BusinessProcessFramework/1647/home.html`

The TeleManagement Forum—`www.tmforum.org`—is responsible for eTOM.

IAF

`http://architectes.capgemini.com/communauteDesArchitectes/laMethodologieIAF/b_Architecture_and_the_Integrated_Architecture_Framework.pdf`

iGrafx

`http://www.igrafx.com/products/flowcharter/`

Indication of Transformation

`www.TurningUpforLife.com`

Kaizen

The Japanese word for improvement. In business it means continuous improvement.

LEAN/Six Sigma

`http://en.wikipedia.org/wiki/Six_Sigma`

Location Model

If you want to get a complete list of associations, go to the free resources at `www.enterprisedesigner.com` and download the Excel spreadsheet of the framework.

Motorola change process

www.margaretwheatley.com/articles/life.html

Shirlaws

Shirlaws is a leading business coaching company. They coach timing, balance, and the power of context to create businesses that are aware, successful, happy and decisive.

www.shirlaws.com.au

Starberry Accounting

Enterprise Designer members can download the complete Starberry ProVision® model from www.enterprisedesigner.com/starberry.

Turning up for Life

Turning up for Life, by Bill Aronson, from the publisher Enterprise Designer Institute www.TurningUpForLife.com

Value Driver Tree

Value driver: Any variable that significantly affects the value of an organization. In his development of shareholder value analysis, Alfred Rappaport identified seven key drivers of value:

- Sales growth rate
- Operating profit margin
- Tax rate
- Fixed capital investment
- Working capital investment
- Planning period
- Cost of capital.

Of these, the first five can be used to forecast the future cash flows of a business, whereas the remaining two can be used to calculate the present value of these cash flows. In practice, different companies will have different value drivers. For example, Sony is a company that produces high-quality products for which customers are prepared to pay a relatively high price. Maintaining a high operating profit margin is therefore more important for Sony than sales growth. For another company, however, the sales growth may well be the more important factor. (Source: www.encyclopedia.com)

Young America

```
http://32nd.americascup.com/en/acclopaedia/circlinggalaxy/profil.
php?idContent=4482
```

Zachman, John

Zachman's work, first published in 1987, *A framework for information systems architecture,* published in the *IBM Systems Journal.* Zachman is considered the founder of Enterprise Architecture.

Zappos

```
www.zappos.com/
```

Index

System Interaction Models, building 144
workflow models, building 135
model
about 44
hierarchical 44
navigator 44, 45
non-hierarchical 44
Motorola change process
references 231
steps 162

N

Navigator Model 85
network 99
New 104
Notebooks 46

O

Open Group Architecture Framework. *See*
   TOGAF
operations 93
organizations, Enterprise Designer frame-
   work
about 108
comments 109
naming convention 109
permitted models 109
permitted objects 109
relationships 109
organization models, building
about 148
business rule models 150
critical elements 148
event models 151
Organize 104
outside-in approach 217-227

P

Pay 104
personal context, Metastorm ProVision®
responsibility 12-14
scope 14
scope, enterprise scope 15
scope, project scope 15

time 12
platform 99, 100
processes, Enterprise Designer framework
Collect 103
comments 103
Help 103
Inform 103
Join 103
Logistics 103
Market 104
naming convention 102
New 104
Organize 104
Pay 104
permitted models 103
permitted objects 102
Quit 104
relationships 103
process modeling
tips 199-204
process modeling, tips
automation 204
backward, modeling 204
Enterprise Designer processes, using 204
handoffs, reducing 201
high volume processes focus 203
how aspect 200
non-essential checking, eliminating 202,
   203
people, communicating with 200
process owner, engaging 200
process owner, identifying 200
process simplification 201
right process, implementing 203
what aspect 200
products, Enterprise Designer framework.
   See **service, Enterprise Designer**
   framework
project implementation
about 20
components, lists 21
information, gathering 22
information transfer, from Metastorm Pro-
   Vision® 26
lists, building 22
model publishing, process 25
object maintainance, ensuring 24

.

[PACKT] PUBLISHING enterprise
professional expertise distilled

Thank you for buying
Open Text Metastorm ProVision® 6.2 Strategy Implementation

About Packt Publishing

Packt, pronounced 'packed', published its first book "Mastering phpMyAdmin for Effective MySQL Management" in April 2004 and subsequently continued to specialize in publishing highly focused books on specific technologies and solutions.

Our books and publications share the experiences of your fellow IT professionals in adapting and customizing today's systems, applications, and frameworks. Our solution based books give you the knowledge and power to customize the software and technologies you're using to get the job done. Packt books are more specific and less general than the IT books you have seen in the past. Our unique business model allows us to bring you more focused information, giving you more of what you need to know, and less of what you don't.

Packt is a modern, yet unique publishing company, which focuses on producing quality, cutting-edge books for communities of developers, administrators, and newbies alike. For more information, please visit our website: www.packtpub.com.

About Packt Enterprise

In 2010, Packt launched two new brands, Packt Enterprise and Packt Open Source, in order to continue its focus on specialization. This book is part of the Packt Enterprise brand, home to books published on enterprise software – software created by major vendors, including (but not limited to) IBM, Microsoft and Oracle, often for use in other corporations. Its titles will offer information relevant to a range of users of this software, including administrators, developers, architects, and end users.

Writing for Packt

We welcome all inquiries from people who are interested in authoring. Book proposals should be sent to author@packtpub.com. If your book idea is still at an early stage and you would like to discuss it first before writing a formal book proposal, contact us; one of our commissioning editors will get in touch with you.

We're not just looking for published authors; if you have strong technical skills but no writing experience, our experienced editors can help you develop a writing career, or simply get some additional reward for your expertise.

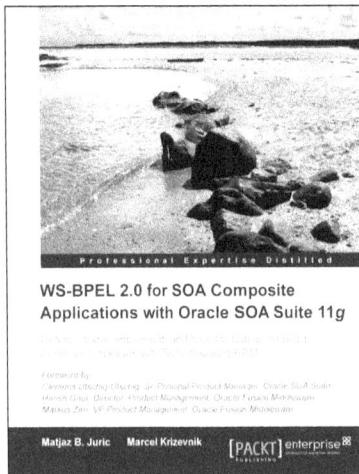

WS-BPEL 2.0 for SOA Composite Applications with Oracle SOA Suite 11g

ISBN: 978-1-847197-94-8   Paperback: 616 pages

Define, model, implement, and monitor real-world BPEL business processes with SOA powered BPM.

1. Develop BPEL and SOA composite solutions with Oracle SOA Suite 11g

2. Efficiently automate business processes with WS-BPEL 2.0 and develop SOA composite applications.

3. Get familiar with basic and advanced BPEL 2.0.

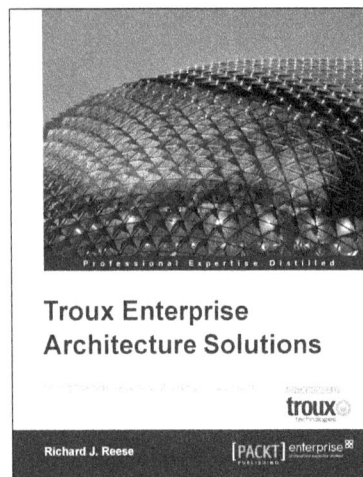

Troux Enterprise Architecture Solutions

ISBN: 978-1-849681-20-9   Paperback: 248 pages

Driving business value through strategic IT alignment.

1. Gain valuable insights about the role of Enterprise Architecture in today's dynamic business environment.

2. Learn about the Troux Transformation Platform and how it supports the disciplines of Enterprise Architecture, transformation planning, and project-goal alignment.

3. Understand the value of integrating metadata from many sources to deliver new management insights about IT effectiveness

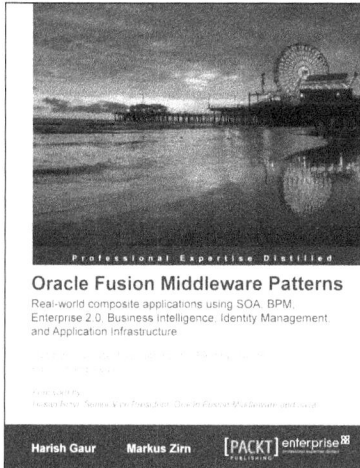

Oracle Fusion Middleware Patterns

ISBN: 978-1-847198-32-7   Paperback: 224 pages

10 unique architecture patterns powered by Oracle Fusion Middleware

1. First-hand technical solutions utilizing the complete and integrated Oracle Fusion Middleware Suite in hardcopy and ebook formats

2. From-the-trenches experience of leading IT Professionals

3. Learn about application integration and how to combine the integrated tools of the Oracle Fusion Middleware Suite - and do away with thousands of lines of code

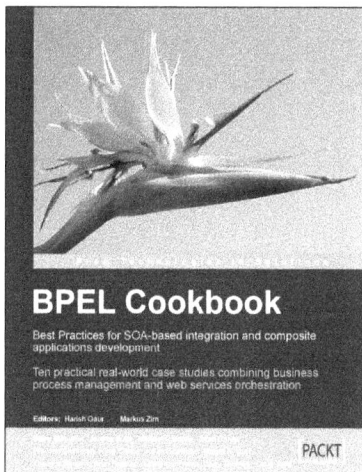

Oracle Fusion Middleware Patterns
Real-world composite applications using SOA, BPM, Enterprise 2.0, Business Intelligence, Identity Management and Application Infrastructure

Harish Gaur   Markus Zirn   [PACKT] enterprise ⊠

BPEL Cookbook: Best Practices for SOA-based integration and composite applications development

ISBN: 978-1-904811-33-6   Paperback: 188 pages

Ten practical real-world case studies combining business process management and web services orchestration

1. Real-world BPEL recipes for SOA integration and Composite Application development

2. Combining business process management and web services orchestration

BPEL Cookbook
Best Practices for SOA-based integration and composite applications development

Ten practical real-world case studies combining business process management and web services orchestration

Editors: Harish Gaur   Markus Zirn

PACKT

Please check **www.PacktPub.com** for information on our titles

www.ingramcontent.com/pod-product-compliance
Lightning Source LLC
Chambersburg PA
CBHW061400210326
41598CB00035B/6050